T5-DHJ-217

5th Edition

Business
Records
Control

Ernest D. Bassett
Analyst/Consultant, Records Systems
Santa Barbara, California

David G. Goodman
Professor, Business Education
University of Wisconsin—Whitewater

Joseph S. Fosegan
Professor, Executive Secretarial Department
Agricultural and Technical College
State University of New York—Alfred

K13

Published by

SOUTH-WESTERN PUBLISHING CO.

CINCINNATI   WEST CHICAGO, ILL.   DALLAS   PELHAM MANOR, N.Y.   PALO ALTO, CALIF.

Copyright © 1981

Philippine Copyright 1981

by

South-Western Publishing Co.
Cincinnati, Ohio

All Rights Reserved

The text of this publication, or any part thereof, may not be reproduced or transmitted in any form or by any means, electronic or mechanical, including photocopying, recording, storage in an information retrieval system, or otherwise, without the prior written permission of the publisher.

ISBN: 0-538-11130-5

Library of Congress catalog card number: 79-67724

1 2 3 4 5 6 7 8 9 10 11 D 1 0 9 8 7 6 5 4 3 2 1

Printed in the United States of America

Preface

The spectacular trends toward the use of electronic means to produce business records and the use of mechanical devices to handle and store business papers have continued into the 1980s. In addition, the growth of computer assisted retrieval (CAR) of records and information, the rapid growth in the use of micrographics for both active records systems and information storage systems, and the blending of electronic data processing systems with word processing systems have added a new dimension to records processing and control.

One result of these trends is that business records continue to expand in form, variety, and quantity. This expansion requires an ever-increasing application of records control by skilled and well-trained personnel. Since filing as a major portion of the control of records is included in the meaning of the term *records control*, this edition has been retitled *Business Records Control*. The new title reflects current terminology as well as the blending of filing with the other aspects of records control within the total records management function. It emphasizes the overall need of the full control of all records.

Another trend is the positive movement toward professional advancement at the managerial and administrative levels of the records field. This upgrading trend is also extending to the supervisory and clerical occupations. Many new responsibilities and new job titles are emerging.

These changes in the area of records occupations are mirrored in several ways in this Fifth Edition of *Business Records Control*. In addition to the title change, the factors that are basic to records control are presented as are those resulting from changing operations and occupations.

For example, Chapter 13, "Word Processing and Micrographic Filing Systems," has been expanded to include word processing as well as electronic data processing and micrographics. The emphasis in this expanded chapter is on the form of records produced, how these records are stored and retrieved, and how they are controlled. Although the rules for indexing and coding records have not been changed and still reflect actual business usage, their presentation has been improved by a process of consolidation in order to form only 14 basic rules that have an increased coverage of indexing problems. The increased use of color in records systems is reflected in Chapter 8, "Use of Color in Alphabetic Filing Systems," as well as in other appropriate chapters.

These changes and others in the revised text material are presented in six parts. *Part 1* includes a dynamic overview of the records control field and the checks and balances that are included in the field. *Part 2* supplies the information needed to process business information in a controlled manner. *Part 3* gives details about the structure of alphabetic filing systems and explains the charge and transfer procedures that must be used in maintaining order in filing systems. *Part 4* shows and describes the various types of filing systems that are in common use. *Part 5* presents the elements of and the procedures used in micrographics as well as the factors in word processing and data processing that affect records operations and controls. *Part 6* gives an overview of the types of equipment that are used in the field and how these contribute to the efficiency of filing operations. The final chapter deals with specific practices and procedures that keep filing systems manageable and operational.

Ernest D. Bassett
David G. Goodman
Joseph S. Fosegan

Contents

Part 1
Introduction to Records Control

The Shaw – Walker Co.

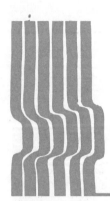

CHAPTER 1

A Preview of Records Control

Section 1 The Importance of Records Control

I can't find it!

"I can't find it! I know it's here . . . somewhere!" Who said that? A cook looking for a favorite recipe? A mechanic looking for a tool in the garage? A taxpayer looking for a receipted bill? Perhaps it is you looking for your favorite record album in a heap of records. Or is it a business executive looking for a letter, a report, or a statement of how much George Andrews owes? "I can't find it! I know it's here . . . somewhere!" Who said that? Just about *everybody* at one time or another.

At work, disorder is a CO$TLY matter.

Although we may tolerate a good deal of disorder in our personal lives, we are often annoyed at the time and energy wasted in looking for misplaced items. At work, disorder is another matter—a CO$TLY matter. A bank may handle 500,000 or more depositor cards. An airfreight line may generate 150,000 freight documents *a month*. An insurance company may handle over *a million* policies. Even a *small* hospital may

Get a Head Start on a Career in Records Control

2

maintain medical histories on 5,000 or more patient admissions a year. A staggering number of records, wouldn't you say? The offices in these organizations are responsible for maintaining and handling these important records so they are not lost, misplaced, or accidentally destroyed. Any disorder in handling these records would be costly, if not disastrous—costly in terms of the time spent in search of a misplaced record, and perhaps disastrous if any records are lost or accidentally destroyed.

Many different kinds of records are kept.

Equally amazing are the different kinds of records kept by various companies. Letters and memos, blueprints and maps, reports, inventory and price lists, purchase orders, shipping receipts, newspapers and catalogs, sales and personnel records, and computer printouts are just some familiar types of office records. New office techniques and equipment have created new kinds of office records—the *paperless* records! Some of these paperless records include computer tapes, magnetic cards, floppy disks, diskettes, cassette tapes, microforms (film on which a printed page is photographed in miniature), and X-rays. Although these records are paperless, they must be held under control in filing systems. Illustration 1-1 shows how paperless records in the form of reels, tapes, cards, and disks are stored in filing systems.

Filing is the process of storing records for reference purposes.

The variety and quantity of information and records handled in an office will vary from one organization to another. Common to all organizations, however, is the need to *store* and *protect* these records and to *find* them when they are needed. *Filing* is defined as the process of storing many kinds of records for present and future reference purposes. *Records control* is defined as the *procedures and systems* used to make filing a reliable and systematic process.

Filed information can be found quickly and easily when it is classified or arranged in an orderly manner. Remember the last time you used the telephone directory? Without realizing it, perhaps, you made use of filing principles to find the information you needed. Telephone numbers are presented in the *alphabetic* listing of subscribers' names. Businesses and services that advertise in the classified directory (Yellow Pages) are grouped *alphabetically* by occupation or subject. The area code numbers are listed in an *alphabetic* arrangement by state and city. So you see, you are already familiar with *alphabetic* indexing, the most frequently used filing classification in an office.

Section 2 Career Opportunities in Records Control

The extent of records control work that is performed in business, industry, government, and professional offices is surprisingly great. In some organizations, records are controlled in a large *centralized* filing department by a full-time files supervisor and staff. The staff includes

TAB Products Company

a. DATA MEDIA Cabinet

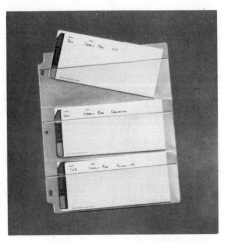

C-Line Products, Inc.

b. Magnetic Tab Card Holder

Ring King Visibles, Inc.

d. Diskette Rotary File

C-Line Products, Inc.

c. Floppy Disk Holder

illus. 1-1, Paperless Records Stored in Filing Systems

trained personnel in such jobs as records supervisors, code clerks, files operators, records assistants, records librarians, and clerical workers in methods analysis.

Over 90 percent of all office workers do some filing work.

In other organizations, *departmental* files staffed by records personnel are maintained in various offices and departments. Also, secretaries, stenographers, bookkeepers, and general office workers all do some filing work and are a part of the overall records control system in the organization. Many office employees whose work is related to electronic data processing and microfilming are directly involved in indexing and filing the records that are produced in their departments. In fact, studies show that filing and records control ranks in the top 10 percent of all office activities and that over *90 percent of all office workers do some filing work.*

There are a variety of career opportunities in records management.

The field of records control is an expanding area. As more records are produced, more jobs are opened to qualified, well-trained people. A knowledge of filing may be a key factor in obtaining an office job or advancing in a job you already have. The person who recognizes the importance of the filing function and chooses to study the field further may enjoy a variety of career opportunities in records management. The *Dictionary of Occupational Titles*, published by the U.S. Department of Labor, lists over 160 jobs that relate to records and records control. These titles range from clerical to managerial.

Although salaries for records managers may range from $15,000 to $40,000, those who seek records management positions must possess more than a desire for a good salary. Records managers are highly trained professionals who are familiar with all filing systems, equipment, and procedures. They keep up to date on all new developments in the field of records management and control. They are responsible for training files operators to be accurate, neat, and orderly in their work. Records managers must convey enthusiasm and interest in this important office function. More than anything, they must appreciate and understand the need for order.

This textbook is about order in records control and how to create it. This textbook is for those who have experienced delight and satisfaction in exclaiming "Eureka! I found it!"

Section 3 Understanding Records Control

As a student of records control, you undoubtedly expect to do filing work someday. In order to establish or maintain a filing system, you will want to be familiar with the following aspects of records control:

Systems of Filing
Equipment and Supplies
Controls for Maintaining Order in the Filing System
Receiving, Retrieving, Releasing, and Returning File Materials
Efficiency and Economy Controls
Transfer and/or Disposal of Inactive Materials

The SECRET of filing.

The "SECRET" of filing lies in understanding each of these important areas. *Systems of Filing* and *Equipment and Supplies* are essential to establish the file. *Controls* are necessary to maintain order in any filing system. Following is a preview of these three major topics that you will study in this course.

Systems of Filing

The term *filing system* refers to the orderly or systematic arrangement of office records in suitable containers so that information can be found quickly and easily. Office records are most commonly classified by alphabet or by number. You will study alphabetic and numeric filing systems, as well as systems organized around geographic names and subject titles. You will learn how these filing systems contribute to the information storage and retrieval (finding) needs of an organization.

Equipment and Supplies

The kinds of filing equipment and supplies that are needed to maintain a filing system are many and varied. This is true because business operations differ from one company to another. Records systems must be geared to the needs of each company. Office layout and design, the kinds and volume of records kept, and an ever-increasing concern for reducing filing costs all affect the filing equipment and supplies to be used. You will want to become familiar with some of the equipment and supplies that support the filing system.

Filing equipment and supplies are many and varied.

The vertical file cabinet is still the most common piece of filing equipment in the office. However, the traditional manila file folders in the familiar file drawers are making way for a new look: colored folders (sometimes plastic, reusable folders) on open shelves. (See Illustration 1-2.)

Available to protect and hold the paperless records created by computers, power typewriters, and microform printers are: filing cabinets, fan-styled albums, pocket folders and binders, rotary stands, and divided tray files. (See Illustration 1-3, page 8.)

"Spin your files, not your heels," claim manufacturers of the power files. Mechanical filing equipment comes in a variety of shapes and sizes: revolving tubs, wheel files, oval track rotating shelves, and movable aisle files (yes, movable aisles!). Illustration 1-4, page 9, shows several designs of mechanical filing that have brightened and lightened the lives of records people.

Vertical File

Open-Shelf File

Shaw-Walker

illus. 1-2, Types of Files

**Controlling
the Filing
System**

A filing system, no matter how carefully planned and set up, is only as good as the people who use it. The files need controls, and the files users need to follow the control procedures in order to make the best use of the filing system. The usefulness and the completeness of the filing system are assured when these controls are consistently and strictly applied. The three controls that you will study are:

*Files users need
to follow control
procedures to
make the best
use of the filing
system.*

1. how materials are processed as they enter, leave, and finally return to the system.
2. how efficiency/economy controls affect system changes.
3. how inactive materials are removed from the system.

Receiving, Retrieving, Releasing, and Returning File Materials.
Receiving and preparing records to be placed in the filing system is the first step in the control process. Once materials have been received for filing, the files operator must determine *where* they are to be placed in the file. For example, the filing department receives for filing a letter from Logan C. Horton, of Astroline of New York, inviting your company to participate in a business show sponsored by the Business and Commerce Association of Greater New York. Where would that communication be filed? Under H for Logan C. Horton? Under A for Astroline of New York? B for Business and Commerce Association of Greater New York? Or B for Business Show? It is much like looking in a cookbook for Applesauce Loaf. Will you find it under A for Applesauce? L for Loaf? Or

*Where to place
materials in the
file is the impor-
tant beginning
of the control
process.*

a. Magnetic Card Easel Binder

b. Diskette Desk Stand

Ring King Visibles, Inc.

Ring King Visibles, Inc.

d. Floppy Disk Binder

C-Line Products, Inc.

c. Microfiche Rotary Stand

Ring King Visibles, Inc.

e. Fiche Finder

Ring King Visibles, Inc.

illus. 1-3, Filing Equipment for Paperless Records

KARDEX Systems, Inc.

KARDEX Systems, Inc.

*White Power Files, Inc.,
Union, New Jersey*

illus. 1-4, Mechanical Filing Equipment

C̲ for C̲ake? Where to place materials in the file is the important beginning of the control process.

How filed materials will be retrieved from the file, how they will be released (checked out) to the person or department needing them, and how they will be returned to the file are other procedures included in your study of controlling office records. Where were the records originally filed? Where are the released materials now? How long have the materials been gone from the file? Have the records been returned to the file? These are questions the files operator must be able to answer. Rather like being a detective, isn't it? Or maybe more like being a guard, because the movement of information in and out of the files must be carefully *guarded*.

The movement of information in and out of the files must be carefully guarded.

Placing materials in the files, retrieving them for further use, and following up to assure their safe return to storage are three closely related control functions. Each is dependent on the successful handling of the other. Neglect in any one of these control areas will soon break down a filing system, and the system will slowly become useless to the organization.

An Efficiency/ Economy ratio is a helpful tool.

Efficiency and Economy Controls. An Efficiency/Economy ratio (E/E) is a helpful tool when considering changes in a filing system. Basically, the ratio shows the benefits of a possible change divided by the cost of providing the change. The outcome must be greater than 1. The formula looks like this:

$$\frac{\text{Efficiency (Benefits)}}{\text{Economy (Cost)}} = \text{Greater than 1}$$

For example, you may suggest the purchase of a simple desk rotary-wheel file that costs $50. If the wheel file saves you just 12 minutes throughout a day, the file will save you 1 hour each week. If you are paid $3 an hour, using the file for only 1 year can save your company $150 (50 hours × $3 per hour = $150). The formula looks like this:

$$\frac{\text{Benefits: Labor saved in using equipment}}{\text{Cost: Price of equipment}} = \frac{\$150}{\$\ 50} = 3 \text{ (greater than 1)}$$

In the foregoing example, the investment looks like a good one. The company saved $150 while spending only $50. The wheel file pays for itself in less than one year, and the company continues to benefit from its use long after it is paid for. The Efficiency/Economy ratio shows what a company receives in return for money it has spent. Who can argue with that? If a firm did not get back more money than it invested, it could not pay your salary.

A filing system becomes either more efficient or less efficient.

The files operator who is aware of the benefit/cost factor better understands the rapid changes taking place in filing and records control. Remember, a filing system becomes either *more* efficient or *less* efficient. The system cannot remain the same when change is taking place all around it. Wages and other operating expenses are soaring. New equipment becomes available. More information is needed to operate the business. And top speed is required in handling the information. "I need it yesterday!" might be a common exclamation from a busy executive. The filing system must meet the growing demands placed on it.

Increase efficiency! Reduce costs!

Increase efficiency! Reduce costs! If you understand these goals, you will remain adaptable and flexible. You will be prepared for change. You will be able to evaluate, explore, and recommend changes. For example, what steps can your organization take to minimize or eliminate the cost of misfiled or lost records? What new procedures or equipment will your organization consider in order to streamline its retrieval (finding) process? What can be done to reduce time and fatigue in the filing process? How can the misuse of valuable office storage space be minimized? To what extent can your organization afford the installation of power files or mechanical retrieval systems? microform records? computers? A knowledge of the E/E ratio provides you with a realistic approach to your study of filing. You will not study *just* equipment and supplies, or *just* filing controls, or *just* space requirements for stored records. You will study each part in terms of how that part will increase the efficiency and reduce the cost of the total filing system. An awareness of efficiency/economy control will make you a vital part of an information system in a rapidly changing environment.

Transfer and/or Disposal of Inactive Materials. Records are classified as *vital, important,* or *useful* according to their importance to the company. Records that are essential in order for the company to survive are the *vital* records. Vital records, such as patents, formulas, legal papers, or corporate documents, must be kept in fire-resistant and waterproof storage areas. Accounts receivable records (how much customers owe) could not be replaced. If these records were destroyed, a company might not be able to survive the loss. Some organizations store their vital records safely with commercial storage companies located in underground caves and abandoned mines.

Most office records are *important* and *useful* to an organization for a certain period of time only. Some, however, may have to be kept, even though the records are seldom used. The organization itself usually determines when records have outlived their usefulness. However, in some instances, state or federal government regulations will determine how long records must be retained.

A retention-destruction schedule should be established for every type of record.

A *retention-destruction schedule* should be established for every type of record in a filing system. The retention-destruction schedule lists all kinds of records kept, where they should be kept, the length of time they must be saved, and when they should be destroyed. You will learn the methods of removing inactive (no longer used) materials and semiactive (sometimes used) materials from the active files. Too many offices ignore this transfer, or disposition, control. A file jammed with useless information costs a company time and money. Valuable office space is used to store useless records, and time is wasted plowing through these records to find what is needed. Attention to this "housekeeping" function will enable the other filing functions to operate at top efficiency.

"I can't find it! I know it's here . . . somewhere!" Who said that? When you complete your study of *Business Records Control*, that person won't be YOU!

Questions for Discussion

1. Why is disorder in handling records a costly matter?

2. What are some of the kinds of records kept in business, at home, and at school?

3. What are paperless records?

4. What is filing?

5. Can filing lead to a high-paying career?

6. What is the SECRET of filing?

7. What is a filing system?

8. What are three kinds of filing equipment that you have seen or used?

9. What is the first task in controlling filed materials?

10. How is the Efficiency/Economy ratio used in records control?

11. Why is transfer or disposal control a necessary and important control function?

12. What is a retention-destruction schedule?

Part 2
Alphabetic Indexing

The Shaw – Walker Co.

CHAPTER 2

Alphabetic Card Filing and Indexing

Section 1 Alphabetic Card Filing

Alphabetic card filing is a basic filing method in which cards are arranged according to alphabetic order and are placed in a container. An *alphabetic card filing system* consists of a file tray or box or cabinet in which are kept, in alphabetic order, cards showing information of various kinds. The information may be names and addresses of persons or businesses, book titles, types of supplies, or many other items.

Alphabetic card filing is one of the simplest filing systems. It has many uses in both business and personal filing situations. For these reasons, we shall begin our study of business records control with alphabetic card filing.

Uses of Alphabetic Card Filing
Almost all of us have used an alphabetic card file. For example, when you go to the library to find a book to read, you can save time by using the "card catalog." The card catalog is just an alphabetic card file that tells you if your library has the book you want and where the book is stored. You can then quickly find the right book among the thousands of other books stored on the library shelves. (See Illustration 2-1.)

Many other people use card files to keep information available for quick and easy reference. A few of these users and some of the types of information they keep are:

1. Secretaries: The names, addresses, and occupations of all frequent office callers. One card may contain the name of the caller, the name of the company represented, the time of the usual call, and the length of time spent in the office.
2. Office supervisors: The names of potential employees and their addresses, telephone numbers, and special abilities.
3. Stenographers: The names and addresses of frequent correspondents.
4. Typists: The names and addresses of persons who receive copies of company reports.
5. Club secretaries and treasurers: The name, address, and dues-payment status of each member of the organization.

Ohio National Life Insurance Company

illus. 2-1, Card File

A card file may be based on an alphabetic, geographic, numeric, or subject system. Card files ordinarily are used to store current records, but they may be used also to store seldom-used or less up-to-date records.

6. People at home: The names and addresses on a holiday card list, dates of birthdays, a tool list, and a household goods inventory.
7. Salespeople: The names and addresses of potential clients for the products they sell.
8. Supply clerks: The names and addresses of suppliers of various office items and the names and addresses of machine repairers and other service suppliers.

Alphabetic Card Filing System

Cards. The cards in a card file are usually 5 inches wide by 3 inches high (5″ x 3″). Other standard sizes are 6″ by 4″ and 8″ x 5″. These cards are usually white, but they may be of different colors in order to help find the right one more rapidly. The cards may or may not be ruled. If the information to be placed on the card is to be handwritten, the cards may be ruled because the horizontal lines make it easier to write in a straight line and in the same place on each card. If the information is to be typed on the cards, the typist may find it easier not to have to follow a ruled line, so unlined cards are often used. When the cards are not ruled, the typist begins to type on the third line from the top of the card. The left margin is 3 or 4 spaces wide. This arrangement makes it easier to file as well as to find the desired card. (See Illustration 2-2.)

Guides. *Guides* are special cards or partitions that divide the file drawer into convenient alphabetic sections. The guides are usually made of material heavier than that of the cards so that they will help support the cards and also withstand the long use given them. (See Illustration 2-3.)

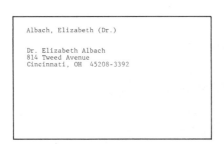

illus. 2-2, File Card

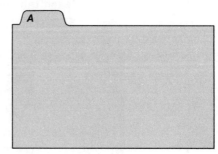

illus. 2-3, Card Guide

Tabs. A *tab* is a projection at the top of a guide. The tabs enable a person to see the guides above the other materials in the file. The tabs may be made of the same material as the guides, may be made of plastic, or may be made of metal with a plastic "window" through which information on the tabs can be read. Some tabs are bent slightly backward so that they can be read easily when the files operator is looking down on the drawer.

Captions. *Captions* are titles or alphabetic divisions of the file that are written, typed, or printed on the tabs of card guides.

Illustration 2-4 shows a caption (A   1) on the tab. The illustration also shows the tabs on two other card guides to be used farther back in the file drawer. In this illustration the tabs are cut one third the width of the guides with each tab the same size. Tabs of this width are called *third-cut tabs*. They vary in position at the top of the guides so that they are staggered across the file drawer from left to right. In this way three different positions are provided. This staggering of position enables the files operator to read the captions more easily.

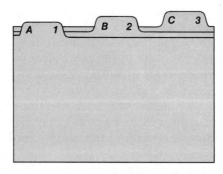

illus. 2-4, Third-Cut Card Guides

It is possible to obtain guides with tabs cut in different positions. The most common, in addition to third-cut, are *fifth-cut* (five tab positions), *half-cut* (two tab positions, each one half the width of the guide), or *full-cut* (each tab covering the entire width of the guide).

Numbers are sometimes included in the captions to indicate the order for placing guides in the file drawer.

Organization. Cards are placed in a file tray, box, or drawer so that the names are arranged in alphabetic order from front to back. Illustration 2-5 shows a drawer from a card file cabinet. In studying the illustration, notice the use of the guides with third-cut tabs on which names are printed as captions and fifth-cut tabs on which letters of the alphabet are printed as captions.

Shaw-Walker

illus. 2-5, Alphabetic Card File

The guides (*Med* to *My*) that appear in a row at the left are called *primary guides* and indicate the principal alphabetic sections into which the drawer is divided.

The guides *(Medina, Miller,* and *Moreno)* that appear in a row at the center are called *auxiliary* or *secondary guides*. They divide the principal alphabetic sections into subsections according to frequently used last names.

The guides appearing in a row at the right are *special auxiliary guides* that divide a single surname section into subsections according to the initial letters of the first names. An "End" or "Stop" guide is used to show the end of a subsection. Notice the alphabetic guides *E, G, J, M, R,* and *W* after *Miller* and the END guide following the last card after the special auxiliary guide *W* in Illustration 2-5.

The cards are placed behind the appropriate identifying guides. The captions on two consecutive guides indicate the alphabetic range of the names to be filed between the two guides. In Illustration 2-5, for example, the first guide is captioned *Med* and the second, *Medina*. Thus, cards bearing names from *Med* through *Medina* would be filed behind the first and second guides in this file drawer. The special section for *Medina* would stop at the "END" guide. The *Med* section would continue with such a name as *Medinger*. A card bearing the name *Meyer* would be found between the guides labeled *Mey* and *Mic*.

For guides to be effective in an active file, one guide should be provided for about every 20 cards. For a less active file, one guide should be provided for about every half inch or inch of cards.

To aid in locating the correct file drawer, a *drawer label* is placed on the outside front of the drawer. In Illustration 2-5, this label reads *Med-My*, which tells the files operator that the cards in this drawer range from those bearing last names beginning with the letters *Med* to those cards bearing names beginning with *My*.

Purpose of Filing Rules

If cards in an alphabetic card file are to be filed quickly and found easily, definite rules must be followed when the files operator is determining the order in which materials are to be filed. These rules are known as the *rules for alphabetic indexing*. The same rules are used in filing correspondence or other materials in alphabetic files. Four of these rules are presented in Section 2 of this chapter. The rest of the rules are given in Chapters 3 and 4.

Section 2 Alphabetic Indexing of Personal and Business Names

Need for Procedures and Rules

The purpose of filing is to be able to store your records so that they can be found immediately and easily whenever they are needed. Imagine, in an emergency, trying to find the telephone number of your family doctor in a telephone directory that has no logical arrangement of names. Some large city directories have almost two thousand pages of names in small print. Even small city telephone directories have many pages of names. It would be almost impossible to locate the information you needed unless the directory followed a consistent, planned system of listing that you knew how to use. Business and personal lists and files would also be difficult to use unless materials were stored in a planned, organized manner that was known by everyone using them. In order to have such a planned system of filing and finding records, it is necessary to use indexing rules.

Indexing Rules

Indexing rules are the commonly accepted rules that are followed in alphabetic filing systems so that a filed record may be located quickly and easily when it is needed. They can generally be explained in this manner: to "index" is to point out. Your "index" finger is aptly named since it is the one that "points out." In much the same manner, you will learn to file by using indexing rules so that each name under which something is to be filed will be "pointed out" because you have applied a rule to it. Thus, each indexed name will have a special place in the file that will make it distinct from all other names in the same filing system. So, when a record is requested from the file, you will be able to find it without undue delay.

The most commonly used indexing rules are presented in this chapter as well as in Chapters 3 and 4. Although these rules are followed by many businesses, others may change some of the rules to fit their own unique filing requirements. A good records control program, however, requires that once the indexing rules are adopted, they must be followed consistently by everyone using the files.

Indexing Names for Filing Purposes

The process of indexing is made up of two steps: (1) dividing names into units and (2) alphabetizing names. Since a name must be divided into units before it can be placed in alphabetic order, this procedure will be considered first in the explanation of indexing practice.

Dividing Names into Units. Two steps must be taken before a name can be placed in alphabetic order in relation to other names. First, the files operator must notice how many units a name contains and, second, the operator must determine which of the several units is the most important one to be used for filing purposes. This unit is the *key unit*.

An example of this process is as follows: If the name "Mary Miller" is to be indexed for filing, the operator would first notice that the name has two units—"Mary" and "Miller." Next, it must be determined which of these two units is the key unit—the one under which this name will be filed first. In this case, the key unit is the surname, "Miller." The operator would mark it or rewrite it to point it out as the key unit.

If the name is to be rewritten on an index card, for example, the name will be written in this order—Miller, Mary. The card on which this name appears would be filed in the "M" section of the card filing system being used. If the name appears in a letter, on a printed or typed page, or as a signature, the name is not rewritten but is *coded* to show the key unit and the second unit. *Coding* (marking of the units in a name) consists of (1) separating the units by diagonal lines, (2) underlining the key unit, and (3) writing numbers above the remaining units to indicate their rank in the filing order:

2
Mary/ <u>Miller</u>

This code marking indicates that the name is to be filed under the key unit, "Miller," and that the given name, "Mary," is to be used secondarily if it is needed in order to place the name in alphabetic order in relation to other names on cards or papers in the file.

Alphabetizing. If you wish to file alphabetically the two names "Sue Abbott" and "Sam Barden," your procedure would be as follows:

1. Notice that "Sue Abbott" is a two-unit name and determine that "Abbott" is the key unit.
2. Notice that "Sam Barden" is a two-unit name and determine that "Barden" is the key unit.
3. Compare the key units in the two names.
4. File the name "Sue Abbott" before the name "Sam Barden" because "A" comes before "B" in the alphabet.

The following tabulation illustrates the indexing of the two names:

Names	Index Order of Units	
	Key Unit	**Unit 2**
Sue Abbott	<u>A</u>bbott	Sue
Sam Barden	<u>B</u>arden	Sam

How to Study Indexing Rules

The manner in which you study the indexing rules in Chapters 2, 3, and 4 is very important. First, read a rule twice to be sure that you understand it. Second, study all the names in the list below the rule. Finally, restudy the names in the list, comparing each name with the names above and below it. In this way, you will discover the reason for the order of a name in an alphabetically arranged list of names. You will know this because you will have found the unit or letter in a name that fixes its position above or below other names in a list. This last step is very important because the comparison of the names in the list shows how the rules are applied even when names vary from a standard pattern. *Names are sometimes so complex and varied that scores of rules could not cover every possible way of indexing all types of names.*

Therefore, example names are sometimes presented in a manner designed to show many ways of applying a single rule.

Rule 1   Order of Indexing Units

Business names as well as names of institutions and organizations usually are indexed as they appear in written form unless they start with two or more units of a personal name. A personal name is indexed in this manner: (1) the surname is the key unit; (2) the given name or initial is the second unit; (3) the middle name or initial is the third unit.

Why Rule 1 Is Needed. Personal names must be indexed by considering surnames as key units because last names are the ones commonly used first for identification. If surnames were not considered first, individual names would not be grouped under family names and would not be easy to locate. Names of businesses, institutions, and organizations *usually* are referred to by the first word in the name, and this word is the key unit. Exceptions to this rule are given in Rules 2 and 10.

Examples of Rule 1.

	Names	Index Order of Units in Names		
		Key Unit	**Unit 2**	**Unit 3**
1.	Antonia L. Cardona	Cardona	Antonia	L.
2.	Cardona Discount Stores	Cardona	Discount	Stores
3.	Thomas J. Carlson	Carlson	Thomas	J.
4.	Thomas James Carlson	Carlson	Thomas	James
5.	Chicago National Bank	Chicago	National	Bank
6.	Christian Church	Christian	Church	
7.	Jane Christie Appliances	Christie	Jane	Appliances
8.	Clayton High School	Clayton	High	School
9.	Clayton Hotel	Clayton	Hotel	
10.	Clayton News Press	Clayton	News	Press
11.	George Clinton School	Clinton	George	School
12.	Computer Dealer Magazine	Computer	Dealer	Magazine
13.	Credit Managers Association	Credit	Managers	Association
14.	CRYOVAC Corporation	Cryovac	Corporation	
15.	Crystal Plastics Company	Crystal	Plastics	Company

Note: In each example in the list given above, the letter of the unit that determines the alphabetic sequence is underlined. This practice will be used in illustrations of each of the rules.

Rule 2   Minor Words in Business Names

Such minor words as *and, the, of, by, to,* and *for* do not add meaning to a business name and are not used as indexing units. When such other words as *a, at, on,* or *in* appear as *meaningful first units* in names, they are used as key units.

> **Note:** Minor words disregarded as units may be enclosed in parentheses to avoid confusing them with units considered in indexing.

Why Rule 2 Is Needed. Unless this rule is used, when papers are being coded for filing purposes, papers bearing similar names might be coded in differing ways. For example, when coding the name "The Inside Lounge," one person might use the word "The" as the key unit while another person might use the word "Inside" because it is considered by that person to be the most important word. The use of Rule 2 helps prevent this from happening.

Examples of Rule 2.

	Names	Key Unit	Unit 2	Unit 3	Unit 4
			Index Order of Units in Names		
1.	Aaron and Egan Attorneys	Aaron (and)	Egan	Attorneys	
2.	The Abbey Motel	Abbey	Motel (The)		
3.	Akita and Kato Importers	Akita (and)	Kato	Importers	
4.	Arnold on the Mall	Arnold (on the)	Mall		
5.	At Home Motel	At	Home	Motel	
6.	In Town Auto Repair	In	Town	Auto	Repair
7.	The Inside Lounge	Inside	Lounge (The)		
8.	Inside and Outside Paint Company	Inside (and)	Outside	Paint	Company
9.	Northwoods Auto & Boat Storage	Northwoods	Auto (&)	Boat	Storage
10.	Northwoods at the Boat Service	Northwoods (at the)	Boat	Service	

Rule 3 Single Letters and Abbreviations

Single letters (with or without hyphens and with or without spacing between them) in business names, and initials in personal names, are treated as separate indexing units. Abbreviations of commonly known words (*Co.* and *Inc.*) and abbreviations of personal names (*Wm., Jos., Thos.*) are considered to be written in full. Brief personal names (*Liz, Jon, Rod*) are used as they are spelled.

Why Rule 3 Is Needed. When a nickname or a brief personal name is to be coded for filing, the change to an assumed different form of the name should not be made. For example, the name "Kate" may be a nickname for "Katherine" or "Kathleen," or it may be the person's full name. To assume that it is Katherine may be incorrect, and the material filed could be misplaced. In the case of abbreviations, only a very few words are accepted as being universally known. For example, the abbreviation "AMA" could stand for American Medical Association, American Marketing Association, or merely a convenient series of letters. On the other hand, some abbreviations are distinctive and well known and should be coded as if written in full. For example, *Pres.* for *President, N.Y.* for *New York, St.* for *Street, Sat.* for *Saturday,* and *N.E.* for *Northeast.*

Examples of Rule 3.

Names		Index Order of Units in Names			
	Key Unit	Unit 2	Unit 3	Unit 4	Unit 5
1. JAL, Inc.	J	A	L	Incorporated	
2. J-S Markets	J-	S	Markets		
3. J & U Electronics, Inc.	J (&)	U	Electronics	Incorporated	
4. Juanita Apartments	Juanita	Apartments			
5. John Jukowicz	Jukowicz	John			
6. Jon Jukowicz	Jukowicz	Jon			
*7. KLM-TV	K	L	M	Television	Station
8. K-Mart Stores	K-	Mart	Stores		
*9. KNX Radio Station	K	N	X	Radio	Station
10. Al Kahn	Kahn	Al			

* A company doing business with several radio or television stations might index these names first by the title *Radio Station* or *Television Station*, then by the call letters.

Rule 4   Possessives

When "apostrophe s" ('s) is added to a name to form a possessive (as in "Johnson's"), the added "s" is not considered in alphabetizing. When the ending is "s apostrophe" (s'), the "s" is considered part of the word.

Why Rule 4 Is Needed. If the "s" were considered a part of the name, the key word, "Johnson('s)," would be separated in the file from names of other persons or businesses bearing the same name, "Johnson," thus making retrieval difficult.

Examples of Rule 4.

Names		Index Order of Units in Names		
	Key Unit	Unit 2	Unit 3	Unit 4
1. Bank's Portable Coaches	Bank('s)	Portable	Coaches	
2. Sam A. Bank	Bank	Sam	A.	
3. Bank's Window Washing Co.	Bank('s)	Window	Washing	Company

(continued on page 24)

Names	Index Order of Units in Names			
	Key Unit	**Unit 2**	**Unit 3**	**Unit 4**
4. Bankers Book Printers, Inc.	Bankers	Book	Printers	Incorporated
5. C. Joseph Bankhead	Bankhead	C.	Joseph	
6. Arnold M. Banks	Banks	Arnold	M.	
7. Banks' Dump Trucks	Banks'	Dump	Trucks	
8. George R. Banks	Banks	George	R.	
9. Banks & Georgi	Banks (&)	Georgi		
10. Barb & Betty's Diner	Barb (&)	Betty('s)	Diner	
11. Bauer's Furniture Mart	Bauer('s)	Furniture	Mart	
12. Geo. C. Bauer	Bauer	George	C.	
13. Sarah A. Bauer Company	Bauer	Sarah	A.	Company
14. Bauers' Bathing Suits	Bauers'	Bathing	Suits	

Typing Index Cards

The rules you have just studied and those you will be studying are illustrated by lists of names, but in actual filing, such names usually are typed on index cards or on folder labels. Since your first filing job will involve the use of index cards, the following explanation and illustration will show how index cards are prepared and arranged.

As shown in Illustration 2-6, an index card includes (1) the name typed or written in indexed form on the second or third line from the top edge of the card and 3 or 4 spaces from the left edge and (2) the name and address typed or written 3 or 4 lines below the name. Carefully read each card in Illustration 2-6. Observe how names and titles are typed and how they are spaced on cards. This arrangement looks neater and makes it easier to file as well as to find the desired card.

Either all capital letters or capital and lowercase letters may be used for the name. Some records supervisors prefer to have the first indexing unit typed in all capital letters and the other indexing units typed in capital and lowercase letters.

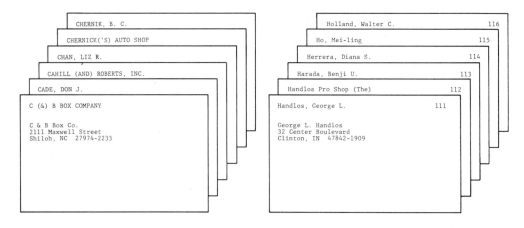

illus. 2-6, File Cards Typed in Index Form

If the name contains a minor word or words, such as "and" or "the," which are to be disregarded in filing, type the minor word or words in parentheses. If a minor word such as "The" is the first word of a name, type it in parentheses at the end of the name.

If the file card is to be filed according to a numeric system, the name is given a code number. The code number is then typed in the upper right-hand corner of the file card. (See Illustration 2-6.)

Questions for Discussion

1. What is an alphabetic card filing system?

2. What are some of the types of information kept in an alphabetic card file by (a) a secretary? (b) an office supervisor? (c) a stenographer? (d) a typist? (e) a club secretary? (f) a person at home? (g) a salesperson? (h) a supply clerk?

3. What types of cards are usually used in a card file?

4. What is a guide? a tab? a caption?

5. What is a third-cut tab?

6. What are the most common cuts for tabs?

7. In what order are cards placed in a file tray of an alphabetic card file?

8. How close together should guides be placed in an alphabetic card file?

9. What is a drawer label on an alphabetic card file?

10. Why are filing rules necessary?

11. Why is it necessary to use a planned system of filing?

12. What does the term "indexing" mean?

13. How does the indexing of names help filing and finding?

14. What are the two steps in the indexing process?

15. As an example, divide your name into units. What is the key unit in your name?

16. If names are not rewritten in transposed form, how are the units in these names marked (coded) for filing purposes?

17. How is alphabetic order determined between two names?

18. When would it probably be better to index broadcast stations under the key units of "Radio Station" or "Television Station" than alphabetically by call letters?

19. What is the key unit in each of the following names?

a. Alma Lois Curran
b. Curran Industries, Inc.
c. John Dix Corporation
d. Drost and Hamilton Architects
e. The Sunshine Resorts
f. Jon C. Ellis
g. St. John's Taxi Service
h. At Home Rug Cleaners
i. PDQ Pizza
j. Wm. Torres Furniture

20. What are the second units of the names in question 19?

21. Is the alphabetic order of the two names in each of the following pairs correct?

a. Jane R. Brick
    Fire Brick Engineers
b. George A. Vendor
    G & A Vendors, Inc.
c. Wilma C. Hands
    Wm. J. Hands
d. B. Charlotte Hoye
    The Hoye Barber Supply Company
e. Sims' Custom Cleaners
    R. P. Sims
f. Point of View Paints
    Point's View Cabins
g. Jos. Sax
    Joseph A. Saxe
h. Charles A. Pike
    Charlene J. Pike
i. The Olsen Realty Co.
    Olson's Real Fruit Pies
j. One Hour Cleaners
    One Hour Muffler Service

22. What is the correct order in which each of the names within the following groups of three would be arranged in an alphabetic file? Indicate the order by writing on a separate sheet of paper the numbers representing the correct order. For example, the first problem would be arranged with (2) first, then (1), then (3). Your answer sheet for question (a) will be marked 2 1 3.

a. (1) Melvin E. Meyer (2) Cathy J. Meyer (3) Meyer's Milk Bar
b. (1) Lang and Lang Builders (2) L. B. Lang (3) Alice Lange
c. (1) Enami Auto Imports (2) The Enami Photo Shop (3) Mary S. Enami
d. (1) Jos. Johnson (2) J. A. Johnson (3) Joe L. Johnsen
e. (1) The By Pass Motel (2) Theresa V. Bye (3) Byer's Dress Boutique
f. (1) Lifetime Fences (2) The Fence Builders (3) Mario A. Fence
g. (1) ABC Heating Co. (2) A-B Cleaners (3) A. B. Cardona
h. (1) Donald M. Caine (2) Doris L. Cain (3) David J. Cane
i. (1) Turks Auto Repair (2) Jos. P. Turk (3) Turk's Dance Studio
j. (1) David's Scenic Tours (2) David C. Brown (3) David J. Brown

Job 1   Card Filing

At this time complete Job 1 in OFFICE FILING PROCEDURES, Fifth Edition. The instructions and supplies for this job and the following jobs are included in the practice set.

CHAPTER 3

Alphabetic Indexing of Names with Unique Characteristics

Unique Characteristics of Names

In Chapter 2 you learned the order of indexing units in business and personal names so that you could file and find the names easily. In addition, you learned how to index minor words in business names, single letters in a name, abbreviations, and possessives. In this chapter you will learn how to index several types of unique names. These will include names with such titles as Reverend, Doctor, and Senator. Names of married women and names with articles and particles will also be studied. Identical names, including those with such seniority titles as Jr., Sr., II, and III, and numbers in names will also be considered.

The more complex a name is, the more difficult it is to index the name and the more necessary it is to use definite indexing rules. As you study this chapter, follow the same study procedure suggested in Chapter 2: Read a rule twice. Study the list of examples. Then restudy the examples in detail, comparing each name with the names above and below it.

Patient Information Is Close at Hand when Records Are Properly Filed

Rule 5   Titles

A title in a business name is considered to be an indexing unit. A title used with a personal name is not considered to be an indexing unit unless it is used with only one name (*Brother John*). The units in such a name are indexed in the order in which they are written.

Note 1: A title or degree not considered in indexing is written in parentheses at the end of the name for identification purposes.

Note 2: When the titles *Mr., Mrs., Miss,* and *Ms.* are used in business names, they are indexed as written. Other titles, such as *Dr.* and *Prof.,* are indexed as if they were spelled in full.

Why Rule 5 Is Needed. In the case of personal names, titles change frequently as a person's education, job, or marital status changes. For example, a senator holding political office may use the title "Senator" while in office but not afterwards. Or a minister may sometimes write to a company using the title "Reverend" but on other occasions may omit the title. If only the name is considered and the title is not used as an indexing unit, all correspondence with the same person will be filed in the same place.

In the case of titles in business names, the titles do not change and the use of the titles as indexing units helps to separate the personal correspondence from the business correspondence in the files.

Strict use of Rule 5 will insure that both personal and business correspondence are filed in the proper locations consistently for easy and accurate retrieval.

Examples of Rule 5.

	Names	Index Order or Units in Names			
		Key Unit	**Unit 2**	**Unit 3**	**Unit 4**
1.	Brother John	Brother	John		
2.	C. Lewis Brothers	Brothers	C.	Lewis	
3.	Judge Gordon E. Docter	Docter	Gordon	E. (Judge)	
4.	Dr. Pepper Bottling Co.	Doctor	Pepper	Bottling	Company
5.	Doctor's Rest Home	Doctor('s)	Rest	Home	
6.	Brother Robert J. Fath	Fath	Robert	J. (Brother)	
7.	Father & Son Painters	Father (&)	Son	Painters	
8.	Senator Carlos G. Fernandez	Fernandez	Carlos	G. (Senator)	
9.	Dr. Carmen Fernandez	Fernandez	Carmen (Doctor)		
10.	Barbara L. Garcia, M.D.	Garcia	Barbara	L. (M.D.)	
11.	General Julian A. Garcia	Garcia	Julian	A. (General)	
12.	Rev. Renee J. Godo	Godo	Renee	J. (Reverend)	
13.	Professor David L. Mayer	Mayer	David	L. (Professor)	
14.	Everett S. Mayor, D.D.	Mayor	Everett	S. (D.D.)	
15.	Mister Oliver Imports	Mister	Oliver	Imports	

(continued on page 29)

Names	Index Order of Units in Names			
	Key Unit	**Unit 2**	**Unit 3**	**Unit 4**
16. Mr. James Hairdresser	Mr.	James	Hairdresser	
17. Mrs. Wedding Gowns	Mrs.	Wedding	Gowns	
18. Ms. Perfumes	Ms.	Perfumes		
19. Professor's Book Sales, Inc.	Professor('s)	Book	Sales	Incorporated
20. St. Charles Greeting Cards	Saint	Charles	Greeting	Cards
21. Sister Yvonne	Sister	Yvonne		

Rule 6 Married Women

A married woman's name is filed as she writes it. It is indexed according to Rule 1. The surname is the key unit; the given name or initial is the second unit; the middle name or initial is the third unit. If more than one form of a name is known, the alternate name may be cross-referenced, if necessary. (The cross-referencing procedure is explained in Chapter 4 on page 44.)

Why Rule 6 Is Needed. Some married women prefer to use their first name and their maiden surname with their husband's surname. Others use their first and middle names or initials with their husband's surname. Still others may prefer to use their husband's first name, initial, and surname. And some continue to use their maiden names after marriage for business or personal reasons. A woman's preference should be accepted. When more than one form of the person's name is used, and other forms are known, cross-referencing to the original form keeps all material for the same person together. Consistent use of this rule makes this possible.

Examples of Rule 6.

Names	Index Order of Units in Names		
	Key Unit	**Unit 2**	**Unit 3**
1. Mrs. Jane Larkin Miller * (Mrs. Kenneth T. Miller)	Miller	Jane	Larkin (Mrs.)
2. Mrs. Janet Sue Miller	Miller	Janet	Sue (Mrs.)
3. Mrs. Jason C. Miller	Miller	Jason	C. (Mrs.)
4. Mrs. Joan Wilson Miller * (Ms. Joan Wilson)	Miller	Joan	Wilson (Mrs.)
5. Ms. Judi Miller * (Mrs. Judi Miller Paxton) * (Mrs. Arthur Paxton)	Miller	Judi (Ms.)	

---

* These names should be used for cross-references (see page 44).

Rule 7   Articles and Particles

A foreign language article or a particle in a business or personal name is combined with the part of the name following it to form a single indexing unit. The indexing order is not affected by a space between a prefix and the rest of the name.

Note: Examples of articles and particles are *D', Da, De, Del, De la, Della, Den, Des, Di, Du, El, Fitz, L', La, Las, Le, Les, Lo, Los, M', Mac, Mc, O', Te, Ten, Ter, Van, Van de, Van der, Von, Von der.*

Why Rule 7 Is Needed. Foreign language articles and particles appear in many forms as prefixes to names. Sometimes there is a space in the prefix. Sometimes there is a space between the prefix and the rest of the word. Sometimes there are no spaces. In some cases, the first letter of one or more parts of the prefix is capitalized; sometimes not. This rule is necessary to insure that file materials concerning a certain name are all kept together regardless of how the article or particle is written.

Examples of Rule 7.

	Names	Key Unit	Unit 2	Unit 3	Unit 4
1.	Dr. August T. Damian	Damian	August	T. (Doctor)	
2.	Professor Maria D'Amico	D'Amico	Maria (Professor)		
3.	Damico Match Company	Damico	Match	Company	
4.	De La Camp Sports Wear	De La Camp	Sports	Wear	
5.	Delano Meat Market	Delano	Meat	Market	
6.	Miss Evelyn K. Della	Della	Evelyn	K. (Miss)	
7.	Oliver W. Della Maria, M.D.	Della Maria	Oliver	W. (M.D.)	
8.	Brother Joseph E. Dell'Armi	Dell'Armi	Joseph	E. (Brother)	
9.	Henry H. Fitzgerald	Fitzgerald	Henry	H.	
10.	Rev. Loretta C. FitzGerald	FitzGerald	Loretta	C. (Reverend)	
11.	LaSalle Interior Designers	LaSalle	Interior	Designers	
12.	La Salle Mfg. Representatives	La Salle	Manufacturing	Representatives	
13.	Mack's Corner Market	Mack('s)	Corner	Market	
14.	Mitchell D. Macks	Macks	Mitchell	D.	
15.	Dana Maclean Art Supplies	Maclean	Dana	Art	Supplies
16.	Donald S. MacLean	MacLean	Donald	S.	
17.	McLain Trucking Company	McLain	Trucking	Company	
18.	Obrien's Flowers	Obrien('s)	Flowers		
19.	W. J. O'Brien Engineering	O'Brien	W.	J.	Engineering
20.	Gerald Q. Van Den Berg, Ph.D.	Van Den Berg	Gerald	Q. (Ph.D.)	
21.	Vandenberg Hospital Supplies	Vandenberg	Hospital	Supplies	
22.	Vanden Berg Moving & Storage	Vanden Berg	Moving (&)	Storage	
23.	Van den Berg Office Supplies	Van den Berg	Office	Supplies	

Rule 8   Identical Names

When names of businesses, institutions, organizations, or persons are identical, addresses are used to determine filing order. Cities, states or provinces, streets, and house numbers or building numbers are used, as needed, in that order. Seniority titles (Jr., Sr., II, III, IV) can be used to determine the filing order of otherwise identical personal names even when addresses are different.

Note 1: Numbered streets are considered to be in spelled-out form. House and building numbers are used in ascending order.

Note 2: The titles "Junior" (Jr.) and "Senior" (Sr.) are used in alphabetic sequence. The titles "II," "III," and "IV" are used in numeric sequence.

Note 3: Postal ZIP Codes are *not* considered in determining the filing order of identical names.

Why Rule 8 Is Needed. Identical names occur frequently; therefore, a consistent method of indexing such names must be used to make sure that materials with identical names are properly filed. Rule 8 provides the required directions for the consistent indexing of *all types* of identical names.

Examples of Rule 8.

Names	Index Order of Units in Names				
	Key Unit	**Unit 2**	**Unit 3**	**Unit 4**	**Address**

(Names of Cities Used to Determine Filing Order)

Names	Key Unit	Unit 2	Unit 3	Unit 4	Address
*1. John Adams School Concord, Vermont	Adams	John	School		Concord, Vermont
*2. John Adams School Manchester, Vermont	Adams	John	School		Manchester, Vermont

(Names of States and Provinces Used to Determine Filing Order)

Names	Key Unit	Unit 2	Unit 3	Unit 4	Address
3. Beechmont Hotel Freeport, Illinois	Beechmont	Hotel			Freeport, Illinois
4. Beechmont Hotel Freeport, New York	Beechmont	Hotel			Freeport, New York

5.   Cranleys Bank
       Vancouver,
       British Columbia
	Cranleys	Bank			Vancouver, British
					Columbia

6. Cranleys Bank Vancouver, Washington	Cranleys	Bank			Vancouver, Washington

(continued on page 32)

---

* Notice that the key unit for this name is "Adams." The address is not the key unit; it is used only to determine the filing order of the two names concerned. The address is also used only to determine the filing order for names 3 and 4, 5 and 6, and 7 to 10.

Names	Index Order of Units in Names				
	Key Unit	**Unit 2**	**Unit 3**	**Unit 4**	**Address**

(Names of Streets and Building Numbers Used to Determine Filing Order)

		Key Unit	Unit 2	Unit 3	Unit 4	Address
7.	Diamond Markets 913 Arch St. Dayton, Ohio	Diamond	Markets			913 Arch Street
8.	Diamond Markets 174 Baker St. Dayton, Ohio	Diamond	Markets			174 Baker Street
9.	Diamond Markets 212 Park Ave. Dayton, Ohio	Diamond	Markets			212 Park Avenue
10.	Diamond Markets 439 Park Ave. Dayton, Ohio	Diamond	Markets			439 Park Avenue

(Seniority Titles Used to Determine Filing Order)

		Key Unit	Unit 2	Unit 3	Unit 4
11.	George R. Edwards 358 Coleridge Atlanta, Georgia	Edwards	George	R.	
12.	George R. Edwards, Jr. 933 Ross Way Atlanta, Georgia	Edwards	George	R.	Junior
13.	George R. Edwards, Sr. 3434 Decatur St. Atlanta, Georgia	Edwards	George	R.	Senior
14.	Thomas Flores 1221 Juniper St. San Mateo, California	Flores	Thomas		
15.	Thomas Flores II 111 Hermosa Drive San Mateo, California	Flores	Thomas	II	
16.	Thomas Flores III 2210 Cypress Street San Mateo, California	Flores	Thomas	III	

Rule 9   Numbers in Business Names

A number written in digit form in a business name is considered to be in written-out form and, despite its length, is used as a single indexing unit. Four-digit numbers are considered to be written out in hundreds (3060 is considered to be Thirty hundred sixty). Larger numbers are written in thousands, ten thousands, etc.

Why Rule 9 Is Needed. If this rule were not followed, different files operators would use different indexing patterns for the same types of names with numbers. This would, of course, waste much time when searching for materials. For example, 2410 Century Company could be indexed and filed under "Twenty-four hundred ten," or "Two thousand four hundred ten," or "Twenty-four ten"—three different titles that could be filed many drawers apart in a large filing system.

Examples of Rule 9.

	Names	Index Order of Units in Names			
		Key Unit	**Unit 2**	**Unit 3**	**Unit 4**
1.	Eight Bells Room	Eight	Bells	Room	
2.	8 Dollar Motel	Eight	Dollar	Motel	
3.	8 Track Recording Co.	Eight	Track	Recording	Company
4.	1894 Palm Gardens	Eighteen hundred ninety-four	Palm	Gardens	
5.	1812 Records, Inc.	Eighteen hundred twelve	Records	Incorporated	
6.	18th and Indiana Currency Exchange	Eighteenth (and)	Indiana	Currency	Exchange
7.	18th Street Businessmen's Association	Eighteenth	Street	Businessmen('s)	Association
8.	The 18,000 Apartments	Eighteen thousand	Apartments (The)		
9.	The Eighth Day, Inc.	Eighth	Day	Incorporated (The)	
10.	8th Ward Headquarters	Eighth	Ward	Headquarters	
11.	8th and Western Garage	Eighth (and)	Western	Garage	
12.	The 800 Daniels Shop	Eight hundred	Daniels	Shop (The)	
13.	Eight-Thousand Club	Eight-Thousand	Club		
14.	81st Street Cleaners	Eighty-first	Street	Cleaners	

Questions for Discussion

1. Why is a title used with a personal name not considered to be an indexing unit while a title used with a business name is considered an indexing unit?

2. Is a married woman's name filed differently than a single woman's name or a man's name?

3. Why are articles and particles treated the same in indexing order regardless of the spacing between the prefix and the rest of the name?

4. When two or more business or personal names are identical, is the state name or the city name considered first as the location unit for indexing purposes?

5. How are seniority titles used in determining filing order?

6. How are numbers written in digit form considered in indexing?

7. What is the *key unit* in each of the following names? What is the *second* indexing unit in the same names?

   a. De la Salle Furniture Mart
   b. Dr. Shirley Samuelson
   c. 21st Century Builders
   d. Brother Paul
   e. Mr. Anthony Restaurant
   f. Mrs. Debra Flores Ramos
   g. Rev. Charles TenBroek
   h. Brother Peter Garcia
   i. The Sixth Street Theater
   j. Doctor Sun's Lotion

8. Is the order of the names in each of the following sets of names correct or incorrect?

    a. Ms. Sally A. Schwartz (Boston)
        Mrs. Sally A. Schwartz (Cleveland)
    b. Top's Radio Supplies (Boston)
        Top's Radio Supplies (Baltimore)
    c. Father & Son Plumbing
        Father Timothy Aiken
    d. H and D Specialties, Inc.
        Herbert D. MacDougal IV
    e. Dr. Michael A. Curtis, Jr. (St. Paul)
        Michael A. Curtis, Sr., M.D. (Minneapolis)
    f. Brother's Kitchen Ware
        Brother Louis Wojek
    g. Harry L. Davies
        Harry L. Davis
    h. The Thos. Winter Shoe Shop
        Dr. Will S. Thomas
    i. 1018 River Road
        10 Terrace Lane
    j. Ramond D. Anzio
        D'Anzio Meat Wholesalers

9. What is the correct order in which each of the names within the following groups of three would be arranged in an alphabetic file? Indicate the order by writing on a separate sheet of paper the numbers representing the correct order.

    a. (1) Bill R. Kimura (2) William A. Kimura (3) Wm. Kimura and Sons
    b. (1) Mrs. Penny S. Canton (2) Mrs. Canton's Bakery (3) Mrs. Charles A. Canton
    c. (1) Second Street Barber Shop (2) Secondhand Clothing, Inc. (3) Secure Zipper Company
    d. (1) O'Hare's Shipping Lines (2) Fred C. Ohare (3) James O. Hare
    e. (1) Maj. Jack W. Edwards (2) Maj. Jack's Investment Service (3) Major Motor Repairs
    f. (1) Bert T. Sanfelippo, Jr., 329 W. Poplar Street, Salem, Oregon
        (2) Bert T. Sanfelippo, Sr., 197 W. Oak Street, Portland, Oregon
        (3) Bert T. Sanfelippo, 26 W. Pine Street, Salem, Oregon
    g. (1) Lo Bue Studios (2) Greta M. Lo'Breglio (3) Gerry Lobus and Assoc.
    h. (1) 1263 Fourth Avenue (2) 126 Fourth Avenue (3) 26 Fourth Avenue

Job 2   Card Filing

At this time complete Job 2 in OFFICE FILING PROCEDURES, Fifth Edition. The instructions and supplies for this job and the following jobs are included in the practice set.

CHAPTER 4

Alphabetic Indexing of Specialized Names

The indexing order of the more common types of individual and business names was presented in Chapters 2 and 3. The rules in Chapter 2 covered the order of indexing units, minor words, single letters and abbreviations, and possessives. The rules in Chapter 3 covered titles, names of married women, articles and particles, identical names, and numbers.

Chapter 4 now completes the indexing rules by presenting rules for indexing specialized names of organizations and institutions, separate single-word names, compound names, government names, and unusual names. The importance of cross-referencing is also explained.

© *Charles Harbutt, Magnum Photos, Inc.*

Businesses Rely on Accurate Files

The types of names to be considered in this chapter are specialized in the sense that they require special attention during the indexing process. For example, a name such as Association of Accountants can be correctly indexed in either of two ways:

2
Association (of)/Accountants   (descriptive method)

OR   2

Association (of)/Accountants   (as-written method)

Since this is true, the indexing method a person uses depends either on experience and training or on the indexing policy that has been established by the company for which the person is working. If no company policy exists, each person might use a different method of indexing and thus create confusion in the records system.

Indexing Methods   The way out of this dual indexing problem is, first, to know that there are two possible ways of indexing certain types of names and, second, to select one of the methods and use it instead of the other. If this is not done, one person will index a name like "The Bank of Toronto" first under "Bank," while another person will index it first under "Toronto." In this situation, papers concerning this bank will be lost or difficult to find.

Because there are many types of names in the general category of organizations, institutions, and agencies, the indexing problem cited is critical and must be resolved before accurate, dependable records control can exist.

The two methods of indexing identified above—the descriptive method and the as-written method—are discussed in the following paragraphs.

Descriptive Method of Indexing. In this method, the most identifying unit in a name is used as the key unit. For example, in the name "Association of Accountants," the term "Accountants" most accurately defines this organization. Thus, in the descriptive method of indexing, the word "Accountants" is used as the key unit and the word "Association" is used as the second unit. Names of other organizations, institutions, and agencies are indexed in this manner. Of course, all the indexing rules presented in Chapters 2 and 3 are followed when names of organizations, institutions, and agencies are being indexed. The descriptive method only *assists* in determining the *key unit* to be used.

As-Written Method of Indexing. In this method, names of organizations, institutions, and agencies are considered, for indexing purposes, in the form in which they are written and are read. Thus, the name "Association of Accountants" is coded with "Association" as the key unit and "Accountants" as the second unit. Again, the indexing rules presented in Chapters 2 and 3 apply to the indexing of names of organizations, institutions, and agencies. The as-written method is used as an assist in determining the key unit to be selected for filing purposes.

Selecting the Indexing Method

The decision about which indexing method to use, the descriptive method or the as-written method, must be made by the records manager or supervisor in each office. Once such a decision is made, all records personnel must follow it so that confusion will not result from two methods being used in the same office.

The basis for deciding to use one or the other method is usually governed by the nature and extent of operations in a given company. If, for example, the operations of a business involved only limited contact with organizations, institutions, and agencies, the as-written method of indexing would prove adequate. On the other hand, if business contacts included many organizations, institutions, and agencies, the descriptive method of indexing would provide better control over records because this method is the more comprehensive and accurate of the two. *It is for these reasons that the descriptive method of indexing will be used in showing examples and in presenting rules for study in this textbook.* Also, all practice materials will be based on the descriptive method.

Rule 10 Organizations and Institutions

When names of organizations and institutions (such as associations, societies, religious and educational institutions, and certain business organizations) are indexed by the descriptive method, the most identifying unit in a name, wherever it might appear, is used as the key unit.

Why Rule 10 Is Needed. A consistent method of applying indexing rules is necessary in order to make filing and finding easy, quick, and accurate. Certain types of names of organizations and institutions sometimes present special indexing problems. Rule 10, when adopted by a company, will provide the safeguard that is needed for consistent indexing of such names.

Note 1: Denominational names of churches, if known, are used as the most descriptive units. Words such as "Church" or "Cathedral" are not used as key units even if they appear as the first words in church names. Because names of synagogues and temples vary in form, each company should determine its own policy on whether to use the descriptive method or the as-written method in filing such names.

Note 2: The words "College," "University," and "School" are not used as key units.

Examples of Rule 10.

	Names	Key Unit	Unit 2	Unit 3	Unit 4
1.	Association of Architects	Architects	Association (of)		
*2.	Bank of Atlanta	Atlanta	Bank (of)		
*3.	Atlanta Savings Bank	Atlanta	Savings	Bank	
4.	National Audubon Society	Audubon	Society	National	
5.	Foundation for the Blind	Blind	Foundation (for the)		
6.	National Federation for the Blind	Blind	National	Federation (for the)	
7.	Eastern Association of Food Chains	Food	Chains	Eastern	Association (of)
8.	Western Association of Food Chains	Food	Chains	Western	Association (of)
9.	Council on Foreign Relations	Foreign	Relations	Council (on)	
10.	Independent Order of Foresters	Foresters	Independent	Order (of)	
11.	Society of Illustrators	Illustrators	Society (of)		
12.	Committee for Justice	Justice	Committee (for)		
13.	Bethel Lutheran Church	Lutheran	Church	Bethel	
14.	Lutheran Church of Our Savior	Lutheran	Church (of)	Our	Savior
15.	Church of Mental Science	Mental	Science	Church (of)	
16.	Motel Roberts	Roberts	Motel		
17.	Rochester Motel	Rochester	Motel		
18.	Union of State Employees	State	Employees	Union (of)	
19.	University of Texas	Texas	University (of)		
20.	Texas Wesleyan University	Texas	Wesleyan	University	
21.	Hotel Victoria	Victoria	Hotel		
22.	Washington Hotels	Washington	Hotels		

---

    * In this list of examples, certain pairs of names are bracketed in order to show that, when indexed by the descriptive method, these related names are held together as well as being in alphabetic order. This would not be true if these names had been indexed entirely by the as-written method. For example, under the as-written method "Bank of Atlanta" would have been placed in the "B" section of a filing system, while "Atlanta Savings Bank" would have been in the "A" section.

Rule 11   Separated Single Words

    When a single word (*southwest*) or a word and a prefix (*nonstop*) is separated into two or more parts in a business name (*south west; non stop*), the parts are considered to be a single unit. Hyphens in such names are disregarded.

Note 1: Examples of words that are sometimes separated into two words are *airport, carload, crossroads, downtown, eastside, goodwill, halfway, railroad,* and points of the compass words such as *northeast, northwest, southeast,* and *southwestern.*

Note 2: Examples of words that are sometimes separated from their prefixes are *antiacid, biannual, midlands,* and *noncorrosive.*

Note 3: A recent dictionary should be used to determine if one word is acceptable. If so, the name should be indexed as one word. For example, *drugstore* is one word in the dictionary and thus is coded as one word even when written as two words.

Why Rule 11 Is Needed. Unless this rule is followed, firm names that seem to have identical key units may be widely separated in the filing system. The problem can be seen in the names "South East Credit Bureau" and "Southeast Motor Sales Company." If "South" is considered as the key unit of the first firm name, it would be separated from "Southeast" by such names as *South* Dental Laboratory, *South* Park Shop, and Sam *South*ard. If Rule 11 is followed, these two firm names will be located in the same section of the files.

Examples of Rule 11.

Names	Index Order of Units in Names		
	Key Unit	**Unit 2**	**Unit 3**
1. Airport Florists	Airport	Florists	
2. Air Port Golf Range	Air Port	Golf	Range
3. Dr. Rita F. Antic	Antic	Rita	F. (Doctor)
4. Anti-Cruelty Society	Anti-Cruelty	Society	
5. Anti-Mite Termite Control	Anti-Mite	Termite	Control
6. Antioch Insurance Agency	Antioch	Insurance	Agency
7. Wm. J. Good, D.D.S.	Good	William	J. (D.D.S.)
8. Good Will Copy Service	Good Will	Copy	Service
9. Goodwill Industries	Goodwill	Industries	
10. Goodwill Mfg. Co.	Goodwill	Manufacturing	Company
11. Mrs. Natalie C. Goodwill	Goodwill	Natalie	C. (Mrs.)
12. Ms. Zelda P. South	South	Zelda	P. (Ms.)
13. Southeast Sales Corporation	Southeast	Sales	Corporation
14. South East Veterans Cab	South East	Veterans	Cab
15. Southland Drug Store, Inc.	Southland	Drug Store	Incorporated
16. South-Side Electric Co.	South-Side	Electric	Company
17. Southside Glass Company	Southside	Glass	Company
18. South Side Pharmacy, Inc.	South Side	Pharmacy	Incorporated
19. Stanley's Drugs	Stanley('s)	Drugs	
20. Suburban Drugstore	Suburban	Drugstore	

Rule 12   Compound Names

The separate parts of compound personal names (*St. John*), of compound geographic names (*New York*), and of compound business names, either coined or actual, are treated as separate indexing units. Hyphens are disregarded.

Note 1: Foreign equivalents of the English word *Saint* are *Sainte, San, Santa, Santo,* and *São*. They follow the rule governing the English word *Saint*. The name *Robert St. Clair*, therefore, would be indexed as three units. Other examples of compound and hyphenated names are *Mary Armstrong-Jones* (3 units), *Lu-yin Ho* (3 units), and *Robert P. San Galli* (4 units). Examples of *coined* compound business names are *Coca-Cola Bottling Co.* (4 units), *La-Z-Boy Chair Co.* (5 units), and *Frito-Lay, Inc.* (3 units).

Note 2: Examples of *actual* compound business and geographic names are *Trans World Airlines, Inc.* (4 units), *Mid America Coach Lines, Inc.* (5 units), *New York Life Insurance Company* (5 units), *Zurich-American Insurance Co.* (4 units), and *Anheuser-Busch, Inc.* (3 units).

Why Rule 12 Is Needed. Compound personal surnames are becoming more common, as are compound coined or actual words, names, or word substitutes in business names. Unless all names of this kind are treated the same way each time they are indexed, they can be filed in widely separated sections of the files. By using Rule 12, all types of compound names will be indexed in the same way and will be easily filed and located.

Examples of Rule 12.

	Names	Key Unit	Unit 2	Unit 3	Unit 4
1.	A-1 Pizza Shop	A-	One	Pizza	Shop
2.	Al-Rite Typewriter Co.	Al-	Rite	Typewriter	Company
*3.	Alan-Baker Manufacturing Co.	Alan-	Baker	Manufacturing	Company
4.	All-American Boat Co.	All-	American	Boat	Company
5.	All Star Leather Co.	All	Star	Leather	Company
*6.	Sandra M. Allen-Bennet	Allen-	Bennet	Sandra	M.
7.	E-Zee Lounge Chairs	E-	Zee	Lounge	Chairs
*8.	Erie-La Salle Body Shop	Erie-	La Salle	Body	Shop
9.	St. Louis Mills	Saint	Louis	Mills	
10.	Sainte Marie Park	Sainte	Marie	Park	
11.	San-Dee Chemical Products	San-	Dee	Chemical	Products
12.	San Jose Pharmacy	San	Jose	Pharmacy	
13.	Santiago J. Sanchez	Sanchez	Santiago	J.	
14.	Santa Fe Transport	Santa	Fe	Transport	
15.	Sta-Brite Paint	Sta-	Brite	Paint	
*16.	Sweeney-Thomas Insurance Agency	Sweeney-	Thomas	Insurance	Agency

---

* Names such as *Alan-Baker Manufacturing Co., Sandra M. Allen-Bennet, Erie-La Salle Body Shop,* and *Sweeney-Thomas Insurance Agency* usually require cross-referencing under the second units as explained on pages 45-47 of this chapter.

Rule 13 Government Names

The name of a foreign or domestic government agency is indexed by (1) the name of the government unit—*United States* (country), *Virginia* (state or province), *San Diego* (city or county); (2) the principal words in the name of the department; (3) the principal words in the name of the bureau, division, or agency. The various units are considered in the descending order of importance, from highest to lowest.

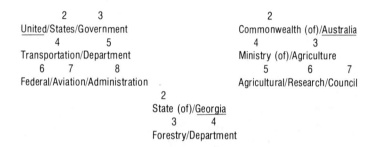

Note 1: If the key name, *United States Government*, does not appear on the material as part of the name, it is written in for filing purposes.

Note 2: Two titles are usually sufficient for identifying state, county, and city names because these names are usually less complex than those in the federal government.

Note 3: If the key name does not appear on the material as a part of the name, it is written in for filing purposes.

Note 4: National names used as key titles can be made as informal as distinctive identification will permit. For example, the shorter title *Kingdom of Great Britain* may serve in place of the exact title *Kingdom of Great Britain and Northern Ireland*. The title *Republic of Mexico* may be used in place of the formal title *United States of Mexico (Estados Unidos Mexicanos)*.

Why Rule 13 Is Needed. Most organizations correspond with several government offices. The trend toward multinational business has increased the correspondence with foreign government offices. Frequently the divisions, bureaus, and/or departments within various political divisions and subdivisions of both the United States Government and foreign governments use similar or identical titles. The only way to keep correspondence with these offices properly separated is through complete, consistent indexing as presented in Rule 13.

Note: The *U.S. Government Organization Manual* and the *Congressional Directory,* published annually, report a current list of United States government agencies and offices. The *State Information Book,* by Susan Lukowski, provides an up-to-date list of state departments and their addresses. The *World Almanac and Book of Facts* is an illustration of a reference for translations of foreign names into English and for identifying relations between governments.

Examples of Rule 13.

Names	Index Form of Names
1. Department of Commerce State of Alabama Montgomery, Alabama	Alabama, State (of) Commerce, Department (of) Montgomery, Alabama
2. Department of Public Welfare State of Arkansas Little Rock, Arkansas	Arkansas, State (of) Public Welfare, Department (of) Little Rock, Arkansas
3. State Protocol Hospitality and Conference Section Operations Division Department of the Secretary of State Government of Canada Ottawa, Canada	Canada, Government (of) State, Secretary (of), Department (of the) Operations Division Hospitality (and) Conference Section State Protocol Ottawa, Canada
4. Department of Public Works Hartford, Connecticut	Hartford, City (of) Public Works, Department (of) Hartford, Connecticut
5. Leon County Department of Public Welfare Tallahassee, Florida	Leon County Public Welfare, Department (of) Tallahassee, Florida
6. Department of Safety Tallahassee, Florida	Tallahassee, City (of) Safety, Department (of) Tallahassee, Florida
7. Management Divisions Agricultural Research Service U.S. Department of Agriculture	United States Government Agriculture, Department (of) Agricultural Research Service Management Divisions
8. Patent Office U.S. Department of Commerce	United States Government Commerce, Department (of) Patent Office

9. Bureau of Enforcement
Food and Drug Administration
U.S. Department of Health and
    Human Services
	United States Government
	Health and Human Services,
	    Department (of)
	Food and Drug Administration
	Enforcement, Bureau (of)

Rule 14   Unusual and Obscure Names

Unusual and obscure business, geographic, and political names are indexed as written. The last unit in the as-written form of an unusual personal name is used as the key unit.

2   3
Koningryk/der/Nederlanden

2   3
Mohamed/Ayoob/Cía.

2   3 4
Tapia/Zamora, /S./A.

2
David/George

Note 1: The abbreviation "Cía." stands for "Compañia" and means "Company."

Note 2: The letters "S.A." are the abbreviation of "Sociedad Anónima" and mean "Incorporated." If the files operator does not know the meaning of the abbreviation, the individual letters "S." and "A." would be considered to be separate units.

Why Rule 14 Is Needed. Use of the as-written form for unusual or obscure business names is consistent with the order for business names that was given in Rule 1. Filing personnel should not attempt to translate foreign business names, since not all those concerned with records control in a company may be able to translate such names and the translated names might therefore be lost.

Obscure personal names also require a consistent application. For example, although in Japan and China family names appear first, most Japanese and Chinese people in the United States write their names in the common form, given names first and family names last. Rule 14 follows the order established for personal names in Rule 1 and thus insures consistent filing and finding.

Examples of Rule 14.

	Names	**Key Unit**	**Unit 2**	**Unit 3**	**Unit 4**
			Index Order of Units in Names		
1.	A-B-L Printers	A-	B-	L	Printers
2.	A-1 Travel Agency	A-	One	Travel	Agency
3.	Able Auto Cleaners	Able	Auto	Cleaners	
*4.	Akita Akira Company	Akita	Akira	Company	
5.	B-29 Club	B-	Twenty-Nine	Club	
6.	Bodega Latina Cía.	Bodega	Latina	Cía.	
*7.	Carol June Designs	Carol	June	Designs	
8.	Carol Photo Studio	Carol	Photo	Studio	
9.	D's TV Repair	D('s)	T	V	Repair
10.	Dai-Ichi Restaurant	Dai-	Ichi	Restaurant	
11.	DaLite Windows	DaLite	Windows		
12.	Kim-Lee, Ltd., Imports	Kim-	Lee	Limited	Imports
13.	Cheong Lee	Lee	Cheong		
14.	Adam Louis	Louis	Adam		

---

* Names like *Akita Akira Company* and *Carol June Designs* are usually cross-referenced.

Cross-Referencing

When names are properly indexed and arranged alphabetically in a card file, there is usually little difficulty in locating a card bearing a particular name. In some cases, however, difficulties are encountered because (1) the unit in the name that was given second position for filing purposes is not known to the person looking for the card or (2) the name that is thought of by the person looking for the card is not the name under which the card is filed, even though the two names may be related.

Business names, like individuals' names, sometimes present difficulties in filing because someone requesting information about a certain company may not remember the exact name of the company or may remember only part of it. Such difficulties are overcome in filing practice by using cross-reference cards. The index form of a name is used as the basis for filing the original card. Another form or arrangement of the name is used as the basis for the preparation of a second card, known as the *cross-reference card*.

The extent of cross-referencing is determined primarily by the needs of the office or business the card file serves. If it is probable that more than one name will be associated with the same information or material, cross-reference cards should be used. Unnecessary cross-referencing should be avoided because it may create confusion and it is a time- and space-consuming operation.

Married Women. (See Rule 6.) The name of a married woman is written in index form on the original card in a card file, followed by the name as she writes it. The title "Mrs.," "Ms.," or "Miss," if known, is used for identification purposes. If other forms of her name are known, a cross-reference card is prepared for each of the other forms so that all forms of the name are on file for reference purposes. (See Illustration 4-1.)

```
Wegner, Carol A.  (Mrs.)

Mrs. Richard C. Wegner
2317 Mountain Road
Clearfield, UT  84015-3672
```

```
Wegner, Richard C.  (Mrs.)

See Wegner, Carol A.  (Mrs.)
```

Original Card   Cross-Reference Card

illus. 4-1, Cross-Reference for the Name of a Married Woman

Unusual Names. (See Rule 14.) Even though the last part of an unusual name of an individual is considered to be the surname, it is wise to prepare a cross-reference card for the name to show the name in the way in which it is written. This procedure insures that if the name is referred to by either of the two units, the card can be readily found. For example, for the name *Mai Soong* two cards would be prepared as shown in Illustration 4-2.

```
Soong, Mai

Mai Soong
153 Flores Street
San Mateo, CA  94403-1033
```

```
Mai Soong

See Soong, Mai
```

Original Card   Cross-Reference Card

illus. 4-2, Cross-Reference for an Unusual Name of an Individual

Compound Names. (See Rule 12.) When a business name includes two or more individual surnames, it is often desirable to prepare a cross-reference card for each surname other than the first. For example, if an original card is made out for Beck-Arnley Company, a cross-reference card for the name should be prepared. The two cards would appear as in Illustration 4-3.

```
Beck-Arnley Company

Beck-Arnley Company
842 Water Street
Atlantic City, NJ  08401-1189
```

```
Arnley-Beck Company

See Beck-Arnley Company
```

Original Card   Cross-Reference Card

illus. 4-3, Cross-Reference for a Hyphenated Business Name

If an original card is made out for Lorna Dorst & John Olsen, Manufacturing, the original card and the cross-reference card should be made out to show the information in Illustration 4-4.

```
┌─────────────────────────────────────────┐   ┌─────────────────────────────────────────┐
│ Dorst, Lorna (&) Olsen, John, Manufacturing │ │ Olsen, John (&) Dorst, Lorna, Manufacturing │
│                                           │   │                                           │
│ Lorna Dorst & John Olsen, Manufacturing   │   │ See Dorst, Lorna (&) Olsen, John,         │
│ 14 Industrial Park                        │   │     Manufacturing                         │
│ Columbus, AR  71831-4531                  │   │                                           │
│                                           │   │                                           │
│                                           │   │                                           │
│                                           │   │                                           │
│                                           │   │                                           │
└─────────────────────────────────────────┘   └─────────────────────────────────────────┘
```

Original Card   Cross-Reference Card

illus. 4-4, Cross-Reference for a Compound Name

If an original card is made out for O'Neill, Fletcher, and Buss, Attorneys, the two cross-reference cards should look like those in Illustration 4-5.

```
┌─────────────────────────────────────────┐   ┌─────────────────────────────────────────┐
│ Fletcher, Buss, and O'Neill, Attorneys    │   │ Buss, O'Neill, and Fletcher, Attorneys    │
│                                           │   │                                           │
│ See O'Neill, Fletcher, and Buss, Attorneys │  │ See O'Neill, Fletcher, and Buss, Attorneys │
│                                           │   │                                           │
│                                           │   │                                           │
│                                           │   │                                           │
│                                           │   │                                           │
└─────────────────────────────────────────┘   └─────────────────────────────────────────┘
```

First Cross-Reference Card   Second Cross-Reference Card

illus. 4-5, Cross-References for a Three-Name Firm

When a business name such as Bakers-Ritelite Company (a surname and a coined name) occurs in a filing system, materials may be requested by the name "Ritelite" only as well as by the complete company name. In such a situation, if the original card is made out for Bakers-Ritelite Company, the cross-reference card should be made out to show the following information:

Ritelite-Bakers Company
See Bakers-Ritelite Company

There are several circumstances under which a business may be known by more than one name:

1. A business operating under a long name may be popularly referred to by a shortened name, such as "Rossing's" for "Rossing's Restaurant and Pizza Shop."

2. A business may have its own name, but it may actually be a subsidiary of another company. For example, a firm with the name of "Alfonso Business Forms" may be a subsidiary of the firm "Southern Industries, Inc."

3. A store (for example, "Aurora Distributors") may be a branch of a large organization ("Mountain Wholesale Group") that gives to each branch the name of the city in which the branch is located.

The name used on the original card should be either (a) the better known or more commonly used name or (b) the name appearing on the letterhead.

	Original Card	Cross-Reference Card
1.	Rossing's	Rossing's Restaurant and Pizza Shop <u>See</u> Rossing's
2.	Alfonso Business Forms	Southern Industries, Inc. <u>See</u> Alfonso Business Forms
3.	Aurora Distributors	Mountain Wholesale Group <u>See</u> Aurora Distributors

Abbreviations and Single Letters in Company Names. (See Rule 3.) Many companies and associations are referred to by titles in abbreviated form or by letters rather than by full titles. When both forms are known, cross-references should be prepared for all names or titles of this type.

AAA

   <u>See</u> American Automobile Association

ABC

   <u>See</u> American Broadcasting Company

ARMA

   <u>See</u> Association of Records Managers and Administrators

ITT

   <u>See</u> International Telephone & Telegraph Corporation

WPS

   <u>See</u> Wisconsin Physicians Service

Newspapers. (See Rule 1, name 10.) If the city of publication of a newspaper is not the first word or words in the name of a newspaper, a cross-reference should be prepared under the city name.

Original Card	Cross-Reference Card
1. Christian Science Monitor (The)	Boston: Christian Science Monitor (The) <u>See</u> Christian Science Monitor (The)
2. Des Moines Register	(No cross-reference necessary)
3. Long Island Press	New York: Long Island Press <u>See</u> Long Island Press
4. Wall Street Journal (The)	New York: Wall Street Journal (The) <u>See</u> Wall Street Journal (The)
5. Washington Post (The)	(No cross-reference necessary)

Magazines. (See Rule 1, name 12.) Since a file card is prepared for the name of a magazine, a second card may be prepared for the name of the publisher and, if necessary, for any other name closely associated with the name. For example, *Farm-Home Magazine,* published by the Rahe and Dawson Magazine Publishers, may have been printed formerly under the name *Rural Home*. A new card prepared for a card file would show the name "Farm-Home Magazine" and the date or approximate date the change was made. In addition, two cross-reference cards would be prepared: one for the name of the publishing company and another for the former name of the magazine. (See Illustration 4-6.) This system of cross-referencing makes it possible to locate the desired information easily and rapidly regardless of the name that first comes to mind, for each cross-reference card refers to the original file card.

```
Farm-Home Magazine


Farm-Home Magazine
Rahe and Dawson Magazine Publishers
1225 Euclid Avenue
Cleveland, OH  44102-5562


Until 10/10/-- published under the name
   Rural Home
```

Original Card

```
Rahe (and) Dawson Magazine Publishers


Rahe and Dawson Magazine Publishers
1225 Euclid Avenue
Cleveland, OH  44102-5562


See Farm-Home Magazine
```

Cross-Reference Card for
Publisher

```
Rural Home


See Farm-Home Magazine
```

Cross-Reference Card for
Former Name of Magazine

illus. 4-6, Cross-References for a Magazine

Similar Names. When several surnames are identical or similar in pronunciation but different in spelling, permanent cross-references should be made to each of the various spellings of the name as shown below.

Meyer, <u>See also</u> Maier, Mayer, Mair, Mayr, Meier, Myer

Maier, <u>See also</u> Meyer, Mayer, Mair, Mayr, Meier, Myer

Mair, <u>See also</u> Meyer, Maier, Mayer, Mayr, Meier, Myer

Mayer, <u>See also</u> Meyer, Maier, Mair, Mayr, Meier, Myer

etc.

Foreign Language Names of Companies and Foreign Government Agencies. (See Rules 13 and 14.) When a translation is given for a foreign language business or a foreign language government name, the original card is prepared under the translated name and the cross-reference card is prepared under the foreign name. Otherwise index the name as shown.

Original Card	Cross-Reference Card
1. Uruguay, Republic of Public Education, Secretary of	Republica Oriental del Uruguay Secretaria de Educacion Publica <u>See</u> Uruguay, Republic of Public Education, Secretary of
2. Aluminum Corporation of Belgium (The)	L'Aluminium Belge Societe Anonyme <u>See</u> Aluminum Corporation of Belgium (The)

Subjects as Primary Titles

Sometimes the use of a certain subject title is preferable to the use of names as titles for indexing purposes. In such a case, a company's filing rules must authorize the specific subject title to be used. The subject title is then used as a key unit, and personal or business names are used as secondary and subsequent indexing units. If the subject title does not appear on material being coded, it should be written in.

Applications for employment and bids on construction, as examples, are usually filed according to the subject titles rather than by correspondents' names. In such a subject breakdown, names of correspondents are arranged alphabetically within the subject classification.

Examples of Indexed Names When Subjects Are Used as Key Units.

Key Unit		Unit 2	Unit 3	Unit 4	Unit 5
	Names				
Applications (for employment)	Sally A. Gregory	Gregory	Sally	A.	
Applications (for employment)	Geo. C. Hahn	<u>Hahn</u>	George	C.	

(continued on page 50)

Key Unit	Names	Unit 2	Unit 3	Unit 4	Unit 5
Automobile Rental Service	Avis Rent A Car	Avis	Rent	A	Car
Automobile Rental Service	Budget Rent-A-Car	Budget	Rent-	A-	Car
Insurance Agencies	Abbott & Adams, Inc.	Abbott(&)	Adams	Incorporated	
Insurance Agencies	Aetna Ins. Co.	Aetna	Insurance	Company	

Questions for Discussion

1. What are the names of two commonly used indexing methods?

2. What is the key indexing unit of the name "The Society of Archivists" according to the descriptive indexing method? The as-written method? Which is the correct method to use in this case?

3. If your filing operations were concerned with papers from local businesses, institutions, and organizations in a city of less than 50,000 population, would your indexing system *probably* be the descriptive or the as-written method? Why?

4. Why would it not be advisable to use both the as-written and the descriptive methods of indexing in one filing system?

5. If your filing system included materials about schools located in several different states, would you be more apt to use the descriptive or the as-written method of indexing?

6. What is the difference between the indexing of two words separated by a hyphen and a single word separated into two parts?

7. How would you determine if two or more words should be considered as one word or as a series of separate words?

8. How are the separate parts of compound personal names indexed? Compound geographic names? Compound business names?

9. Give four examples of types of names that probably should be cross-referenced.

10. Give two examples of subject titles that would probably be used as key units instead of names of businesses or of persons.

11. What is the *key unit* in each of the following names when the *descriptive* method of indexing is used? What is the *second indexing unit*?

a.   The Minneapolis Bank
b.   New Jersey Milk Producers
c.   Crossroads Restaurant
d.   Julius V. Angus-Scott
e.   John St. Charles
f.   Chao-cheng Sun
g.   Biannual Flower Show
h.   Bay City Rotary Club
i.   Top-of-the-Rock Parking Co.
j.   Third Presbyterian Church

12.   What is the *key unit* in each of the following names when the *as-written* method of indexing is used? What is the *second indexing unit*?

a.   WCQU Radio Station
b.   The Motel Midway
c.   University of Nebraska, Lincoln, NE
d.   Panama City Optimist Club
e.   Union Bank of Dayton, Ohio
f.   <u>The Daily Herald</u>, Kansas City, MO
g.   Second Methodist Church
h.   Association of Accountants
i.   St. Ann's Elementary School, Salem, ME
j.   John Thomas

13.   Is the order of the two names in each of the following pairs correct or incorrect according to the *descriptive method* of indexing?

a.   Northeast Antique Shops
     Sally A. North
b.   B-4 Dinner Treats
     Arnold Q. Befour
c.   KVLY Radio Station
     KMTN Television Station
     (File contains many broadcast
     stations)
d.   Non-stop Water Softeners
     Nonstop Power Generators
e.   King George Hotel
     Hotel King Edward
f.   Kool-Lite Luminaries
     Kooling Coils, Inc.
g.   Peter L. St. Francis
     Saint Francis Monastery
h.   First State Savings, Colby, KS
     First State Savings, Evansville, AR
i.   George M. Street III
     3rd Street Arcade
j.   The Airport Restaurant
     The Air Port Hotel

14.   What is the correct order in which each of the names within the following groups of three would be arranged in an alphabetic file using the *descriptive indexing* method? Indicate the order by writing on a separate sheet of paper the numbers representing the correct order.

a.   (1) The In-Town Store (2) In and Out Cleaners (3) Introductions, Inc.
b.   (1) Sara M. De La Cotera (2) Sam's Delicatessen (3) Vinny C. Dela
c.   (1) The RTE Company (2) R-T-E Shops (3) Jos. Riteman, M.D.
d.   (1) Benj. F. Soga (2) Benjamin A. Soga (3) Soga Beauty Shoppe
e.   (1) Two-Brothers' Sandals (2) Brother Tom (3) Clarence Brothers-Smith
f.   (1) University of Art (2) Artist's Hotel (3) Association of Artists
g.   (1) Mrs. Jane M. Carpenter (Charles E., Jr.) (2) Carpenter's Hobby House (3) Charles E. Carpenter, Sr.
h.   (1) The Quick-Cote Paint Co. (2) The Quick House of Tools (3) C. H. Quick
i.   (1) San Francisco Appliances (2) Frank San (3) Bay High School, San Francisco
j.   (1) Hotel Miami (2) <u>The Miami Tribune</u> (3) Miami Beach Swim Suits

15.   Write the following names in correct *descriptive indexing* order. If a name or address is incomplete, add the words required to complete it.

a. Research Division
U.S. Department of Housing and
   Urban Development
451 7th Street NW
Washington, DC 20410-1177

b. Thiel College
Greenville, PA 16125-1292

c. Peoples National Bank
Dover, DE 19901-1080

d. The Clarion-Ledger
Jackson, MS 39210-1565

e. Bureau of Dairy Industry
Idaho Commissioner of Agriculture
Boise, ID 83725-2559

f. Martin Luther King High School
Detroit, MI 48221-3147

g. Life Magazine
Time, Inc.
New York, NY 10003-4590

h. Butler County Sheriff's Department
El Dorado, KS 67042-1330

i. Department of Naturalization
Republic of Ireland
Dublin, Ireland

j. Department of Public Safety
Grand Forks, ND 58201-6321

16. For some of the following names, cross-reference cards may be needed; for other names, a cross-reference card is not needed. On a separate sheet of paper, after the number of the name listed, indicate by a letter "x" those needing cross-references. Then write the information as it would be written on a cross-reference card. For those that, in your opinion, do not need a cross-reference, write "No cross-reference needed" after the number of the name. Follow the example of the first two names on the list.

1. C. M. Ames and T. L. Maxwell Medical Center
   (1x. Maxwell, T. L., and Ames, C. M., Medical Center
         See: Ames, C.M., and Maxwell, T. L., Medical Center)
2. Sportland Arena
   (2. No cross-reference needed)
3. Mrs. Sara T. Greene (Mrs. Thomas C. Greene)
4. The Clinton-Reed Company
5. The Johnstown Inn
6. Sackner, Marion, and Gordon Agency
7. Mark S. Braun
8. The Philadelphia Bulletin
9. The American Plumbing Supply Company
10. Explorers Association of Texas
11. The Information Manager Magazine (Information and Records Management, Inc., Publishers)
12. Semco Products (Division of Safety Envelope Mfg. Co.)
13. TAC Floor Coverings
14. Northeast Paper Distributors, Inc. (stationery supplies)
15. Johnson's Klear-Site Windows, Inc.

Job 3 Card Filing

Job 4 Card Filing—Indexing and Filing Review (Optional)

At this time complete Job 3, and Job 4 if desired, in OFFICE FILING PROCEDURES, Fifth Edition. The instructions and supplies for these jobs are included in the practice set.

Part 3
Alphabetic Filing Procedures and Controls

The Shaw – Walker Co.

CHAPTER 5

Alphabetic Systems and Filing Procedures

There are four different ways to file business papers: by alphabet, by number, by location, by subject. It probably wouldn't take more than one guess to tell which is most frequently used in business offices. Alphabetic, of course. This is true because a filing system based on divisions of the alphabet is relatively simple and easy to use—that is, when you know how. The "know-how" follows in this chapter.

In order to understand how an alphabetic filing system is formed, you need to know two things: (1) what equipment is needed in order to hold business papers in storage and (2) how papers are handled (processed) during the time they are being prepared for filing.

Section 1 Equipment Needed for a Filing System

Cabinets and Shelves

Naturally, the first thing needed for a filing system is a container of some sort that can be used to hold or store business papers in an orderly

Proper Coding Leads to Successful Records Control

54

The two major types of equipment are filing cabinets and filing shelves.

manner. For this purpose, there are two major types of equipment: (1) filing cabinets and (2) filing shelves. Illustrations 5-1 and 5-2 show these two types.

Filing cabinets, like the one shown in Illustration 5-1, have pull-out drawers in which to place the sets of guides and folders that are used to hold papers in a filing system. Illustration 5-2 shows the type of equipment that is used for shelf-filing purposes. This is an open-faced shelf unit that holds all the guides and folders needed to form a system for holding business papers.

TAB Products Company

illus. 5-1, Filing Cabinet   illus. 5-2, Filing Shelf Unit

Guides and Folders

Guides mark sections and folders hold papers.

Now we come to the most important parts of a filing system: the guides that are used to mark sections in a system and the folders that are used to hold papers.

Guides. The guides used in a filing system can be compared with street signs. Guides show the names of areas within a filing system just as street signs show names of streets in a city. A file without guides would be like a city without street signs. Everyone would live on (?) street. It would take a door-to-door search to find anyone.

Guides are used to mark the location of folders that hold papers in a filing system. Some guides show where folders in major alphabetic sections can be found. Other guides are used to point out the location of folders that hold papers related to special names or to special subjects.

A guide like the one shown in Illustration 5-3 is made from a single piece of heavy pressboard. The small piece that rises above the top of the guide is called a *tab*. Either a letter of the alphabet or a name of some sort appears on the tab of a guide in an alphabetic filing system. This letter or name is known as a *caption*. Captions are there to show which folders are to be found behind a particular guide.

Folders. If papers are placed in loose stacks between two guides, it is very difficult to find a particular paper. A files operator may have to sort through as many as 50 sheets of paper to find the one sheet needed. In addition, a stack of loose papers tends to sag and slide into a "U" shape. Folders are designed to prevent such chaos as this.

Folders are made of a heavy paper known as manila or craft paper. A sheet of this material is folded into a "V" shape, with the front part about ½" shorter than the back part. This folding forms a pocket into which papers can be placed. Generally, several score marks are made at the bottom of the "V" so that the folder can be refolded into an expanded "U" shape. Thus, this permits the storage of more papers in an orderly manner.

In Illustration 5-4, notice that the folder has a tab piece like that used on the top edge of a guide. Also, like tabs on guides, folder tabs have captions that show letters of the alphabet, names of one sort or another, or numbers. Such captions tell which papers should be filed in or can be found in a folder.

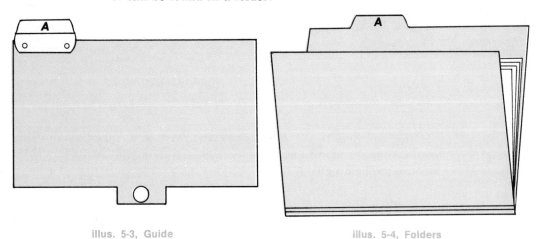

illus. 5-3, Guide   illus. 5-4, Folders

The "Cut" of Guide and Folder Tabs. When guides and folders are placed in file drawers or on shelves, they must be located so that each guide and each folder can be seen to best advantage. When this is done, the finding of a certain section and the locating of a needed folder will be made as easy as possible. Manufacturers of guides and folders know this and have made provision for it by cutting the tabs of both guides and folders into different positions across the top edge. Because of this, guides and folders can be purchased in any of five or more positions so they can be arranged the best way in a cabinet drawer or on shelves. (See Illustration 5-5.)

Illustration 5-6 shows how guides and folders are used in various positions across a file drawer. The colored illustrations of filing systems that are included in Chapter 8 show several alphabetic systems in greater detail than the partial system in Illustration 5-6. Turn to Chapter 8 and look at the colorful systems pictured there. They will help you understand the positions of guides and folders in various types of filing systems.

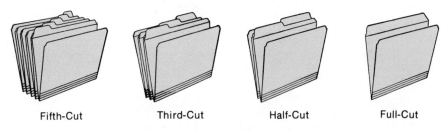

Fifth-Cut   Third-Cut   Half-Cut   Full-Cut

illus. 5-5, Standard Tabbing on Folders

Section 2 Study of an Alphabetic Filing System

Now that you know about cabinets, guides, folders, tabs, and captions, it is time to see and study these in an alphabetic filing system. As you read the material that follows, look at Illustration 5-6 and locate the parts of the system that are being described.

Positions of Guides and Folders

Positions of guides and folders make tabs as easy to see as possible.

The first thing to notice in Illustration 5-6 is that the tabs on guides and folders are spread across the top in four different positions. This has been done to make the tabs as easy to see as possible. Each of the four positions is reserved for one type of guide or folder. In this system, the positions are used as follows:

1. *First position* (on the left side) is reserved for a series of folders called *miscellaneous folders*.
2. *Second position* (from the left side) is used for *primary guides*.
3. *Third position* is filled by *special guides*.
4. *Fourth position* is used for *individual folders* and *special folders*.

Why are various guides and folders given these names? How are they used in the system? Read on!

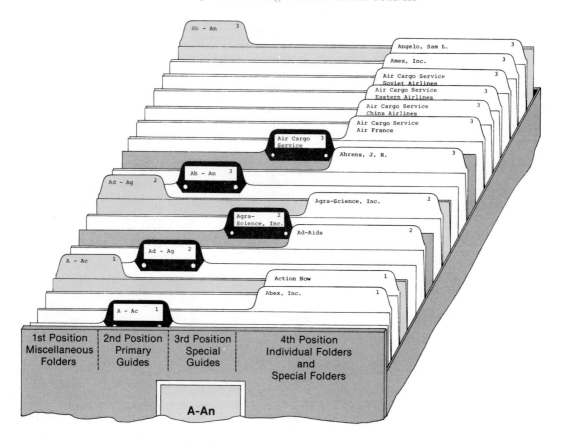

illus. 5-6, Three Sections of an Alphabetic Filing System

Primary Guides. The three primary guides in *second position* are the "street signs" referred to earlier in this chapter. They guide the eye to the main alphabetic sections of the filing system. They are placed in second position because it is near the center of the file drawer. In this location, the primary guides are most readily seen as a file drawer is opened.

Miscellaneous Folders. The tab on each of these *first-position* folders bears the same alphabetic caption as that which is shown on the primary guide in each alphabetic section in the filing system. A primary guide opens an alphabetic section in the filing system, and a miscellaneous folder closes the section. These folders are given the name "miscellaneous" because each is used to hold papers from more than one person or company with whom there is not enough correspondence to justify the use of individual folders. For example, in Illustration 5-6, the miscellaneous folder for the alphabetic section, *A-Ac 1,* would hold papers from these correspondents: Aames Tire Co., J. C. Abbott, and Acosta & Sons.

Individual Folders. When correspondence or other material relating to persons or companies increases in volume or is considered to be very important, individual folders are prepared for those persons or companies. Then, all their papers are removed from the miscellaneous folders and are refiled in the newly prepared individual folders. The folders for "Abex, Inc.," and "Action Now" (in fourth position in Illustration 5-6) are examples of individual folders. Notice that the tabs on these individual folders are double the width of the tabs on the other folders and guides in order to provide typing space for long company and personal names.

Individual folders are also used to hold correspondence about *subjects* that are vital to the operation of a business organization.

Special Guides and Folders. In the system shown in Illustration 5-6, *special guides* are located in third position. The guide for "Agra-Science, Inc.," is an example of a special guide. It pinpoints the location of a fourth-position individual folder for this company. This special guide was added to the filing system because of frequent requests for papers from the "Agra-Science, Inc.," folder. The special guide makes this folder easier to find.

At other times, a special guide is used to mark the location of a single folder, or a series of folders, holding papers related to a special subject. The third-position guide "Air Cargo Service" in Illustration 5-6 is an example of a special guide that shows the location of a series of special subject folders relating to the rates and schedules of air freight carriers. Special guides and folders might also be used for such subjects as Taxes, or Contracts, or Applications for Employment.

Why Alphabetic Sections Are Numbered

Look again at Illustration 5-6 and notice that there are three complete sections in this system. Each section is opened by a primary guide and is closed by a miscellaneous folder. Also, note that every item in a particular section is given the same number. All guides and folders within a section are thus identified as a group. This numbering plan makes it easier to locate a specific section. It also makes it easier to replace borrowed folders in their correct sections after they have been returned to the records department.

Section 3 How to File Papers So They Can Be Found Again

What You Must Know and Do

It might seem like a simple thing to file papers so that they can be found when they are needed. Actually, it is—but not unless you know and use a few rules and follow certain procedures.

*To file papers so
they can be
found when they
are needed, you
must know and
use indexing
rules and
procedures.*

1. You must know and use indexing rules. These you learned in Chapters 2, 3, and 4.
2. You must learn how to choose the one name in a letter that must be used as the key title for filing purposes.
3. You must know how to code the key title name. This you learned in Chapter 2 and in Jobs 1, 2, and 3. More about coding names in letters is given in this chapter.
4. You must be orderly and use the same procedures every time you prepare letters or other materials for filing. You will learn these things in this chapter.

How Letters are Processed (Handled) Before They Are Filed

Using a Time Stamp. When mail is first received, many companies have a mailroom clerk open it and mark each letter with a dated rubber stamp or a time stamp machine. This mark is known as a *time stamp*. It records the date, and sometimes the time, of the receipt of each piece of mail. (See Illustration 5-7 for an example of a time stamp mark.)

Making a Release Mark. After mail is time stamped, it is sorted according to names of individuals or departments and is delivered to them. After a letter has been read and answered, both the original letter and a copy of the reply to it are released to the records department for filing. Before the original incoming letter is sent to the records department, it is marked to show that it has been released for filing. The release mark is made on the letter by a secretary or by the person who received the original incoming letter. The initials of either person are written in the upper left part of the original letter. (See Illustration 5-7 for an example of a release mark.) A copy of an answering letter does not need a release mark because it can be assumed that such a copy would not have reached the records department without the knowledge and approval of the person who wrote it.

Inspecting Papers for Filing. When the records department receives material for filing, a files operator inspects it to find out if it has been released in the proper manner. The files operator also determines whether or not the paper has been pre-coded. Pre-coding will be explained as you continue studying this chapter.

Making Key Title Decisions. In most letters and related materials, it is possible to find two or more names that might be used as key titles. Because of this, a decision must be made regarding which of several names is to be used as the key title for filing purposes.

In making such decisions, the files operator must know and use a set of coding rules. If these rules were not known or not used, the way of selecting key titles might not be the same from one time to another or between one code clerk and another. This would make the finding of papers in a filing system more difficult and, because of wasted time, more costly.

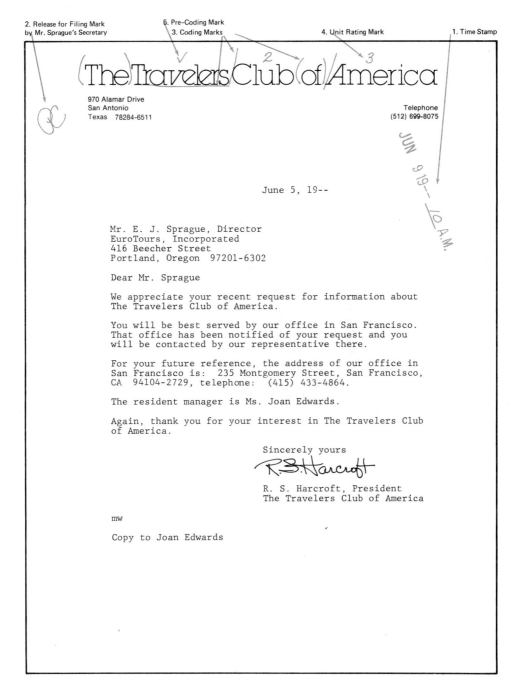

2. Release for Filing Mark
by Mr. Sprague's Secretary

5. Pre-Coding Mark
3. Coding Marks

4. Unit Rating Mark

1. Time Stamp

The Travelers Club of America

970 Alamar Drive
San Antonio
Texas   78284-6511

Telephone
(512) 699-8075

JUN 9 19-- 10 A.M.

June 5, 19--

Mr. E. J. Sprague, Director
EuroTours, Incorporated
416 Beecher Street
Portland, Oregon 97201-6302

Dear Mr. Sprague

We appreciate your recent request for information about
The Travelers Club of America.

You will be best served by our office in San Francisco.
That office has been notified of your request and you
will be contacted by our representative there.

For your future reference, the address of our office in
San Francisco is: 235 Montgomery Street, San Francisco,
CA 94104-2729, telephone: (415) 433-4864.

The resident manager is Ms. Joan Edwards.

Again, thank you for your interest in The Travelers Club
of America.

Sincerely yours

R. S. Harcroft

R. S. Harcroft, President
The Travelers Club of America

mw

Copy to Joan Edwards

**illus. 5-7 Incoming Letter Time-Stamped, Released for Filing,
Pre-Coded, Coded, and Rated**

*Correspondence
is filed under
the most impor-
tant name in it.*

Rules for Selecting Key Titles. In general, correspondence is filed under the most important name in it. That name must be the one which will most likely be used when letters are being requested from the files. When selecting this name as the key title, code clerks should use the following rules:

1. When an incoming (original) letter is being coded, the name to be used as the key unit is the *name of the company* that appears on the letterhead. When there is no letterhead, the *name of the person who signs the letter* is used as the key unit.
2. The key unit that is used for a copy of an outgoing letter is the *company name* that appears in the inside address. If no company name is given in the inside address, the *name of an individual* in the inside address is used as the key unit.
3. If a *subject* or a *name* that is written *in the body of a letter* is considered to be of greatest importance to filing and finding, that subject or name is used as the key title. This key title is rewritten by the code clerk on the top right side of the letter.
4. When *special sections* with *special titles* are used in a filing system, a code clerk uses these as key units. The code clerk must then write these titles in exact form on the top of letters or other materials being coded for filing in special sections. For example, if a letter concerning advertising rates was being coded and there was a special section in the filing system for Advertising Rates, the letter would be coded by writing the title Advertising Rates at the top of the letter.

Coding and Rating Key Titles. Once the key title is selected, it is coded and rated by the code clerk to show the proper filing order. Marking the key title is called *coding*. Marking the order in which the various parts of the title are to be considered for filing purposes is called *rating*.

*The most impor-
tant unit is un-
derlined; other
units are
marked off by
diagonal lines
and given a
rating number.*

When you write a note to someone, you probably underline the most important part in order to be sure that the person "gets the message." This is what is being done when papers are coded for filing. After a name has been chosen as the key title, the most important unit in it is underlined. This underlined unit is the primary (first) one under which a name will be filed. Any other units in the name are marked off by diagonal lines. Each of these units is given a rating number that shows its place in the indexing order of the name in relation to other names in a filing system. For example, when the name "Chicago Art Center" is selected as the key title, it is coded and rated as: Chicago/Art/Center. The underlined word, Chicago, is the key unit under which the name will be filed. *Art* is the second unit. *Center* is the third unit in this name.

Pre-Coding. Sometimes before a letter has been released to the records department, a secretary or the person to whom the original letter was addressed will not only release it but also will check or underline a name in it that should be used as the key title. Such a check mark is shown in the letter in Illustration 5-7.

If there is no indication of a checked name, a code clerk or a files operator must scan the letter and select the name in it that is to be used as the key title.

At the time of this inspection, the code clerk or files operator must also decide if a cross-reference is needed. Cross-referencing is explained later in this chapter.

Section 4 How to Make Filing and Finding Easier

To prevent overgrowth, transfer less active papers and folders to a storage location.

Over a period of time—for example, one year—an active filing system will grow considerably as papers are being added to it. More papers need more folders. More folders need more guides. Of course this situation can't go on unchecked because, if it did, there would be nothing except filing cabinets in an office.

The principal way to prevent overgrowth is to continually "weed out" unneeded papers (dead papers) and, about once a year, to transfer the less active papers and folders to a storage location. Chapter 7 will tell you how to handle transfer problems. However, from day-to-day you must watch your files to see that miscellaneous folders do not become overcrowded. One way to do this is to prepare and use individual folders.

How and Why Individual Folders Are Added to a Filing System

Individual folders make papers much easier to find.

When the filing system shown in Illustration 5-6, page 58, was started, there might not have been any individual folders in the first alphabetic section, *A-Ac 1*. Thus, for a while, all letters would have been filed in the miscellaneous folder for this section. Then, over a period of time, more and more letters and papers were received from and sent to a number of individuals and companies whose names fell within the range A to Ac. These tended to overcrowd the *A-Ac 1* miscellaneous folder and make papers difficult to locate. Therefore, it was decided that when six or more letters or other papers concerning an individual or a company had been received for filing purposes, an individual folder would be prepared and used. Thus, when six papers accumulated for Abex, Inc., an individual folder was prepared and all papers concerning this company were removed from the miscellaneous folder and refiled in the new individual folder. This relieved the overcrowded condition in the miscellaneous folder and made Abex, Inc., papers much easier to find. This same procedure was followed when each of the other individual folders in the system was started (opened).

How Special Guides and Folders Are Used in a Filing System

Special guides and folders are used in several ways to make filing and retrieval an easier process than it otherwise would be. You can use special guides to show the exact place a very active folder is to be found. In addition to this, you can use a special guide to point out where a subject folder can be found in the filing system. Special title folders can also be used to advantage, as they were in the "Air Cargo Service" section in the system shown in Illustration 5-6.

Special guides make folders easier to locate.

Used in these ways, special guides and folders not only reduce the number of papers in miscellaneous folders but also make folders easier to locate. And, of course, the papers the folders hold can be found more quickly.

How are special guides and folders added to a system? Let's take a few examples from Illustration 5-6. In section *Ad-Ag 2*, over a period of time, correspondence with Agra-Science, Inc., became very active. That is, many letters and other papers were exchanged with this company and there were many requests to the records department for papers concerning Agra-Science, Inc. Although there was an individual folder for Agra-Science, Inc., it was decided that this folder could be more easily located if a special guide leading to it was added to the system.

In section *Ah-An 3*, a subject section with a special guide and a series of special folders was added to this alphabetic section. Before the subject section was added, each airline had an individual folder without the title *Air Cargo Service* appearing on it. Each folder was filed according to the name of the airline. Thus, each folder was located in a different alphabetic section of the filing system. In time, there were many requests for letters, rate sheets, and schedules that were held in the different individual folders. Thus, a files operator had to look in four different sections within the system in order to locate needed rate sheets or other papers that related to all the airlines.

Because of this problem, it was decided to bring all the folders for airlines into the same section of the filing system. This was accomplished by adding a special guide bearing the title "Air Cargo Service." This guide was followed by four special folders. Each of these folders showed the same subject title as that appearing on the special guide, and, in addition, each folder tab showed the name of an airline. In this way, a special subject section was added to the filing system. This section made material from the four airlines much easier to find and therefore reduced the time for filing and finding needed papers from these airlines.

Kinds of Papers Held in Alphabetic Filing Systems

As you might suspect, alphabetic filing systems are not limited to the holding of letters. Many other types of papers are filed along with letters. Depending on the kind of department where the files are located, many types of papers and documents are held in alphabetic filing systems. Examples are credit records, personnel records, magazine and newspaper clippings, catalogs, market reports, sales reports, corporate papers, and interoffice memorandums or messages. Illustration 5-8 shows how an interoffice memorandum is coded for filing purposes.

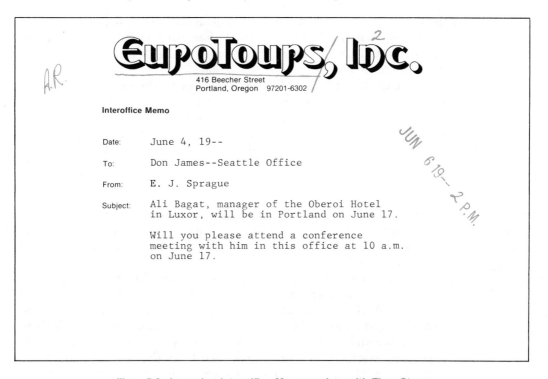

EuroTours, Inc.

416 Beecher Street
Portland, Oregon 97201-6302

Interoffice Memo

Date: June 4, 19--

To: Don James--Seattle Office

From: E. J. Sprague

Subject: Ali Bagat, manager of the Oberoi Hotel
in Luxor, will be in Portland on June 17.

Will you please attend a conference
meeting with him in this office at 10 a.m.
on June 17.

illus. 5-8, Incoming Interoffice Memorandum with Time Stamp,
Release Mark, Coding Marks, and Rating Marks

How Cross-Referencing Makes Filing and Finding Easier

Sometimes the key title of a letter may have an alternate name under which the correspondence may be requested. Or a letter may contain another important name or topic by which the correspondence may be asked for. A cross-reference makes it easier to locate a letter of this kind. To *cross-reference* means to file so that a letter can be located in two or more places in a filing system.

When there is a possibility that a letter may be called for by a name other than the one selected as the key title, two steps are taken in preparing a cross-reference. First, a wavy line is drawn under the cross-reference name if it appears in the letter, or the cross-reference name is written in the margin of the original letter if the name does not appear in the letter. In the former case, the name to be cross-referenced is indicated by an "x" in the margin opposite the name. The wavy line under the cross-reference name distinguishes it from the straight line used to code the key title. Second, a *cross-reference sheet* is prepared, which will be filed under the name selected as the cross-reference.

The letter is filed under the key title and the cross-reference sheet is filed under the alternate name.

An example of the need for a cross-reference is when a company name is composed of two personal names. Either of these might be used when someone is requesting papers from the files. For example, if a company name is Long & Richter, correspondence would be filed under the key title "Long," but it might be desirable to cross-reference under the name "Richter." A cross-reference sheet filed under the name "Richter" would tell a files operator looking for Long & Richter papers that these would be filed under the title "Long."

An example of the need for a cross-reference when a letter contains a different but important name is shown in Illustrations 5-9 and 5-10. "Royal Denmark Hotels" is the key title and "Royal Frederikshaven Hotel" is the cross-reference. Illustration 5-9 shows a copy of the outgoing letter with the key title coded and rated and the cross-reference marked. Illustration 5-10 shows the cross-reference sheet prepared for this letter.

How Papers Are Sorted and Why This Is Necessary

After key titles have been coded and necessary cross-references made, material for the files should be sorted. *Sorting* is the process of getting papers into alphabetic order before they are taken to the files and placed in folders.

Sorting serves two purposes: (1) It saves time in filing. If materials are not sorted, the operator would have to move back and forth from one cabinet or shelf section to another in a random manner. Also, movement from the top drawer or shelf to another would be aimless. To do this is to waste time, and since "time is money," money would be wasted. (2) If papers are needed before they have been filed, they can be found more easily when they are held in a sorted order than in a random stack.

Papers may be sorted by using specialized equipment such as sorting trays. (See Illustration 5-11, page 68.) Equipment such as this is composed of a series of guides, labeled alphabetically, that are held together in either a vertical position or in a horizontal (flat) one.

If special sorting equipment is not available, papers can be sorted into alphabetic units in the following manner:

1. Divide materials into stacks of alphabetic units according to the first letters of the key units in key titles. For example, use five alphabetic stacks: A-D, E-H, I-M, N-S, T-Z.
2. In each of these five stacks, papers may be sorted into single alphabetic units. For example, the A-D stack may be sorted into separate stacks for A, B, C, and D.
3. Finally, papers in each stack may be sorted alphabetically.

Steps 1 and 2 are known as *rough sorting*. Step 3 is *fine sorting*.

How to Place Correspondence in File Folders

All correspondence is placed in folders with the letterhead or the inside address at the left side and with writing facing forward.

In an *individual folder*, letters are arranged according to date of writing, with the most recently dated letter at the front.

In *miscellaneous folders* and in a single *special section folder*, correspondence is placed in alphabetic order according to the units in the

CROSS-REFERENCE SHEET

Name or Subject *Royal Frederikshaven) Hotel*

Date of Item *June 3, 19--*

Regarding *adding this hotel to the tour that*

SEE

Name or Subject *Royal Denmark Hotels*

Authorized by *Johnson* Date *6/9/--*

Illus. 5-10, Cross-Reference Sheet for Letter Shown in Illustration 5-9

June 3, 19--

Mr. Stefan Hedstrom
General Manager
Royal/Denmark/Hotels
12 Vester Sogade
Copenhagen, Denmark

Dear Mr. Hedstrom

EuroTours is scheduling six tours next year
for Denmark, Norway, and Sweden.

We would like to continue our contract with
Royal Denmark Hotels and add the Royal/
Fredefikshaven/Hôtel to our list.

Mr. Jon Claybourne, from our Copenhagen
office, will contact you about these matters.

Sincerely yours

E. J. Sprague, Director
EuroTours, Incorporated

EJS/mp

copy to Jon Claybourne

Illus. 5-9, Copy of Outgoing Letter with Key Title Coded
and Rated and Cross-Reference Marked

Yawman & Erbe of Calif. Corp.

illus. 5-11, Using a Correspondence Sorter to Get
Coded Papers into Alphabetic Order

names concerned. Then, within each group of letters from and to the same person, it is placed according to date of writing. The letter with the most recent date is placed in front of all others in the group. For example, in a *miscellaneous folder* captioned *E-Em*, letters would be filed as follows (reading from the front of the folder to the back):

	Order of Letters	Correspondents' Names	Dates on Letters
(Back)	6	2 El Rancho/Brands	October 28, 19—
	5	2 El Rancho/Brands	November 1, 19—
	4	2 El Rancho/Brands	November 6, 19—
	3	2 Ralph/Ekdahl	July 10, 19—
	2	2 (The) Eiko/Corp.	September 26, 19—
(Front)	1	2 (The) Eiko/Corp.	October 5, 19—

Questions for Discussion

1. Why are guides and folders cut to various positions?

2. How are primary guides used in a filing system?

3. How are miscellaneous folders used in a filing system?

4. Are individual folders needed in a filing system? Why or why not?

5. Why are special sections useful in a filing system?

6. Why is it necessary to code the key title in a letter before the letter is filed?

7. What would you do in order to add an individual folder to the system shown in Illustration 5-6?

8. How would you add a special section for the *A & F Stores* to the system in Illustration 5-6?

9. Why would it be advisable to cross-reference a name like *Wilson and Cartwright, Inc.*?

10. What are some reasons for sorting papers before they are filed?

Job 5   Alphabetic Correspondence Filing

At this time, complete Job 5 in OFFICE FILING PROCEDURES. The instructions and the supplies for this job are included in the practice set.

CHAPTER 6

Requisition, Charge, and Follow–Up Controls

A systematic method of charging borrowers for files materials must be used.

In *Hamlet*, Act 1, Scene 3, part of the advice given by Polonius to his son Laertes was, "Neither a borrower nor a lender be . . . ." This might still be good advice for personal behavior, but not so good if you are running a bank or trying to control business records. In these operations, borrowing and lending are vital. Records departments exist in order to lend papers to those who need to borrow them.

However, lending must be strictly controlled because some who borrow have the bad habit of not remembering to return things that are lent to them. Or, they lose control of borrowed things because they re-lend them to others. Left unchecked, the results of forgetting or re-lending files materials are lost papers, frustrated borrowers, and unhappy records personnel. In order to avoid such headaches as these, a systematic method of charging borrowers for files materials must be one of the controls used by records department people.

Records Control at Home Makes Life Easier

A complete system for controlling borrowed papers must include the following steps:

1. *Requisitioning.* There must be a well-known and accepted way for borrowers to request materials from the filing system.
2. *Charging.* There must be a means of charging borrowers (holding them responsible) when they are given papers from the files.
3. *Canceling.* When borrowed papers are returned, there must be a method for canceling charges held against the borrower.
4. *Follow-Up or Tracing.* When papers are not returned on time, there must be a way to follow-up or trace and locate the missing papers.
5. *Reserving.* When papers are needed at a future time, it must be possible for records department people to process requests for reserving these papers.

Each of these parts of a complete charge-out system will be considered in this chapter.

illus. 6-1, Well-Organized Records Department

Section 1 Requisitioning Materials from the Files

The form used to request records is a "requisition."

Usually those who want papers from the filing system can make this known in any of several ways. They can call in person at the records department, make a request over the intercommunications system, or send a request by interoffice delivery. But no matter how the request is made, someone in the records department must make a written record of it.

The form used to request records is known as a *requisition*. Illustration 6-2 shows one style of requisition form that is widely used. This is a *requisition card*.

Usually requisition cards are 5″ × 3″ in size and are printed to show such headings as: the name of the company or person whose papers are needed, the name of the person and department making the request, the date of the papers being borrowed, the date the papers are taken, and the date the papers are to be returned to the records department.

Another style of requisition form that is commonly used is shown in Illustration 6-3. It is called a *requisition sheet*.

Name or Subject	Date Wanted
Johnson, Pearl	*10/26/--*
Re	Date of Letter
Employment	*10/5/--*
Taken by	Date Taken
Mark Brown	*10/26/--*
Signed	Dept.
M B	*Personnel*
REQUISITION	Return Date *11/2/--*

illus. 6-2, Requisition Card

OUT

To Records Dept.
REQUEST FOR PAPERS
Papers Wanted on *6/21/--*
(date)
Description of Papers
Date *1/18/--*
Name *M R Conrad*

Address *Phoenix, AZ*

Subject *Matter concerning Bancroft + Serrano*
Wanted by *Rose Toshiba*
Department *Administration*

For Records Dept. Use
Return Date *6/25/--*

illus. 6-3, Requisition Sheet

Requisition cards and requisition sheets are used in different ways. Depending on the circumstances, requisition forms may or may not be entirely filled out by records department personnel. When a request is made in person or received through office delivery, the borrower fills in a description of the material needed and the date it is wanted. Other parts of the requisition form are filled in by records department personnel. When a request is received by telephone or over an intercom, the entire requisition form is filled in by records personnel. Usually requisition forms are prepared in duplicate.

Section 2 Charging for Borrowed Materials

A charge-out system must handle all kinds of requests.

When you borrow a book from a library, you are "charged" for it in order to make you responsible for returning it within a period of time. The same is true for those who borrow from a filing system. However, some charge procedures that are used in records departments are different from those usually followed by libraries. One reason for this is that some file materials are more difficult to identify than are books in a library. For example, a person might need to borrow a whole folder full of papers, or a series of folders, or papers from only one folder, or papers from several folders. Thus, the records department must have a charge-out system that can handle all kinds of requests.

Charging For Selected Papers

A requisition card is placed in the pocket of an OUT guide.

Requisition Card Method. When a requisition card is used for borrowing selected papers from a file, the marker that is placed in the file folder from which material has been removed is called an *OUT guide.* The two main styles of OUT guides—an OUT guide with a pocket and an OUT guide with printed lines—are discussed below.

OUT guide with Pocket. When an OUT guide with a pocket is used, a copy of the requisition card is placed in the pocket. (See Illustration 6-4.) The files operator then places the OUT guide with the inserted requisition card in the file folder from which the letter or other paper has been taken. When placed there, the OUT guide with the inserted requisition card serves as a substitute for the borrowed paper as well as a marker to show that a paper has been removed from a folder and who has it. The completed requisition card serves as a charge against the person who requested and received the borrowed paper.

A second copy of the requisition card, which was made when the request was received, is placed in a *follow-up file*. The use of this file will be explained later in this chapter.

OUT Guide with Printed Lines. When an OUT guide with printed lines (see Illustration 6-5) is used, only one copy of the requisition is prepared. Information from the requisition is used to fill out the printed form of the OUT guide. Then the OUT guide is placed in a file folder to mark the place from which a paper was removed and to charge the borrower for that paper.

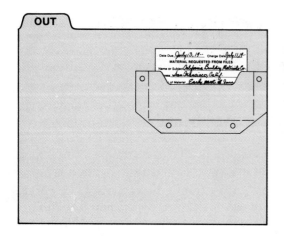

NUMBER, NAME, OR SUBJECT	DATES OF LETTERS	ISSUED TO	DATE ISSUED
C.R. Cramer	May 6, 19--	K. Jones	June 1, 19-
Brooks + Co.	July 9, 19--	D. Towne	Aug. 6, 19--
Huber + Son	Sept. 7, 19--	Ray Smith	Oct. 1, 19--

illus. 6-4, OUT Guide Holding a Copy   illus. 6-5, OUT Guide with Printed Lines
of a Requisition Card

Illustrations 6-6 and 6-7 on page 75 show the use of OUT guides in two types of files: a shelf file and a vertical drawer file. The prominence of these OUT guides makes it easy to relocate the correct position of a borrowed paper when it is being returned to the file.

Both forms of OUT guides are reusable after the paper is returned by the borrower and replaced in the files. If the pocket-type OUT guide is used, the guide is removed from the file and the requisition card is removed from the pocket. When the ruled form of OUT guide is used, the information regarding the borrowed material is crossed off and the guide is ready for use again with new charge information written on the next line.

Requisition sheets are also used as markers in file folders.

Using Requisition Sheets as OUT Sheets in File Folders. When requisition sheets like the one shown in Illustration 6-3 are used to charge for borrowed papers, they are also used as markers in file folders. Two copies of the requisition sheet are prepared. One copy is placed in the file folder from which papers have been removed. The other copy is filed in the departmental follow-up file.

When files materials are returned, the requisition sheet is removed from the file folder and destroyed. Thus, the charge against the borrower is canceled. The requisition sheet held in the follow-up file is saved. It will be used at a later date to check on file activity.

Charging For Borrowed Folders

Using OUT Folders. When an entire folder is requisitioned and removed from the filing system, an *OUT folder* is used to replace it. OUT folders are of two types: (1) a folder with a ruled form printed on the front (see Illustration 6-8, page 76) or (2) a folder with a visible pocket attached to the inside back flap (see Illustration 6-9, page 76). This pocket is used to hold a copy of a requisition card.

Shaw-Walker

Illus. 6-7, OUT Guide in a Vertical File Drawer

Illus. 6-6, OUT Guides in a Shelf File

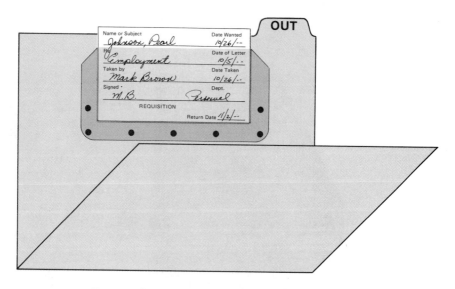

TAKEN BY	NUMBER, NAME, SUBJECT	DATE	TAKEN BY	NUMBER, NAME, SUBJECT	DATE	TAKEN BY	NUMBER, NAME, SUBJECT	DATE
A.A.	*Robertson Co*	*4/10*						
D.F.	*For Carter Bro.*	*4/20*						
R.R.	*Kolm & Kolmer*	*4/21*						

illus. 6-8, OUT Folder with Printed Sections

Name or Subject	Date Wanted
Johnson, Pearl	*10/26/--*
Re: *Employment*	Date of Letter *10/5/--*
Taken by *Mark Brown*	Date Taken *10/26/--*
Signed *M.B.*	Dept. *Personnel*
REQUISITION	Return Date *11/2/--*

illus. 6-9, OUT Folder with Requisition Card in Pocket

The OUT folder is used as a substitute for the folder that is removed.

When the ruled and printed OUT folder is used, information from a requisition card is transferred to the form on the outer face of the OUT folder. The requisition card is placed in a follow-up file.

When the pocket-type OUT folder is used, the requisition card must be prepared in duplicate. One copy is placed in the pocket of the OUT folder. The other requisition copy is placed in a follow-up file.

Regardless of the type, the OUT folder is used as a substitute for the folder that is removed. All materials that are received for filing during the time the regular folder is out of the files are held in the OUT folder. When the regular folder is returned, material accumulated in the OUT folder is removed and filed in proper order in the regular folder. The charge information on the OUT folder is crossed out, or the requisition card is removed from the pocket, and the OUT folder is available for reuse.

The file folder is left in place; the carrier folder is delivered to the borrower.

Using Carrier Folders. When the entire contents of a folder are requested, it is sometimes better to leave the file folder in place and to transfer its contents into a *carrier folder*. The carrier folder is then delivered to the borrower.

Using carrier folders has several advantages over removing regular file folders and sending them to borrowers: (1) Carrier folders are made of heavy manila stock that lasts longer under extra wear than the thinner file folders. (2) Carrier folders usually are of a distinguishing color—one differing from the color of regular manila file folders. Also, they are marked with such phrases as "Return to Files." Therefore, carrier folders are much more apt to be returned to the filing department than are regular file folders. (3) Since regular file folders are not taken from the files, incoming papers can be filed as usual. As a result, there is less disruption of normal filing procedures than there would be if regular folders were removed and OUT folders substituted for them.

Section 3 Canceling Charges when Borrowed Materials Are Returned

Care must be taken to cancel all charges when borrowed papers are returned.

If a charge-out system is to be useful, it must be trusted by those who file and borrow papers. It will not be trusted for long if care is not taken to cancel all charges when borrowed papers are returned to the records department.

The way charges are canceled depends on the kind of supplies used in a charge-out system. If requisition cards are used, these are removed from the pockets of OUT guides or OUT folders and destroyed. Copies of requisition cards in a follow-up file are removed and saved. They are used later in checking on the activity of the main filing system.

If requisition sheets are placed in regular file folders and used as OUT sheets (see Illustration 6-3 for an OUT requisition sheet of this type), these are removed from the file folder and destroyed when borrowed papers are returned. Copies of OUT sheets held in the follow-up file are removed and saved for later use as check sheets. These copies are used at transfer time in order to find out which papers are still active and should be saved.

When lined and printed OUT guides or OUT folders are used, charges written on them are crossed out when papers are returned by borrowers. Also, any copies of requisition cards held in follow-up files are removed so that they will no longer show charges against borrowers who have returned materials to the filing department.

Section 4   Follow-Up Procedures to Trace Borrowed Materials

When you rent a car, you arrange to keep it for a certain number of days. You return it on the due date unless you have asked for, and received, an extension of time. The car rental company keeps an accurate record of all this and starts a tracing procedure (a follow-up) if a car is not returned on time. Exactly the same procedure is also used by a records department in order to control the return of borrowed papers and folders.

Setting Time Limits

Time limits must be established for the return of borrowed items.

In order to establish control over the return of file material, it is necessary first to establish time limits for the return of borrowed items. Such limits vary from one firm to another, largely because of differences in the value of items being held in different filing systems.

Some papers held in files are very valuable and company rules usually determine that these may not be borrowed for a period of time greater than one day, or less. Other less valuable papers may be borrowed over a period of a week, ten days, or two weeks. In general, it is better to allow relatively short periods of time for the return of papers. The longer the time permitted, the less chance there is of having materials returned on time. However, it is necessary to make provision for extending a set time for returning borrowed papers when it is evident that the borrower still needs them. This can be done either by rewriting the due date on the original requisition or by preparing a new requisition and noting a change of date on all OUT forms held in the files.

Follow-Up Methods to Trace Borrowed Materials

A system for checking on out-of-files materials is necessary.

If all borrowed materials were returned on time and if there were no requests for papers that were out on loan, there would be no need for following-up or tracing overdue papers. However, such is not the case. Therefore, the records department must have a system for checking on out-of-files materials.

In checking on the due dates for the return of borrowed papers and folders, any one of three basic procedures may be used: (1) the main files may be scanned, (2) a master control sheet may be used, or (3) a follow-up filing system may be set up.

Scanning the Files. When the filing department is relatively small (for example, when approximately 5 cabinets or sections comprise the filing area), the files operator can check the due dates of borrowed materials by going through the files and reading the due dates written on requisition forms, OUT cards, OUT guides, or OUT folders.

Master Control Sheet. If the filing department has 6 to 15 cabinets or sections, follow-up work can be handled by using a master control sheet or a simple follow-up system. A *master control sheet* is a running record of borrowed file materials and is kept by the files operator at the desk. As requisitions are written or received in the department, data from these are posted to the master control sheet. When borrowed materials are returned, the corresponding charges written on the master control sheet are crossed out.

A follow-up system consists of 12 monthly guides and 31 daily guides.

Follow-Up System. If the filing department is large, a follow-up system simplifies charging for papers and folders taken from the department and tracing them when they are overdue. For this purpose, a *follow-up file*, like that shown in Illustration 6-10, is used. When properly used, a follow-up file is a convenient method of keeping time-related routines up to date and under control.

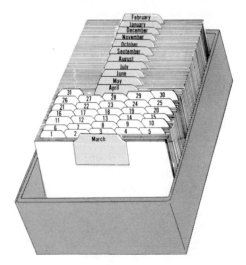

illus. 6-10, Follow-Up File Holding Requisition Cards
that Are Filed by Due Dates

You will recall that requisition cards are filled out when papers are borrowed from the main files. These cards serve as a charge against a borrower. Usually two copies of each card are made. One goes into the main files; the other goes into a follow-up file similar to the one shown in Illustration 6-10. This follow-up file consists of 12 monthly guides in central position and 31 secondary guides captioned for days in the month. Usually only one set of daily guides is needed for a follow-up file.

As the operator checks and processes the requisitions held behind the dated guide for the day, the dated guide is moved out of the current month section and is placed behind the guide for the next month. Thus, the daily guides keep rotating. Unless a large volume of requisitions must be handled, a single set of daily guides is sufficient.

If requisition sheets are used instead of requisition cards, the follow-up file consists of 12 monthly guides and 31 folders captioned for each day in the month.

Follow-Up Procedures

A follow-up file of the type shown in Illustration 6-10 is used in the following manner.

1. Requisition cards are the only materials placed in the file.
2. Each requisition is placed in the follow-up file according to *the date on which the borrowed papers are to be returned*. If that date is in the current month, the requisition is placed behind the day-of-the-month guide that corresponds to that date.
3. Each day the operator of the follow-up system checks to see which borrowed materials are due and notifies the borrowers. If the materials are still needed by the borrower, the operator may extend the due date to a later date. The requisition is changed to conform to the new date and is refiled accordingly.

   The new due date is also written on the face of a lined and printed OUT guide or OUT folder if either is used in the main files.
4. When borrowed papers are returned, the charge against the borrower is canceled by removing the requisition from the follow-up file. This copy of the requisition is held for later use in determining the activity of a filing system.

   If an OUT folder or guide that holds requisitions is used, the requisition is removed and destroyed when papers are returned. If a lined and printed OUT folder or guide is used, notations are crossed out and the folder or guide is brought back to the operator's work station for future use.

Avoiding Follow-Up on Borrowed Materials

Guard against loss by sending an exact copy of the material requested.

No matter how careful the files operator is in charge and follow-up methods, important papers may be lost in transit or may be accidentally destroyed. To guard against such possibilities, many companies avoid releasing certain kinds of original papers from the files.

The removal of material from the files is avoided in many companies by sending the borrower an exact copy of the material requested rather than the material itself. There are on the market a large number of copymaking machines that produce exact copies in a matter of seconds. When this technique is used, the requested paper is removed from the folder only long enough to be put through the copying machine. The original is then refiled, and the exact copy is sent to the borrower with instructions to destroy it after use. This method is used most frequently when a single letter or a few related pieces are needed.

Some firms, in order to prevent the loss of an entire folder, have established rather rigid rules on who may borrow a folder. In some organizations, authorized persons are required to come to the records department to examine the contents of the folder rather than having it sent to them. If selected pieces are needed for further study, exact copies can be made at that time.

Section 5 Reserving Files Materials

The records department frequently receives requests to reserve files materials that are desired at a future date. In such situations, follow-up procedures are needed that will assure the delivery of the requested papers on the date that they are needed.

Methods of Requesting Future Delivery

Requests for the future delivery of papers can reach the records department in any of three ways: (1) A request may be made by writing a note on a letter when it is being released to the records department. In this case, the person who is releasing the letter would write the note in this manner: "Wanted by S.A.R. on 5/21/—." (2) A request may be made over the telephone or through the intercom system. (3) A requisition card or a sheet may be used to make a future reservation by writing an advanced date on the "Papers needed by _____" line on a requisition form.

When a request is made by methods (1) or (2), the files operator prepares the requisition form and files it in the follow-up file according to the future date that the material is needed. If method (3) is used, the files operator files the requisition in the follow-up file according to the future date specified on the requisition sheet or card.

Using Dated Folders in a Follow-Up File

Follow-up files are used to avoid overlooking important matters at a future date.

Folders specially printed for letter-size follow-up files sometimes are used in the records department as well as in other departments. Such departments as purchasing, accounting, shipping, production, and sales are all concerned with matters that require future attention. Follow-up files are used to avoid overlooking important matters at a future date.

The folders used in follow-up files have straight-cut tabs (see Illustration 6-11). The left side of the tab can be labeled to show the name under which the folder is filed. This might be the name of a department, a person, a company, or an order number, depending on where and how the file is being used. In the records department, dated follow-up folders are filed by date only.

The center section of the tab shows the months of the year. A movable signal in this section can be moved to any desired position to

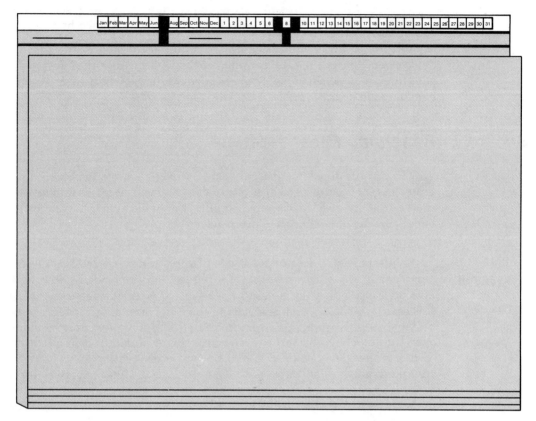

illus. 6-11, Dated Follow-Up Folder with Two Movable Signals

mark the month required. The right side of the tab shows a series of numbers for the days in a month. These can be marked by another movable signal for this section of the tab.

The folder in Illustration 6-11 holds a requisition sheet which shows that a paper is needed on July 8. Signals have been moved in order to show this date. At that time, a follow-up clerk will pull this folder, remove the requisition sheet, take it to the main files, and locate the desired paper.

Section 6 Departmental Follow-Up Files

Follow-up files are used in various departments.

Your future job might be related to follow-up procedures in any of several departmental areas of work. These could include purchasing, credit and collection, sales, shipping and receiving, legal, stores (industrial), and industrial production. Therefore, a brief study of follow-up practices in some of these departmental areas of work should prove useful.

Follow-Up Files in a Purchasing Department

A purchasing department buys materials for use by other sections of its company. These other sections make their wants known by sending *purchase requisition* forms to the purchasing department. These forms are similar to the requisitions that are used to request papers from the files.

Upon receiving and checking a purchase requisition, the purchasing department prepares a set of *purchase order* forms. Depending on the size of a company and its operations, from four to six copies of a purchase order are made. Two copies are sent to the vendor (the supplier). One copy is filed in the purchasing department file—usually according to the number of the purchase order. The fourth copy is filed in the departmental follow-up file.

Frequently the date of delivery of an order is vital to the operations of a department that is served by the purchasing department. Therefore, delivery dates must be closely watched. A follow-up file is used for this purpose. Usually it is made up of printed and dated folders like those used in a records department, except that a company name (the vendor's name) is shown on part of the tab of the follow-up folder. Follow-up folders hold a copy of the purchase order, a copy of the original purchase requisition, and any correspondence related to the order. The folders have signals to show the month and the day that an order is to be delivered.

Follow-Up Files in a Credit and Collection Department

Follow-up files in a credit and collection department are used for handling special cases. Such files are very active and sometimes are known as "hot files." For such cases, fast reference is needed and timing is very important.

Follow-up files are used to note dates when action is to be taken on any of the following matters: overdue accounts, pending credit studies, and current claims. The type of folder-tabbing used is similar to that shown in Illustration 6-12.

Folders in the follow-up files of a credit and collection department hold such papers as credit applications, overdue notices, correspondence concerning specific cases, and written results of telephone contacts. Some of this material is requisitioned from the main files and is returned to them when a case has been completed.

Follow-Up Files in Other Departments

In addition to the follow-up files in records departments, purchasing departments, and credit and collection departments previously discussed, various forms of follow-up files requiring the same kind of equipment are used in other departments. For example, production departments in industrial organizations follow the progress of a production order (a schedule of operations) from department to department by using a type of follow-up file. The heading for follow-up folders in such a

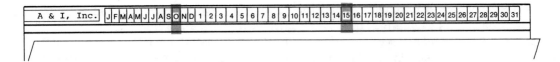

illus. 6-12, Tab on a Follow-Up Folder Used in a Purchasing Department

Signals show that merchandise ordered from A & I, Inc., should be delivered on October 15.

file might show a job number and a listing of department numbers in the manner shown in Illustration 6-13.

Sales departments use dated and signaled follow-up files in several ways. One way is to measure sales performance from month-to-month against past records or against the expected volume of sales for a given period of time (sales quotas).

Almost any type of business, industrial, or professional operation can use some form of the follow-up files just described.

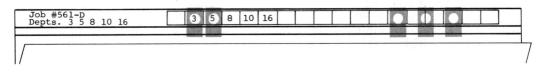

illus. 6-13, Tab on a Follow-Up Folder Used in a Production Department

Signals show that Job #561-D has progressed through Departments 3 and 5. Department 8 should now be working on this job. When 8 has completed its work, a signal will be moved from the right side to a place over the 8. Progress through Departments 10 and 16 will be marked by moving signals over their numbers on the folder tab.

Follow-Up Files for Personal Use

A personal follow-up file can help you to do things on time.

In your business life, a simple follow-up file like that shown in Illustration 6-10 can help you to do things on time. For example, a personal follow-up file at your desk can remind you to prepare certain reports at certain times, to attend meetings, to telephone a customer at a certain time, and to follow up at stated intervals on work in progress.

In your personal life, a follow-up file can also help you to do things on time. For example, your personal follow-up file can help you to meet friends on certain dates at certain times, to pay bills on time, and to keep appointments with doctors and dentists.

In order to use a follow-up file effectively, you must be systematic (orderly) in the way you handle it. On a day-to-day basis, you must prepare and file a card for every future event. You must check the file every day to see what you need to do that day and you must remove cards from the file when they have served their purpose.

Questions for Discussion

1. Why does a records department need to keep a follow-up file?

2. Why is it necessary to fill out a requisition form every time papers are needed from the main files?

3. Usually requisition forms are made in duplicate by records personnel. Why?

4. When entire folders are requested, would you release regular manila folders from the files or would you remove papers from file folders and send them in carrier folders? Why?

5. Once borrowed papers have been returned and placed in file folders, is that the end of the action taken by records department personnel? If not, why not?

6. There are three basic ways to check on the due date of borrowed papers. When could one of these ways be used, and why?

7. Does a card follow-up file need to be equipped with a complete set of daily guides for every month in the year? Why or why not?

8. When it is not possible to release a valuable paper from the files, how can the need for information best be met by the records department?

9. When dated follow-up folders with signals are used in a follow-up file, what arrangement can be made to handle "charges" and "papers wanted" needs?

10. How are follow-up files used in a purchasing department?

Job 6 Requisition and Charge Procedures

At this time complete Job 6 in OFFICE FILING PROCEDURES, Fifth Edition. The instructions and supplies for this job are included in the practice set.

CHAPTER 7

Transfer and Storage Controls

An experience common to many people is the tendency to save almost everything. Then, when the drawer or the closet door will not close, comes the "time of reckoning." Which things to keep? Which to store close at hand? Which to "file" in the attic or basement? Which things to destroy?

Business and industrial organizations must face these same problems as they try to control the volume of records that build up from day to day. If all the papers that accumulate each day were kept, business would soon slow down or stop.

3M Company

The Need for a Records Control System Is Obvious!

You can easily understand how quickly the volume of records can grow when you think about the many sources of papers that find their way into filing systems. For example, papers of one sort or another come from such departments as accounting, advertising, auditing, executive, insurance, purchasing, personnel, production, sales, and shipping. Furthermore, such matters as building maintenance and security add to the amount of records that require filing services. Information relating to taxes is vital and involves a considerable number of records that must be processed in the records control department. Just imagine what would happen if records from all of these sources were not handled in a systematic manner!

Section 1   Procedures and Systems for Transfer and Storage of Records

A complete system of records control includes transfer and storage.

To avoid major problems with filing systems, most business organizations follow a complete system of records control. This includes following certain procedures and using certain kinds of filing systems to make sure that records will always be under control. These procedures and systems, as they relate to transfer and storage, are as follows:

1. *Maintaining permanent files* in which valuable documents and papers are kept under strict security for indefinite periods of time.
2. *Disposing immediately* of certain kinds of papers after they have been scanned or given a single reading.
3. *Filing for immediate reference* those papers relating to active and important matters. Such papers are held in the *active files*.
4. *Filing for semiactive reference* those papers that have limited reference value. When papers are used at a rate slightly less than active, they are usually held in a separate system. Otherwise they are transferred directly from the active system to the storage filing system.
5. *Filing for occasional reference* those materials that are referred to infrequently but still have value. Papers in this class are held in a *storage filing system*.
6. *Destroying unneeded records* according to a predetermined time schedule.

Now we will consider in more detail the six means of controlling records from first reading to final destruction.

Maintaining Permanent Files

Some documents and papers are needed for reference or evidence over an indefinite period of time. Such permanent reference documents and correspondence relating to them come from many sources. A partial list of the kinds of papers in this category includes:

Accident records and reports	Depreciation schedules
Annual reports	Discount rates
Audit reports	Employee contracts and records
Copyrights and related correspondence	Government contracts
	Incorporation records

Leases   Permits
Market research studies   Stock records and reports
Patents and related correspondence Tax records and reports

These and many other similar documents and papers may be kept in departmental files, in a central filing system, or in underground storage centers. Such materials are usually placed in fire-resistant cabinets or vaults. They are not readily available for general reference purposes.

Disposing Immediately of Certain Papers

There is no question at all about the need for destroying certain materials as soon as they have been scanned or read. If this is not done, material of doubtful value will be released for filing. This will add needlessly to the cost of keeping records because files will be crowded with unused papers. Unnecessary filing will result in the purchase of additional supplies and equipment. It will also increase the cost of filing and finding papers because records personnel must search through additional papers in folders in order to locate the ones needed. In most organizations, employees are reminded from time to time to destroy unneeded papers rather than hold them or send them to be filed.

Filing for Immediate Reference

Filing for immediate reference means placing materials in an active filing system. These are the working files—the heart of any records control system.

To be useful, active files must contain only those materials that have a high reference value. This means that materials frequently requested from the files are held in a readily available condition. Because of their value as active sources for reference, the active files are located in areas that are within easy reach of office personnel.

In records departments, active files occupy the most available drawers in filing cabinets or the most reachable shelves in a shelf area. However, this "first-class" treatment cannot be continued indefinitely because, over a period of time, active records become less useful. Also, new material for the files keeps coming in and folders become more and more crowded. Overcrowded folders slow down work in the department because it becomes increasingly more difficult to file and retrieve papers. Overcrowded folders also cause overcrowded file drawers, which in turn slow down departmental work and lead to a generally confused condition. Semiactive files and storage files are therefore used in order to prevent crowding and confusion in the active files.

Filing for Semiactive Reference

Long before active files become overcrowded, procedures are established for transferring papers that are somewhat less useful from the active files into a semiactive filing system. When active records are at first transferred to a semiactive file, they continue to have a limited reference value—that is, they are still requested from the file, but less frequently. To allow for this, many organizations keep semiactive materials close to the location of the active filing system.

One way of doing this is to reserve the two upper drawers of a four-drawer filing cabinet for the active files and the lower two drawers for the semiactive filing system. Or, if five-drawer cabinets are used, the top and the bottom drawers are used to hold the semiactive filing system while the middle three drawers hold the active files. If open shelves are used instead of cabinets, the top and bottom shelves hold the semiactive system and the central shelves hold the active system.

Filing for Occasional Reference

Papers that are needed only occasionally for reference purposes are kept in a storage system. This system is the "final resting place" for papers that continue to have some reference value. However, because that value has reached a relatively inactive stage, storage files are kept in areas where floor space is not as valuable as it is in areas where active files must be located.

Also, because records in storage files are less frequently used, the boxes or cases in which folders are held can be stacked eight or more high. Aisles in storage areas can be relatively narrow—about 30 inches across. Illustration 7-1 shows the office area in a storage center.

*Courtesy of Bankers Box/Records
Storage Systems*

illus. 7-1, Office Area in a Records Storage Center

**Destroying
Unneeded
Records**

Most records do not need to be kept permanently. Imagine how much space and equipment would be needed if *all* records were kept forever. One of the most important services performed by the records department, therefore, is that of finally disposing of all records held in storage.

Records are destroyed only after careful consideration has been given to the future usefulness of each type of record being sent for storage. Usually destruction dates are established after consultation with various department heads and after approval by the executive and legal branches of an organization. The primary concern in a storage center or in a records department is that dates are established for the final disposal of various types of records and that destruction is carried out as scheduled.

Section 2 Transfer Methods

**When To
Transfer**

*When to transfer
depends on a
given situation.*

How often should files materials be transferred from the active files to the semiactive ones? Every day? Once a year? Twice a year? Actually, when to transfer depends on how work is performed and completed in a given situation. For example, in some contractors' offices and in law offices, work is completed in units. When such a job or a case is finished, the file for that job or that case is complete and can be transferred to storage at that time. On the other hand, most business operations require varying times to complete—some long, some short—so that it is difficult to fix an overall period of time for transferring files materials. However, if a semiactive file is close to an active one, semiactive materials can sometimes be cleared from the active file at any suitable time.

Because of the variations in kinds of work performed in different offices, three major ways of transferring records have been developed. These are referred to as perpetual transfer, one-period transfer, and two-period transfer.

**Perpetual
Transfer
Method**

*Perpetual trans-
fer clears the
active files of
unneeded pa-
pers and folders.*

As previously indicated, the perpetual method of transfer is very useful when jobs or cases have been concluded. Then, all folders holding records relating to the completed job or case can be removed from the active file and then refiled either in a semiactive system or in a storage system.

Perpetual transfer is also possible under certain conditions. If the semiactive and active files are held in the same area, files personnel can, as a daily routine, check the active file for "dead" materials—ones no longer being requested for reference. Such a check can be made by saving requisition forms like the ones shown in Illustration 6-2 and 6-3 on page 72. When matched with papers and folders in the active system, these requisitions show which materials are in demand and which are not. The "dead" ones can then be removed and filed in the semiactive filing system.

This kind of checking can be made easier if the files operator makes a tally mark on the upper part of the face of the folder each time a requisition is taken to the active file and materials or folders are removed for reference. A tally mark on the side edge of a paper in a miscellaneous folder will also show the demand for that paper or group of papers.

These methods of perpetual transfer make filing and retrieval easier because the active files are cleared of unneeded papers and folders.

One-Period Transfer Method

All folders are transferred to the storage files in one operation.

Under the one-period transfer method, all folders are removed from the active files and transferred to the storage files in one operation. No semiactive system is used.

Under this method, the transfer usually is made either once a year or twice a year. It is a useful method because, at a set time, all old materials are removed from the active files. The chief objection to this plan is that some recently received material is suddenly sent to storage. There, such material is less available for reference. However, this objection can be partly canceled if frequently requested folders and recently received papers are held for a short time in an auxiliary file near the files operator's desk. Such a file is sometimes called a "hot file." It can be transferred out of use after a short period of time—for example, in a month or less—as the need for the papers in it becomes less critical. These papers can then be transferred to the storage filing system.

Two-Period Transfer Method

The active file and the semiactive file are maintained in the same cabinets or shelves.

When the two-period transfer method is used, two files are maintained in the same cabinets or shelves: the active file and the semiactive file. A storage filing system is also used. It is located in an area that is removed from the active sections in a business office.

The active file uses the most convenient drawers or shelves, for example, the upper two drawers in a four-drawer cabinet or the middle three shelves in a shelf unit. The semiactive system is located in the lower two drawers of a four-drawer cabinet or on the upper and lower shelves in a shelf unit. In five-drawer cabinets the semiactive file is held in the top drawer and the bottom drawer. (See Illustration 7-2.)

Transfer under the two-period method usually is made once a year. At a set date, all folders that have been held in the existing *semiactive* file drawers are removed, boxed, and transferred to the *storage files*.

Following this, selected folders from the existing *active file* are transferred to the drawers formerly occupied by the semiactive file. All guides are left in the active file drawers.

New miscellaneous folders are prepared in advance of transfer day. These are held aside until they can be placed in the drawers of the newly formed active file.

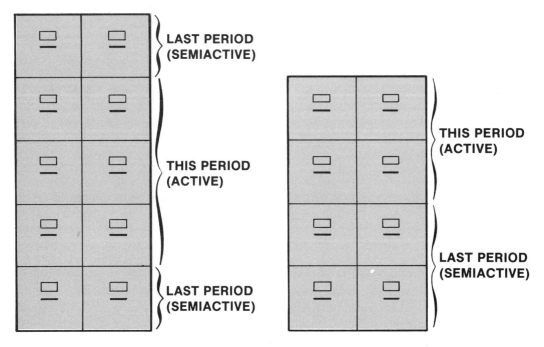

illus. 7-2, Two-Period Transfer Method Using (1) Five-Drawer Cabinets
and (2) Four-Drawer Cabinets

How Folders Are Transferred

There are two ways of transferring folders from an existing *active* file to the *semiactive* sections of file cabinets or shelves: total transfer and dated transfer.

1. *Total Transfer.* At transfer time, *all* folders in the existing active file are transferred to the semiactive file. This total transfer is made without regard to the dates on letters that are held in the active folders.
2. *Dated Transfer.* At transfer time, folders holding *recently dated* papers are kept in the active system. All other folders are transferred to the semiactive file.

The dated way of transferring folders is usually considered to be the better of the two because it keeps the more frequently called for papers where they should be—in the active file. This way of transferring folders prevents frequent searches in both the active system and the semiactive one in order to locate desired papers.

The dated way of transferring folders requires more inspection of the active file prior to transfer time. However, of greater importance is the fact that this way of transferring reduces the time required in the search for papers during the entire period of time between transfer dates.

A simple application of the dated way of transferring folders under the two-period transfer method is presented below. Folders with recently dated correspondence are kept in the active file. All other folders are transferred to the semiactive file.

Procedure when Folders Holding Papers Dated After the Cutoff Date Are Kept in the Active File. Assume that transfer day is June 30. Also assume that folders holding papers dated after April 1 (three months before June 30) *are to be kept in the active file.*

1. *Before* transfer day, take the following action:
    a. Inspect each individual and special folder in the *active file* to find the latest dated paper in it. (This is relatively simple because the first paper in a folder will be the latest one received.) The *date* on this *letter* will tell you how this *folder* is to be processed at transfer time.
    b. Mark the individual and special folders holding *only* papers dated *before* April 1 with a "T" on the upper edge. These folders will be transferred to the semiactive file on transfer day.
    c. Prepare a new set of miscellaneous folders to be used in the new active file that will be started on transfer day.

2. On transfer day, follow these procedures:
    a. Transfer *all* folders from the current *semiactive file* to the *storage filing system*. To do this, remove the folders from the semiactive file and place them in prelabeled transfer boxes. Then send the transfer boxes to the storage files.
    b. Turning to the current *active file*, remove the *miscellaneous folder* in the first primary section. Select from it all papers to be kept in the new active file (because of the latest correspondence being dated *after* April 1). Place these papers in the new miscellaneous folder previously prepared for that section. Transfer the "old" miscellaneous folder and the papers left in it to the front of the recently cleared semiactive file drawer. (Since all guides are left in the active file drawer, the miscellaneous folders serve as guides in the semiactive file.)
    c. Remove from the first primary section of the current active file all the individual and special folders marked with a "T." Put them in the appropriate places behind the miscellaneous folder for that section in the semiactive file.
    d. Repeat Steps 2b and 2c for each section in the current active file. In this way, the old inactive folders from the existing active system are transferred to the newly formed semiactive file. Because of the transferrals, space for a new active file is made available.

In the method presented above, when an individual or special folder contains correspondence dated after the cutoff date, the entire folder is retained in the active system. When an individual or special folder contains correspondence dated only before the cutoff date, the entire folder is transferred to the semiactive file.

Procedure when All Papers Dated Before the Cutoff Date Are Transferred to the Semiactive File. When folders contain numerous papers dated both before and after the cutoff date (mixed dates), it is sometimes desirable to transfer all papers dated *before* the cutoff date to the semiactive file. In such a case new miscellaneous, individual, and special folders for the current active material are prepared before the transfer date and are held in readiness. On the transfer date, the current active material is placed in the new folders in the new active file, and the older correspondence is left in the old folders, which are then placed in the semiactive file.

Section 3 Control of Records in Storage

Need for Control in Storage Files

Controlling stored records requires knowing their exact location.

There is little point in transferring papers to storage unless adequate controls are used for locating stored materials, for releasing them when requested, and for charging borrowers for materials removed from the transfer files. It is evident, therefore, that all the elements needed for records control in the active files are needed also to maintain order in the transfer or storage files. Such control requires that storage areas be identified, that boxes or drawers be labeled, and that central records of these matters be maintained.

The first step in controlling stored records is to know their exact location in the storage area so that they can be found easily. This can be a fairly simple process in a small storage area, but it becomes more complex as the space allotted for storage increases. In large storage areas, the aisles, shelf sections, and boxes or cases are all assigned numbers. These numbers are written on the box labels as well as on storage record cards held at the control desk. Thus, the location of a particular box might be listed as: Aisle: 4 / Section: 12 / Box: 325.

In smaller storage areas, the boxes or cases are given consecutive numbers. These numbers are written on labels affixed to the box fronts or on tags inserted into drawer fronts.

Equipment Used in Storage Files

Files materials in the storage system are held in either of two types of containers specially made for this kind of a filing system: (1) transfer cases or (2) transfer boxes.

Transfer Cases. When transferred records are still used somewhat frequently for reference, these records are usually housed in *transfer cases*.

Transfer cases are made of heavy corrugated fiberboard. They are box-shaped units that are equipped with sliding drawers and plastic handles. This sliding drawer feature permits relatively easy reference to the materials within the case.

If semiactive materials are held in the storage area—as they would be under the one-period transfer method—transfer cases are used to hold materials because of the sliding drawer feature. (See Illustration 7-3.)

Courtesy of Bankers Box/Records Storage Systems

illus. 7-3, Transfer Cases in the Storage Filing System

Transfer Boxes. When transferred records have a relatively low degree of reference value, they are considered to be inactive. In this condition they are usually held in *transfer boxes*.

Transfer boxes do not have sliding drawers but are equipped with lift-up tops or lift-out sides. These tops or sides are held down with a fastener of one kind or another. In Illustration 7-4, notice that string fasteners are used and that tops of boxes have overlapping sections. These features are used to prevent dust from entering the boxes.

Courtesy of Bankers Box/Records Storage Systems

illus. 7-4, Transfer Boxes for Inactive Materials in Storage Files

Labeling Transfer Cases and Boxes

The first order of business in a records storage facility is to locate requisitioned papers quickly and to make them available to those who need them. The first step in this process is to mark each case or box so that it will be distinguished from all others. This is done in either of two ways: (1) by writing identifying marks directly on the case or box or (2) by filling out a label that is then affixed to the case or box.

Each of the transfer cases shown in Illustration 7-3, page 95, is identified by a subject title written on the case. The range of these titles illustrates the types of materials that have been sent to the records storage files. For example the titles include such varied materials as *Sales Correspondence, Advertising Contracts, Bills of Lading, Accounts Receivable, Leases,* and *Operating Control Records.*

In Illustration 7-4, page 96, the transfer box on the table bears several identifying marks. It is Box No. 516 and it holds bills of lading bearing titles ranging from *A* through *Dag*. The boxes on the shelves have titles such as *Accounts Receivable, Cash Sales Slips,* and *Freight Bills*.

Using Guides and Folders in Transfer Files

When materials are transferred from active to semiactive or inactive systems, miscellaneous folders and some individual folders are included in the materials being transferred. However, folders with plastic tabs or other refinements are too expensive to be included in a transfer file. In such a case, less expensive manila folders are prepared in advance of transfer time. These are used in place of the more expensive folders, which are left in the active file.

If manila folders from the active file are transferred to the semiactive file or to the storage system, new folders for a new active file must be prepared in advance of transfer time.

Guides used in the active file are not moved with other materials at transfer time. They are too expensive to be included in a relatively inactive transfer file. In inactive filing systems, notations on miscellaneous folders are adequate for locating folders in a reasonable amount of time.

Illustration 7-5 shows three types of work in a large records storage center.

Using Storage Record Cards

Storage record cards are sometimes known as catalog cards, transfer control cards, or records storage index and destruction control cards. Whatever the name used, these cards are the most vital record kept by a control center (or desk) in a storage department. A storage record card shows when the records were received, by whom they were sent, the contents of the storage box, the exact location of the box, and the date set for the destruction of the contents of the box.

1. Referring to papers held in storage boxes.

2. Placing a storage box in a section.

3. Referring to a control index to locate a particular storage case or box.

illus. 7-5, Three Types of Work in a Large Records Storage Center

Storage record cards are the most vital record kept in a storage department.

The storage record card in Illustration 7-6 is typical of the form used by many business organizations as well as by other types of organizations that maintain records storage centers (sometimes referred to as *archives*).

RECORD TITLE									RECEIVED FROM			
		Correspondence, Purchasing							*Purchasing Department*			
DATE RECEIVED	FILE OR BOX NO.	CONTENTS				LOCATION			DATE TO DESTROY	DATE DESTROYED	CERTIFIED BY	
		ALPHABETIC NUMERIC		DATE		BLDG. OR ROOM	AISLE	SECTION				
		FROM	TO	FROM	TO							
1/5/81	231	A	Az	1/1/80	12/31/80	Base- ment	9	4	1985			
"	232	B	Bi	"	"	"	"	"	"			
"	233	Bj	Bo	"	"	"	"	"	"			
"	234	Bp	Bz	"	"	"	"	"	"			

RECORDS STORAGE INDEX AND DESTRUCTION CONTROL CARD   **BANKERS BOX** 88
record storage systems
DIVISION OF FELLOWES MANUFACTURING COMPANY

FORM 1607

Courtesy of Bankers Box/Records Storage Systems

illus. 7-6, Storage Record Card

Depending on the type of operations in a given organization, storage record cards are prepared by or completed by storage center personnel. The cards usually are made in duplicate.

One storage record card is prepared for every transfer box or drawer in the storage system or one line on a cumulative card like that shown in Illustration 7-6 is used for every box or drawer. When one box or drawer contains more than one type of material, a storage record card is prepared for each kind to be found in that box or drawer.

One of the primary advantages of using a storage record card system is that not all materials sent by one department need be placed in the same section of the storage area. This is possible because information posted on storage record control cards shows exact locations of carefully described materials—regardless of where they are located. This factor saves a great deal of time as papers are being stored, since all papers from one department are not necessarily sent at the same time and future volume cannot be anticipated by storage center personnel.

*There must be
procedures to
control the stor-
ing, finding,
lending, charg-
ing, follow-up,
and final dis-
posal of stored
records.*

Four types of records are required for maintaining order and recording vital statistics in storage operations: (1) a master control file for
locating and retrieving stored papers when they are requested for use by
any department within an organization (such a filing system is known
as a *retrieval control file*); (2) a charge-out system in connection with
storage operations; (3) and (4) records that relate to the final disposition
of stored records. These records and the types of filing systems needed to
maintain them are described below and on pages 101 and 102.

Note that when semiactive papers are kept in the same area as the
active files (as is the case when the two-period method of transfer is
used), there is no need for maintaining separate records when transfer
materials are being processed. Under such conditions, customary procedures in the filing department are sufficient for handling both active
and semiactive file materials. However, when semiactive and inactive
records are stored and processed independently, then all control procedures relating to transferred records become the responsibility of the
storage center. In such cases, there must be procedures and records to
control the storing, finding, lending, charging, follow-up, and final disposal of stored records.

It is in such circumstances as these that the storage center must
maintain the four types of records previously listed. Such records will
now be considered in detail.

Retrieval Control File. This filing system is kept at the control desk
in the storage center. (In Illustration 7-1, the file on the desk is the
control file.) It is composed entirely of storage record cards of the type
shown in Illustration 7-6. These cards are held in a system that is
primarily alphabetic. Primary guides show names of departments from
which file materials have been transferred. Secondary guides show
names of types of records being held for particular departments, for
example, "Correspondence" or "Purchase Orders" or "Accounts Receivable." Finally, series of guides for dates are used to show specific locations within a departmental group. For example, when a requisition is
received from the Sales Department for correspondence material of a
given date, the files operator scans the retrieval control file to locate a
primary guide for "Sales," then a secondary guide for "Correspondence,"
and finally a date guide corresponding to the date shown on the requisition form. Behind the date guide will be found the storage record card
bearing the location information needed. Location data will be transcribed from the card to a routing slip, which will be taken to the storage
section indicated. There, the storage box or case will be opened and the
desired papers withdrawn and sent to the requester.

Charge-Out and Follow-Up File. The use of such a system in a
storage center is exactly the same as that previously described for use in

a filing department. A type of follow-up file similar to that shown in Chapter 6, Illustration 6-10, page 79, is used for tracing as well as charging for borrowed materials that have been removed from the storage center.

Requisition cards or sheets are filed by the "date due" listed on them. The follow-up file is checked daily in tracing due and overdue materials that should be returned to storage.

illus. 7-7, **Releasing Material from the Storage Files**

Tickler File for Destruction Dates. To follow a predetermined time schedule for the destruction of various types of records, it is necessary to keep a reminder or tickler file. The file is checked periodically to determine when destruction dates are scheduled. This filing system is called a *tickler file for destruction dates*. It is also known as a "destruction tickler" or a "destruction follow-up." The file holds only the second copies of storage record cards that are prepared in duplicate when transfer materials are received. These cards are filed according to the destruction date given on them.

The tickler file for destruction dates is used in the same manner that any tickler or reminder type of filing system is used. The follow-up file shown in Chapter 6 on page 79 is typical of the form in which such systems are usually found.

At the time indicated for destruction of a particular group of records, the department head whose papers are to be destroyed is contacted to approve the destruction. Unless complications arise, the records will be destroyed by shredding, burning, selling as scrap, or other approved means.

Destruction File. When materials are destroyed, there must be witnessed or certified proof of this action and a record must be prepared and retained for an indefinite period of time. Destruction of records is a matter of vital importance, and legally acceptable records must be kept by maintaining a *destruction file*.

The primary records held in a destruction file are completed copies of the storage record cards that were held in the tickler file for destruction dates. These cards are pulled from the tickler file when destruction dates are at hand. When destruction and certification have been completed and recorded, these storage record cards are filed according to the name of the department and by the date of destruction.

Cycle of Records Control

A cycle of records control is completed with the destruction of records. This cycle includes all the procedures used in maintaining order during the useful life of those records. These procedures are as follows:

1. Control starts when papers released for filing are coded according to indexing rules and when necessary cross-referencing is completed.
2. Control continues when papers are placed in a filing system according to predetermined coding.
3. Control is extended as papers are released from the files under a charge-out plan and returned under a follow-up system.
4. When papers are transferred from active files to semiactive files to inactive files, control is maintained by keeping records and following procedures designed to preserve order.
5. Control continues as transferred materials are released, borrowers are charged, and return dates for released materials are checked by follow-up.
6. Finally, stored papers are destroyed according to a predetermined time schedule, and records of this action are made. This step represents the final phase of records control.

Questions for Discussion

1. Should a business organization keep and file all the papers that it receives? Why or why not?

2. What kinds of documents are kept in permanent storage?

3. What is an active file?

4. Why are semiactive files sometimes held in the lower two drawers in a four-drawer filing cabinet?

5. Is perpetual transfer a useful way to move business papers from active files to storage files? Why or why not?

6. What does the term "two-period transfer" mean?

7. Why are transfer cases better than transfer boxes for holding semiactive papers?

8. Are guides usually transferred from active files to storage files? Why or why not?

9. What is a storage record card and how is it used?

10. What is a tickler file for destruction dates and how is it used?

Job 7   Transfer Procedures

At this time, complete Job 7 in OFFICE FILING PROCEDURES, Fifth Edition. The instructions and supplies for this job are included in the practice set.

CHAPTER 8

Use of Color in Alphabetic Filing Systems

Section 1 Why Color Is Used in Alphabetic Filing Systems

The use of color improves appearance and increases accuracy.

In this chapter you will be studying filing systems that are constructed around an element that is both beautiful and useful: color. Before you continue reading, look at each of the four-color illustrations in this chapter. They are attractive, aren't they?

The use of color in filing systems not only improves the appearance but also increases the accuracy of filing and retrieving folders and papers. The use of color is not restricted to alphabetic systems. Color is also used in numeric systems and other systems that you will study in Chapters 11 and 13.

Color systems are very effective in reducing the time that it takes to locate a desired folder. Color also prevents the misplacing of folders that are being returned to the system.

How Color Is Used in Filing Systems

Color schemes are used primarily to divide file drawers or shelves into separate sections by using different colors for the different alphabetic or numeric sections in a filing system. This is known as *color coding*.

Another way of using color is to mark each part of a system (guides, folders, etc.) with a different color. This is known as *color accenting*.

Colors are used for color coding or color accenting.

In comparing these two ways of using color, a color-accented system assists filing and finding by such means as showing contrasting hues on various types of guide and folder tabs. A color-coded system uses various hues on guides and folders according to a scheme in which one color is always associated with the same alphabetic unit in a system. Thus, this use of color becomes a code, because a code is defined as a systematic pattern of identification.

**How Color
Systems Are
Presented
in this
Chapter**

*Color is used to
make filing
easier and more
reliable.*

Each of the four filing systems illustrated in this chapter is widely used throughout the country. It is very possible that one of these systems will be used in the office where you will work. It is therefore important for you to know how each of these systems is constructed and how color is used in it to make filing easier and more reliable. To give you this information, each of the filing systems is described first according to the way it has been *designed* and then according to the way that *colors are used* in it. Descriptions of design include the manner or style of arranging the various sections in the system and the types of notations used on guides and folders.

Section 2   Descriptions of Color Systems

As you read about the various features of each of the four color systems described, refer to the illustrations for a better understanding of each system.

**Variadex
System**

The *Variadex System* is shown in Color Illustration A. It is a KARDEX Systems, Inc., color-code system for use in vertical, lateral, and shelf files. The system is based on a definite color plan that is related not only to the identification of sections and items in the system but also to the guiding plan and to names being processed for filing.

System Layout and Guiding Plan. The vertical filing system shown in Color Illustration A is keyed to a color-coding plan. It uses the various positions in the file drawer to advantage for locating color blocks as well as alphabetic subdivisions. Guides and folders are located in an "in-line" arrangement (that is, one directly in back of the other) as follows:

1. All primary guides are in first position. First position is considered by the system designers as the most likely position from which to move across the drawer to other sections in searching for a needed miscellaneous or individual folder.
2. All miscellaneous folders are placed in line in second position. Here they are close to primary guides but are not confused with them because they are in a different position.
3. Individual folders in central position have tabs cut two positions wide (double width).
4. Special guides and OUT guides are placed in fifth position. Here they are readily visible and accessible.

Single-unit notations are used on the primary guide and miscellaneous folder tabs in this system. *Single-unit notations* are formed when two or more single letters of the alphabet are used as a single unit on most of the guide and folder tabs in a system. As Color Illustration A shows, the first guide in an alphabetic section usually is marked with a single letter, in this case "B." It is followed by a series of guides that also show single-unit notations. These divide the "B" section into smaller units. This makes filing and finding easier and more reliable.

Color Scheme. The color plan for the Variadex System is as follows: Five different colors are used for marking five different alphabetic subdivisions between any two primary letters in the alphabet. The colors are shown as strips across the top of the folder tab labels and as solid colors on the tabs of guides. The letter that is used to determine the color is the *second* letter appearing in a name or in a notation. For example, in a name beginning with the letters "Be," the "e" would determine the color used; or, in the name "Bowman," the "o" would determine the color used. The five secondary letters that are used as subdivision breaks are: a, e, i, o, and r. To understand how this plan is used, consult Color Illustration A as you read the following description.

1. The initial letter "B" when followed by "a," "b," "c," or "d" is indicated by a tab with the color *orange*.
2. The initial letter "B" when followed by "e," "f," "g," or "h" is indicated by a tab with the color *yellow*.
3. The initial letter "B" when followed by "i," "j," "k," "l," "m," or "n" is indicated by a tab with the color *green*.
4. The initial letter "B" when followed by "c," "p," or "q" is indicated by a tab with the color *blue*.
5. The initial letter "B" when followed by "r," "s," "t," "u," "v," "w," "x," "y," or "z" is indicated by a tab with the color *violet*.

In the illustration, which shows the "B" to "Bro" portion of the 125-division file, all items in each section are marked with the same color, either by a solidly colored tab or by a colored bar across a tab. Using this color scheme in processing names for filing, the colors for names on materials going into the system illustrated are as follows:

James A. Barton	is filed in the orange section ("Bar" section)
Willis Benson	is filed in the yellow section ("Ben" section)
J. R. Billings	is filed in the green section ("Bi" section)
A. S. Bowman	is filed in the blue section ("Bo" section)
Charles Brown	is filed in the violet section ("Bro" section)

Single-letter names (B-O-A Corp.) are filed in the orange section.

Alpha Code System   The *Alpha Code System*, shown in Color Illustration B, is produced by the TAB Products Company.

System Layout and Guiding Plan. This system is made up entirely of guides and individual folders for use in either shelf or open lateral types of equipment. Because of this use, guides and folders are tabbed and labeled in a vertical style. (See Color Illustration B.) In such an

Color Illustration A

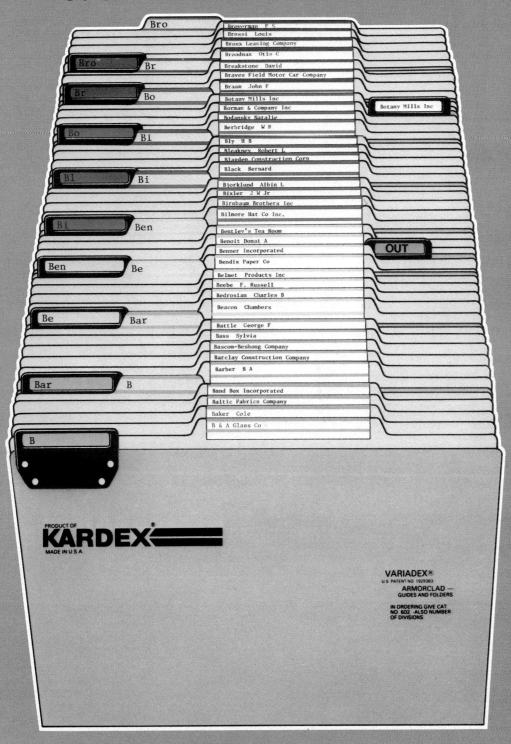

VARIADEX SYSTEM
KARDEX Systems, Inc.

Color Illustration B

ALPHA CODE SYSTEM
TAB Products Company

Color Illustration C

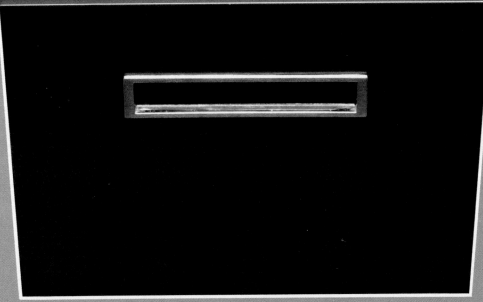

SUPER-IDEAL SYSTEM
Shaw-Walker

Color Illustration D

ALPHA-Z® SYSTEM
The Smead Manufacturing Company

arrangement, first position is considered as being at the top section of the exposed edge of a guide or folder. Second position is the next lower cut. Third position and others are in successively lower positions. Folder tabs are used as follows:

1. *First position* (the top position) is used for primary guides ("A," "B," "C," etc.).
2. Individual folder tabs are located below the primary guides. These tabs are one and one quarter the length of primary guide tabs and are used for three different purposes, so they are divided into three positions: second, third, and fourth.
3. *Second position* is used for individual folder titles (on white labels).
4. *Third position* is used for coding purposes. The letters appearing in this position on folder tabs identify the *first letter* in the key unit of a name—for example, "A" for Anderson and "B" for Browning.
5. *Fourth position* also is used for coding purposes. The letters showing on folder tabs in fourth position are used to identify the *second letter* in the key unit of a name—for example, "N" for Anderson and "R" for Browning. (Note: Although the second letter in these names is written in lowercase as "a," "b," "c," etc., capital letters are shown on folder tabs because such letters are more easily seen.)

There are no miscellaneous folders in this system. Each folder is for an individual correspondent and is labeled with the name of that person or company.

There are several ways of arranging the alphabetic notations that appear on the tabs of guides and folders. The style used in the Alpha Code System shown in Color Illustration B is the *single-letter* method. This type of notation usually consists of single letters, but occasionally two letters are combined to form a single notation. Such combinations are made in sections of the alphabet that are not as active as some others. For example, a frequent combination is "U-V" or "X-Y-Z." The more active letters, such as "B" and "S," are not combined with other letters.

Color Scheme. The color plan for the Alpha Code System combines letters of the alphabet with color patterns to form a code for each folder in the system. This is accomplished in the following manner: Each letter in the alphabet has its own color pattern. For example, an "A" is always printed in *red* on a label showing a *solid red patch* of color. The letter "B" is always *yellow* on a label with a *solid yellow patch*.

There are *two* alphabetic-color labels on each folder. The *upper* label of the two (in third position) is used for the *first* letter in the *key unit* of a name. The *lower* label (in fourth position) is used for the *second* letter in the key unit of a name. Thus, the name "Abbott" has a *red upper* label (in third position) and a *yellow lower* label (in fourth position). All names with the first two letters "Ab" have upper red and lower yellow labels. Thus, a red-yellow block of color is formed in the system.

In a system such as the Alpha Code, when folders are accurately filed, all identically coded folders appear in the same section. Any misplaced folder will be out of its color block and will easily be seen as a misfile.

Refer to the illustration of the Alpha Code System and follow these examples of coded names:

1. In the primary H section, in the center part of the lower shelf, notice that *all* folders behind the H guide have upper tabs colored in solid violet. Violet is the color for the letter H, and the pattern used is a solid patch of the color violet. Then notice that the lower tabs of folders in the violet H section show several patterns and colors. These are used to show color blocks for the various second letters in names. For example, the first five folders in the section show solid red lower tabs—the pattern and color for the letter "a." Thus, such names as H̲all and H̲arrison are found in this violet-red (solid) section.

2. In the B primary section, notice that:
   a. All upper tabs are solid yellow—the color and pattern for the letter B.
   b. The first five folders in the B section have solid red lower labels for "a." Such names as B̲ailey, B̲anks, and B̲ates are found in this color block.
   c. The second block of folders has two-part blue labels in lower position because two-part blue is the pattern and color for the letter "o." Such names as B̲ooks, Incorporated, and B̲orden, L. R., are found in this color block.
   d. The next 14 folders have two-part brown labels in lower position because this is the pattern and color for the letter "r." Such names as B̲ridges, B̲reen, and B̲rennan are found in this color block.

3. After the color-coded second letter of the name or title:
   a. Folders are arranged in strict alphabetic order, considering each letter of the key unit according to the filing rules you learned in Chapters 2, 3, and 4.
   b. Key units containing only one letter (B & O Restaurant) are coded in the lower area by using solid red to indicate no second letter in the name. "B" would thus be coded solid yellow and solid red.

Three different patterns and ten colors are used in covering the alphabet from A to Z. The patterns are: (1) *solid-color* labels for letters from A through H; (2) *two-part* colored labels for the letters I through R; and (3) *three-part* colored labels for the letters S through Z. The colors and patterns for each letter in the alphabet are as follows:

Letter	*Color*	*Letter*	*Color*
A	Solid red	D	Solid light green
B	Solid yellow	E	Solid dark green
C	Solid orange	F	Solid blue

Letter	Color	Letter	Color
G	Solid purple	Q	Two-part violet
H	Solid violet	R	Two-part brown
I	Two-part pink	S	Three-part pink
J	Two-part red	T	Three-part red
K	Two-part yellow	U	Three-part yellow
L	Two-part orange	V	Three-part orange
M	Two-part light green	W	Three-part dark green
N	Two-part dark green	X	Three-part blue
O	Two-part blue	Y	Three-part purple
P	Two-part purple	Z	Three-part violet

These colors and patterns need not be memorized because, if records personnel are working with this system (or one similar to it), the *code is always available*. In a relatively short time, anyone who works with a color-coded system becomes familiar with the code and needs only occasional reference to a key sheet or form showing all the colors and patterns that are used.

Super-Ideal System

The 75-division *Super-Ideal System*, one drawer of which is shown in Color Illustration C, is a product of the Shaw-Walker Company. The Super-Ideal System is made in a variety of indexes that range from 25 divisions (of the alphabet) to over 200. A 25-division index would be used in a one- or two-drawer filing system. A 200-division index would divide the alphabet into 200 primary sections and would be used in a 16-drawer system.

The Super-Ideal System is a color-accented system in which various colors and types of tabs are used on guides and folders to make them easier to locate.

System Layout and Guiding Plan. The positioning of guides and folders is very important to the efficiency of the Super-Ideal System. Thus, most major sections are placed in staggered positions in order to gain maximum visibility for the items in each section of the system.

In the Super-Ideal System, the items are arranged in positions across the file drawer as follows:

1. Primary guides are alternated in a slightly overlapped arrangement in first and second positions so that the greatest degree of visibility will be made available to files operators.
2. All miscellaneous folders (blue) are placed in an in-line arrangement in first position so that reference to them can be made quickly by looking down only one position in the file drawer.
3. Individual folders with double-width tabs are placed in alternating arrangement in slightly overlapped positions 3 and 4 and positions 5 and 6. This provision for large numbers of individual folders keeps the use of miscellaneous folders to a minimum. The bulk of material is held either in individual folders or in special section folders.

4. Special guides with tabs somewhat more than double width are placed at the right of the file drawer.
5. OUT guides are placed in the center of the 3-4 position.

Double-closed notations and multiple-closed notations are used on primary guides and miscellaneous folders in the Super-Ideal System. *Double-closed notations* show the beginning and closing letters in each alphabetic section of the file. For example, the notation on the first primary guide in Color Illustration C is read as "Aa-Al." *Multiple-closed notations* show the beginning and ending letters in each alphabetic section of the file. For example, the notation on the second primary guide in Color Illustration C is read as "Am-Ar-As-Ay." This notation tells the person searching the file that this alphabetic section contains material beginning with <u>Am</u> and ending with <u>Ay</u> and that within this range are the important subsections <u>Ar</u> and <u>As</u>.

The Super-Ideal alphabetic system goes one step beyond the alphabetic combinations usually found in double-closed notations. This system shows additional titles that frequently appear on papers being coded. An example of this type of notation is seen on the first primary guide in Color Illustration C. The caption on this guide is:

$$
\text{A} \quad \begin{array}{c|l} \text{A} & \text{Also} \\ & \text{A \&} \\ \text{L} & \text{A -} \end{array} \quad 1
$$

The letters on the left side of the tab indicate that this alphabetic section goes from <u>Aa</u> through <u>Al</u>. The notations on the right side of the tab show that *within* the <u>Aa-Al</u> section of this file are papers bearing names that begin with "<u>A &</u>" (such as <u>A & P</u> Stores) and those that begin with "<u>A-</u>" (such as <u>A-Z</u> Variety Stores).

Color Scheme. The Super-Ideal System has a color-accent plan in which colors are used on guides and folders to make each type of item in the system stand out from all others and thus be more readily located. The color scheme is as follows:

1. Primary guides, which are staggered in first and second positions, show primary section notations in red letters. All other notations are given with black letters on a white background.
2. Miscellaneous folders in first position have blue tabs and thus stand out from other items in the file drawer because of the contrast between colors used on these folders and on guides and other folders. Miscellaneous folders for primary alphabetic sections have red notations that correspond to those on the guides for those sections.
3. Secondary guides staggered in first and second positions show black notations on white backgrounds in contrast to primary guides with red on white.

4. Special section guides are placed in overlapping fifth-sixth position, which lends distinction to these items as does the use of heavy black tabs and black-on-white notations.
5. Individual folders have distinctively colored labels that set them apart from other items in the file drawer. Also, individual folders are staggered in positions 3 and 4 and in positions 5 and 6 in order to provide maximum visibility for those who search the files.

ALPHA Z® System

The *ALPHA* Z® *System* is shown in Color Illustration D. It is produced by the Smead Manufacturing Company of Hastings, Minnesota.

System Layout and Guiding Plan. ALPHA Z® is made up entirely of guides and individual folders for use in vertical, lateral, and shelf equipment. In lateral and shelf units, guides and folders are tabbed and labeled in a vertical style (see Color Illustration D). In such an arrangement the uppermost position is considered to be *first* position. Second position is the next lower cut. Third position and others are in successively lower positions.

The equivalent of seven positions (from top to bottom) are used in order to guide and color code the ALPHA Z® system. These positions are used in the following manner:

1. *First* position (the top position) is reserved for primary guides.
2. *Second* position is occupied by solid color labels that identify each alphabetic section in the system.
3. *Third* position is used for names of correspondents. These are typed on a white section of the label.
4. *Fourth* position shows colored letters on labels that identify the *first* letter in the key unit of a name.
5. *Fifth* position labels show colored sections that identify the *second* letter in the key unit name.
6. *Sixth* position is used to show colors for the *third* letter in the key unit name.
7. *Seventh* position is reserved for OUT guides.

Color Scheme. In the ALPHA Z® color scheme (plan), two different patterns are used to cover the alphabet. The patterns used are: (1) one-part solidly colored labels for the letters A to M and (2) labels that are divided into three parts for letters that range from N to Z.

Colored labels that are used to code the *key units* in names are used in three positions.

1. Colors for primary alphabetic sections and the first letter in the key unit name are in fourth position. (Letters A-M are color-on-white; letters N-Z are white-on-color.)
2. Colors that are used for the second letter in the key unit are located in fifth position.
3. Colors that identify the third letter in the key unit are in sixth position.

The colors and patterns for each letter in the alphabet are as follows:

Solid Label Pattern		*Three-Part Label Pattern*	
Letter	*Color*	*Letter*	*Color*
A	red	N	red
B	blue (dark)	O	blue (dark)
C	green	P	green
D	blue (light)	Q	blue (light)
E	purple	R	purple
F	orange	S	orange
G	gray	T	gray
H	brown (dark)	U	brown (dark)
I	pink	V	pink
J	yellow	W	yellow
K	brown (light)	X	brown (light)
L	violet	Y	violet
M	green (light)	Z	green (light)

These colors and patterns need not be memorized because if a records assistant is working with this system (or one similar to it) *the code is always available.* In a relatively short time anyone who works with this system becomes familiar with the code and needs only occasional reference to a key sheet or form that shows all the colors and patterns being used.

As an example of how a name is color coded in the ALPHA Z® System, a folder for the name "Abbott" would have a *solid red* letter in fourth position for the letter "A." In fifth position there would be a *solid dark blue* label for the second letter "b." This would be followed by another *solid dark blue* label for the third letter in this name.

If you look at Color Illustration D, you will see several folders bearing the code labels red/solid blue/solid blue. Folders with such a code would hold papers from correspondents with such key units as Abbe, Abbey, Abbot, and Abbott.

In a system such as the ALPHA Z®, when folders are accurately filed, all folders with identical color codes appear in the same color section of the filing system. Therefore, any misplaced folder would be out of its color section and would easily be seen as a misfile.

Questions for Discussion

1. What is the most important reason for using colors in a filing system?

2. What are the two general ways of using color in filing systems?

3. What is the difference between a color-accented and a color-coded filing system?

4. What is meant by an "in-line" arrangement of guides and folders?

5. What use is made of the in-line arrangement found in the Varidex System?

6. In the Variadex System, would a folder for "The Blackstone Company" be filed in the same *color* section as a folder for "Bjorklund & Bishop"? Why or why not?

7. Is the Alpha Code System a color-accented or a color-coded system? Explain.

8. What is meant by the term "single-letter" notation style?

9. Is the single-letter notation style used in the Alpha Code System shown in Color Illustration B?

10. In the Alpha Code System, what is the method used for coding names?

11. Is the Super-Ideal System a color-accented or a color-coded method of filing?

12. A "multiple-closed" form of notation is used in the Super-Ideal System. What does this term mean?

13. Is the ALPHA Z® System a color-accented or a color-coded system? Explain.

14. What is meant by the term "single-unit" notation style?

15. Is the single-unit style used in the ALPHA Z® System?

16. In the ALPHA Z® System, what is the method used for coding names?

Filing Problems

1. *Using the Variadex System.* Assume that letters from the correspondents in the following list are to be coded for filing in a Variadex System. Proceed as follows:

   a. On separate pieces of paper or on index cards, write each of the names below and code it for filing. Include the number of the name on the card.
   b. Arrange the papers or cards in alphabetic order.
   c. Prepare a form like that shown in the example below.
   d. Write the number of each name (in alphabetic order) in the first column. Write the *key unit* in the second column.
   e. After each name, write in the third column the name of the color section in which the letter bearing this name will be filed.

Number	Key Unit (in alphabetic order)	Color Section
7	B (&)	orange

List of Names

1. The Battery & Tire Center
2. C. R. Branch
3. The Blue Balloon
4. Bi-Rite Carpet Co.
5. Bates & Carson
6. Ben Booth
7. B & J Pharmacy
8. Brendon's Restaurant
9. Beggs Brothers
10. Baptist Mission Society
11. John T. Blackstone
12. The Beehive

2. *Using the Alpha Code System.* In this problem you are to assume that papers sent to and received from persons and firms whose names are given on the next page are to be filed in an Alpha Code System as described on pages 106-109. Proceed as follows:

   a. On separate pieces of paper or on index cards, list *only* the number and the key unit of each name given below.
   b. Arrange the papers or cards containing the key unit names in alphabetic order.
   c. Prepare a form like that shown in the example below.
   d. Write the number of each name (in alphabetic order) in the first column and the key unit in the second column.
   e. Indicate in the Upper Label column the letter and the color pattern that would be shown on the upper label for each name on the list.
   f. Indicate in the Lower Label column the letter and the color pattern that would be shown on the lower label for each of the names on the list.

Number	Key Unit	Upper Label Color Code	Lower Label Color Code
13	Accountants	A = solid red	C = solid orange

List of Names

1. Firestone Tire Co.
2. Hallmark Card Company
3. Atkins & Ross
4. McCann and Associates
5. Guzman Labor Supply Co.
6. Damon Travel
7. Joseph's TV Repair
8. Betty's Fashion Shops
9. C. Joseph Evans
10. Ila of New York
11. KAM Industries
12. Magic Town
13. Society of Accountants

3. *Using the ALPHA Z® System.* In this exercise you are to assume that papers sent to and received from persons and firms whose names are given below are to be filed in the ALPHA Z® System. Now proceed as follows:

   a. Prepare a form like that shown below as an example.
   b. Write the number of each name in the first column.
   c. List only the key unit of each name in the second column.
   d. Arrange the key unit names in alphabetic order.
   e. List the 4th position color code in the third column.
   f. List the 5th position color code in the fourth column.
   g. List the 6th position color code in the fifth column.

Number	Key Unit	4th Position Color Code	5th Position Color Code	6th Position Color Code
1	Abbey	red	dark blue	dark blue

List of Names

1. Abbey Rents
2. Arendt & Mosier
3. Bercovitz Steel Co.
4. Barton & Gomez
5. Abbott Laboratories
6. Albert-Spaulding Co.
7. Bloch Safety Co.
8. Church of the Assembly
9. American Sportswear, Inc.
10. Anthony's Market
11. The Ad Club
12. Apparel 21

Part 4
Types of Filing Systems

The Shaw – Walker Co.

CHAPTER 9

Geographic Filing Systems and Procedures

Keeping and storing records of business transactions has been a part of world culture for thousands of years. Many ancient peoples, living in various geographic areas, traded with others in widely separated sections of the Old World. We know this because archaeologists have found thousands of written records about debts owed and contracts agreed upon by traders who lived more than four thousand years ago.

You Can Go Far with Proper Filing!

Most of these records were inscribed on small blocks of clay, and we know that some of these were "filed" in shelf-like slots cut into the walls of storage rooms. Others were held in large clay storage vessels. It is believed likely that some of these ancient records were "filed" according to geographic names because many were written in this manner: "Shami-Adad of Ur owes to Sargon of Cappadocia the sum of ten pieces of silver." Also, we know that as early as 1750 B.C., in Hammurabi's kingdom of Babylon, merchants formed companies and established "branch offices" in such cities as Byblos and Ur.

In modern times, we continue to find geographic filing methods very useful, but in far more complex forms.

Knossos—linear writing on stone—about 1500 B.C.

Lear Siegler, Inc./Borroughs Division

Disk packs, microforms, legal papers, and correspondence

illus. 9-2, Types of Modern Business Records

Perseopolis—cuneiform writing on stone—about 600 B.C.

illus. 9-1, Records of Trading in the Ancient World

Section 1 Geographic Filing Systems

A geographic filing system is used when operations are related primarily to locations.

Geographic filing is an alphabetic method based principally on the geographic location of correspondents. A geographic filing system can be useful when the operations of a business are related primarily to locations rather than to names of persons and companies. Examples of such operations are to be found in many areas of social and political life as well as in business and industry. Thus, such social groups as clubs and societies having national or regional memberships use geographic filing systems.

Geographic filing systems are also extensively used by business and industrial organizations. For example, any company with branch offices in several locations can use the geographic names of these branches as titles for primary guides in a geographic system. Also, any company that sells to customers in different areas or that buys from suppliers in various regions can use geographic files in its sales and purchasing departments; it might even arrange its central filing system in a geographic pattern. Many mail-order companies, publishers, air and rail lines, wholesale houses, and travel-related companies use geographic filing systems in one form or another.

Types of Geographic Filing Systems

In a location name guide system, location names are used as captions on all guides and folders.

There are many types of geographic filing systems. Since so many kinds of organizations can use geographic systems, it is easy to see that no one type would be best for every organization. In fact, geographic systems are among the most adaptable systems of all those in general use. They can be "tailored" to fit almost any kind of geographical condition, from districts in a city to regions in the world. However, there are two basic ways of forming geographic systems:

1. *Using location names on all guides and folders.* In this plan, location names are used as captions on all primary and secondary guides as well as on all individual and miscellaneous folders.
2. *Using letters as captions on primary guides and location names on all folders and on special guides.* In this arrangement, alphabetic captions are used on all primary guides. Geographic titles are used as captions on all special guides and folders as well as on all individual folders.

Of the two types of geographic arrangements, the system using location names on all guides and folders is the one most frequently found. We shall therefore examine the structure of such a system.

Analysis of a Location Name Guide System

A geographic filing system using location name guides is shown in Illustration 9-3. There are four major guides in this system, one for each country included in the system: Egypt, England, Ireland, and the United States. These are marked by the four guides in a central position in the file drawer.

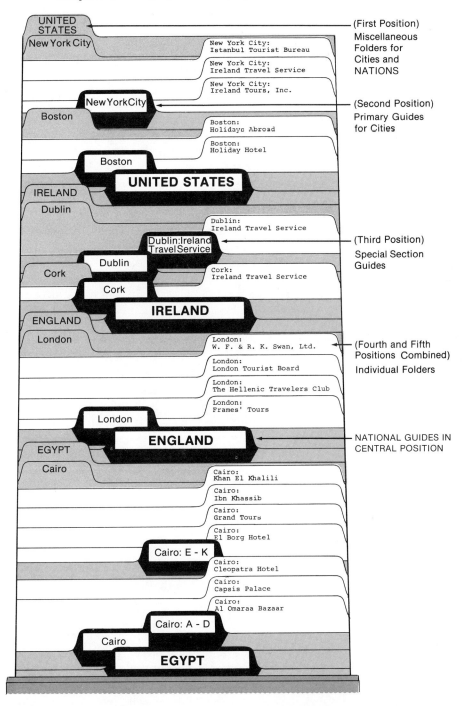

UNITED STATES

New York City

New York City:
Istanbul Tourist Bureau

New York City:
Ireland Travel Service

New York City:
Ireland Tours, Inc.

New York City

Boston

Boston:
Holidays Abroad

Boston:
Holiday Hotel

Boston

UNITED STATES

IRELAND

Dublin

Dublin:
Ireland Travel Service

Dublin: Ireland
Travel Service

Dublin

Cork

Cork:
Ireland Travel Service

Cork

IRELAND

ENGLAND

London

London:
W. F. & R. K. Swan, Ltd.

London:
London Tourist Board

London:
The Hellenic Travelers Club

London:
Frames' Tours

London

ENGLAND

EGYPT

Cairo

Cairo:
Khan El Khalili

Cairo:
Ibn Khassib

Cairo:
Grand Tours

Cairo:
El Borg Hotel

Cairo: E - K

Cairo:
Cleopatra Hotel

Cairo:
Capsis Palace

Cairo:
Al Omaraa Bazaar

Cairo: A - D

Cairo

EGYPT

(First Position)
Miscellaneous
Folders for
Cities and
NATIONS

(Second Position)
Primary Guides
for Cities

(Third Position)
Special Section
Guides

(Fourth and Fifth
Positions Combined)
Individual Folders

NATIONAL GUIDES IN
CENTRAL POSITION

illus. 9-3, A Geographic Filing System Using Location Names on Guides and Folders

Following the national divisions is a series of guides in second position that show the names of six cities: Cairo, London, Cork, Dublin, Boston, and New York City. Each city guide heads a section made up of individual folders, special section guides (if any), and one miscellaneous folder for the particular city section.

Miscellaneous city folders, in first position, hold papers from correspondents for whom no individual folders have been prepared because there are not enough papers from them to warrant such action. Materials held in miscellaneous folders for cities are arranged according to the alphabetic order of the correspondents' names. Then, within a series of papers from the same person or company, filing order is by dates—the most recent date in the front. Filing order within individual folders is also by dates—the most recent date in front.

Third position in the system illustrated is held open so that special sections of one kind or another can be added when they are needed. Usually special sections are necessary when bottlenecks of some kind appear in filing routines. For example, when an accumulation of individual folders makes the finding of a certain one more difficult than it should be, an alphabetic breakdown like that included in the Cairo section should be added to the system.

Third position is also used to mark the location of very active individual folders. The addition of a guide such as that for *Dublin: Ireland Travel Service* allows a files operator to scan third position and quickly locate this very frequently requested folder.

Finally, each national division in this system is closed by a miscellaneous folder for the nation concerned. This is done so that when correspondence not related to any city listed in the system appears for processing, that correspondence can be filed in the national miscellaneous folder. In these types of folders, papers are held in an order based on the alphabetic arrangement of names of cities. Within each city group, papers are placed according to the alphabetic order of names of correspondents. Within name groups, papers are arranged according to dates—the most recent date in the front.

Review of Filing Patterns in a Geographic System

A review of how papers are arranged in the various kinds of folders found in geographic filing systems follows.

Order of Filing Papers in Individual Folders. Letters in individual folders of a geographic filing system are from, and to, one person or company. Therefore, they are filed by dates (chronologically) with the latest dated piece in the front of the folder and the earliest dated piece at the back. Papers that are not dated can be time-stamped with the current date by records department personnel. Such time-stamped papers can then be fitted into the chronological pattern in any of the folders in a geographic filing system.

Order of Filing Papers in City Miscellaneous Folders. City miscellaneous folders hold papers from more than one correspondent in the same city. Therefore, papers are arranged first by the alphabetic order of correspondents' names; then they are arranged by date within a group of papers from the same person or company. Again, dates can be stamped on undated papers.

Order of Filing Papers in Miscellaneous Folders in Major Geographic Sections. The titles of major sections included in a given geographic system will change from one system to another as the areas being covered change. For example, the captions on primary location guides can show any of the following types of names: names of countries, regions, states, cities, or districts in a city. In the international system shown in Illustration 9-3, miscellaneous folders for nations hold papers from correspondents in cities not included in the section. File materials concerning correspondents from unlisted cities are placed in national or state miscellaneous folders according to the alphabetic order of city names. Next, they are arranged by alphabetic order of correspondents' names, and then by date within each group of papers from one person or company.

Use of Card Files to Control Geographic Filing Systems

When geographic filing systems are used, problems sometimes arise because papers are not filed according to the names of correspondents but according to the location of those companies or persons. For example, a person who is requesting materials from the files may have forgotten the address of the correspondent. It is also possible that a correspondent may have written from a location other than the usual business address.

To solve such problems as these, an organization may maintain a supplementary index card file with names of correspondents arranged in alphabetic order. This card file is not needed as an aid in filing materials, but it is helpful in finding filed materials when the correspondent's address is unknown or in doubt.

A supplementary index card file is helpful in finding filed materials when the correspondent's address is in doubt.

Cards for the supplementary index card system are prepared and used in the following manner:

1. *Before a paper is filed*, the files operator refers to the index card file to see if there is a card for that person or company. If there is none, one is prepared by writing the name and the address of the correspondent on a file card. The operator knows that the paper to be filed will be placed in a miscellaneous folder because the correspondent is new and has no other papers in the file. Therefore, the operator types the letter "M" (for "miscellaneous") in the upper right-hand corner of the index card. This shows anyone who might read this card that papers relating to the person or company concerned will be found in a miscellaneous folder.

2. *Later, if the volume of correspondence is sufficient*, an individual folder is prepared for this same correspondent. At that time, the files operator moves all of this correspondent's papers from the miscellaneous folder to a

newly prepared individual folder. The operator also removes the "M" from the index card and in its place types an "I." This signifies that the correspondent's papers are now held in an individual folder.

Section 2 Geographic Filing Procedures

Procedures in geographic filing are similar to those used in alphabetic filing, although there are some differences that will be presented in the following paragraphs.

Inspection

Each incoming letter should be inspected to see that it has been released for filing. Each paper should be checked to see that it has been dated.

Coding

Circle units in the geographic name and number them to show their indexing order.

Since the names of geographic locations are used as the first units for filing papers, these must be clearly marked. An effective way to code is to circle units in the geographic name and number them to show their importance in the indexing order. (See Illustration 9-4 on page 126.)

After the location name has been coded, the name of the correspondent is coded in the usual manner, that is, by using diagonal lines to separate the units, then underlining the key unit, and numbering the others to show their index order.

Cross-References

In a geographic system, cross-references are made from one location to another.

In geographic filing, as in alphabetic filing, there are times when cross-referencing is desirable. For example, if a letter gives useful information about another company, a cross-reference should be prepared. In a geographic system, cross-references are made from one location to another. The name of the correspondent is given second consideration. (See Illustration 9-4 and 9-5 on page 126.)

When desired, a cross-reference can be made in any of three different ways: (1) by using cross-reference sheets or photocopies, (2) by using cross-reference guides, or (3) by making cross-reference notations on folder tabs.

Cross-reference guides are used when there is a more-or-less permanent reason for calling attention to a cross-reference. An example is when a correspondent has offices in several locations. This problem can also be handled by the use of a permanent cross-reference notation on the tab of each folder that contains information relating to materials in other folders. Assume, for example, that a correspondent named "Economy Stores, Inc.," has its main office in Tampa, Florida, and has branches in Macon, Georgia, and in Mobile, Alabama. In the main files, the tab on each folder for each office of this company would show references to the other offices in this manner:

Florida: Tampa
Economy Stores, Inc.
SEE ALSO: Mobile, Alabama
Macon, Georgia

The tabs on the folders filed under Macon, Georgia, and Mobile, Alabama, would also be labeled to refer to the other two branch offices.

Sorting

Letters and other papers are sorted by geographic units, starting with the key unit and continuing until all units involved in the filing process have been used. For example, the first sorting might be on the basis of states, the second sorting might be for cities, and the final sorting would be for names of correspondents.

Filing and Retrieving Papers

The routine involved in filing and retrieving papers in a geographic filing system is about the same as it is in any other type of system. This process is most effective when a well-planned, well-cared-for system is maintained.

In the system shown in Illustration 9-3, a files operator who wants to locate a letter from the Istanbul Tourist Bureau in New York City first scans the drawer labels on the filing cabinets for the appropriate drawer. With the drawer located and opened, the operator scans down the center in order to locate the guide for the UNITED STATES. In the same scanning action, eye direction turns to the right where individual folders are located. Finding the one wanted, the operator pulls the folder partly out of the drawer, thumbs through the papers, and removes the desired letter.

If an individual folder for Istanbul Tourist Bureau has not been included in the system, scanning continues. The operator looks to the far left to find the New York City miscellaneous folder. The desired letter should be found in that folder.

Section 3 Providing for Expansion in Geographic Filing Systems

Need for Expansion

Geographic systems can be expanded with relative ease.

As business operations continue through a year, changes occur that require adjustments in the records control system. For example, a business will be corresponding with new customers and will be buying from new vendors; therefore, new names or sections will need to be added to the filing system. The business may start new programs or manufacture different products from one year to another; then, new titles and divisions must be included in the files. Also, some old customers may be lost or vendors may be changed. If so, some of the current titles or sections in the filing system will have to be eliminated at, or before, transfer time.

CROSS-REFERENCE SHEET

Name or Subject *London, England,*
Claude C. Gilchrist

Date of Item *March 6, 19--*

Regarding *Proposals for Art Tours*

SEE

Name or Subject *Boston, MA*
The Adventure Travel Service

Authorized by *C.T.*   Date *3/8/--*

Illus. 9-5, Cross-Reference Sheet

Notice that this cross-reference sheet was authorized by the secretary whose initials are "C. T." This person was the one who released the letter for filing. At the time of release, the letter (shown in Illustration 9-4) was marked to show how it should be cross-referenced. The files operator then filled out the cross-reference sheet shown above.

The Adventure Travel Service
Specializing in Service to the Travel Industry
4016 International Trade Mall
Boston, Massachusetts 09710[2]-1112
BX 617-0065-5858

March 6, 19--

MAR 8 19--

Ms. Diana Hamilton, Director
ART TRAVEL TOURS
7260 Travel Center Plaza
New York, NY 10020-1901

Dear Ms. Hamilton

It was a pleasure to confer with you during the NATA convention.

Since our meeting, we have been developing the schedules that were discussed. We now are in a position to suggest for your consideration a series of continental plans that can be coordinated with your Famous Art Tours series.

Our resident manager in London, England, Mr. Claude C. Gilchrist, will call you about a series of four proposals. We hope that these plans will meet with your approval.

Your questions concerning the plans will be welcomed by this office and by our London office.

Sincerely,

Melissa Max, President

MM/ac

cc Gilchrist

Illus. 9-4, An Incoming Letter Coded for Filing and Cross-Referencing in a Geographic Filing System

Geographic systems are more adaptable to change than are some other systems of filing. Geographic systems can be expanded or reduced with relative ease.

The first indications of a need for expansion in a system are: (1) an increase in the volume of incoming and outgoing papers being processed for filing, and (2) overcrowding in miscellaneous and individual folders.

Providing for Expansion

Space for expansion is anticipated at transfer time.

If a records department is under efficient management, space for expansion during a period of time (such as one year) will have been anticipated at transfer time. If this is the case, free space will have been left in every file drawer and on every shelf section. This space can then be used during the year to hold additions to the system. For example, as a miscellaneous folder for a state becomes overcrowded with materials from correspondents in various cities in that state, new miscellaneous folders for cities can be prepared. Then, blocks of papers can be removed from the state folder and refiled in the new folders for cities.

If miscellaneous folders for cities begin to bulge with more than about 50 sheets of paper, groups of correspondence can be taken from the city folders and refiled in newly prepared folders for individual correspondents.

In a system similar to the one in Illustration 9-3, a position within the file drawer can be used to set up special sections of some kind. In the illustrated system, the third position has been used in such a manner. With such a position open, it is possible to relieve overcrowding in individual folders by adding guides and folders to form new sections. In these new sections, a series of dated folders or a series of folders bearing special titles can be used to reduce crowding in the individual folders sections. Also, the open position can be used to start new sections that can hold very active materials—ones that are frequently requested.

Section 4 Disadvantages of Geographic Filing

In spite of being very useful and sometimes necessary, geographic filing has certain limitations and problems.

One disadvantage is the need, at times, for using a supplementary index card system along with the geographic system. Having to use a card index means that time must be spent in preparing and maintaining the card system. It also means that occasionally, files operators must search the card system as well as the main geographic system to locate needed papers.

Another disadvantage of the geographic method of filing is that there is no indicated place to file papers relating to the internal operations of a company. For example, where would you file papers relating to the hiring of new employees if you were using the system shown in

Illustration 9-3? Such a problem as this usually is solved by using either a separate alphabetic file or a separate subject filing system to hold all papers relating to a company's internal operations.

It is also possible to reserve a section in the geographic system to use for holding papers relating to internal matters. This can be accomplished by adding a primary guide that has been labeled with the name of the place where a company is located. Then, behind this guide, other guides and folders can be labeled so that they can fill out the section with such titles as "Accounting," "Personnel," and "Purchasing."

Questions for Discussion

1. Several types of companies can use geographic filing systems to advantage. What are some of these types of companies and why do they use geographic systems?

2. What is the difference between a location name guide system and a letter guide system?

3. In Illustration 9-3, how is third position used?

4. In what order are papers arranged in a miscellaneous city folder?

5. How are papers arranged in a miscellaneous state folder?

6. How is a supplementary index card file used in connection with a geographic system?

7. How are cross-references made in a geographic filing system?

8. If some state miscellaneous folders in your filing system are becoming overcrowded, what can you do to relieve this condition?

9. If an individual folder becomes overcrowded, what can you do about it?

10. What is one of the disadvantages of geographic filing?

Job 8   Geographic Correspondence Filing

At this time complete Job 8 in OFFICE FILING PROCEDURES, Fifth Edition. The instructions and supplies for this job are included in the practice set.

CHAPTER 10

Subject Filing Systems and Procedures

We have learned how to file correspondence and other materials in alphabetic order by individual or company name. Thus, a letter from Sue Abbott is located in front of letters from Sam Bardon because Abbott comes before Bardon alphabetically. But what if Sue Abbott's name is not as important to us as the fact that Sue, an accountant, has written about a subject relating to the solution of an important tax accounting question. How can we locate the answer to this accounting question if we do not remember that it was written by Sue Abbott? Many letters from other accountants relating to the same tax question may be in our files. If we were using an alphabetic filing system, we would have to remember the names of all these writers so we could locate all the correspondence on the same question. This chapter discusses subject filing—one way to solve this problem.

Subject Filing Is Another Successful Method of Records Control

Section 1 Subject Filing Systems

Nature of Subject Filing

A system in which information is filed primarily under subject titles is called a subject filing system.

When most of the material in a file is likely to be requested by subject titles rather than by the names of persons or companies, it is better to have a filing system where subject titles are used as captions. A system in which information is filed primarily under subject titles is called a *subject filing system*.

In a subject filing system, the captions on the guides and folders are generally based on subject titles rather than on the names of people or companies. In the case of Sue Abbott's letter concerning the tax accounting question, the letter can be filed under a subject title such as "Accounting—Tax." All other materials concerning this topic will also be placed in the same folder along with Sue Abbott's letter, regardless of who wrote the material. When someone wants to have information on this question, they will find all the related materials, including Sue Abbott's letter, in the same folder or section of the system. They will not have to remember Sue Abbott's name to locate the material. If, on the other hand, there is a large volume of correspondence on this same topic written by Sue Abbott, a separate folder with the caption "Accounting—Tax—Abbott, Sue" can be prepared and filed after the subject folder "Accounting—Tax." This individual correspondence folder would be a part of the subject file and would be located with all folders on the same subject.

The arrangement of a subject file looks like an outline.

Frequently the arrangement of a subject file looks like an outline of the activities of the business. This is true because the titles used as captions on guides are very similar to those that describe the activities, the departments, or the problems of a business or an office. For example, titles used in a subject filing system might be based on the following alphabetic list of activities or departments in a particular company:

Accounting	Manufacturing
Administration	Marketing
Construction	Office
Engineering	Personnel
Insurance	Public Relations
Legal	Purchasing

Each one of the main subject headings listed above would probably be separated into subdivisions. These subdivisions, in turn, could be broken down further into smaller subject areas. For example, a more complete subject breakdown of "Accounting" might be developed, such as the one shown on the following page.

ACCOUNTING

Audits	Credit	Financial

Audits

    Cash Payments
    Cash Receipts
    Management Statements
    Payroll

Budgets

    Branch
    Corporate

Costs

    Administrative
    Manufacturing
    Office

Credit

    Secured
    Unsecured

Expense

    Administrative
    Executive
    Office
    Marketing
    Advertising
    Research
    Sales

Financial

    Bonds
    Investments
    Stocks

Taxes

    Federal
    Local
    State

Uses of Subject Filing

Subject filing groups all material on one subject in one place.

Subject filing can be used to advantage whenever it is desirable to have all material on one subject grouped in one place in the files rather than separated under many different names. This is especially important when all the records related to one product or one activity are needed at the same time. Such a situation is generally more typical of single departments in a business than it is of a centralized file for an entire business. The correspondence of one department is usually concerned with a relatively small number of subjects with few divisions and subdivisions. These subjects fit into a simple classification that everyone in the department who has occasion to use the file understands thoroughly.

Subject files are frequently found in:

1. Research departments where materials are filed under titles describing particular studies. A research director for new products development, for example, may file research reports first by product name and second by the specific report name.
2. Executive offices where the interest is not so much in a particular correspondent as in the overall picture. A purchasing agent for office equipment, for example, may be more concerned with the types of office equipment available than with the names of the manufacturers of such equipment.
3. Offices that keep instructional information. In teachers' files, for example, information relating to various subjects is filed under topic headings.
4. Companies and institutions where work is handled first by group titles and then by name. Art galleries, museums, libraries, and commercial supply houses are examples.

Subject Filing in a Centralized File

A centralized records department must handle materials relating to customers as well as to business operations.

Some businesses operate a central records department. In such a department, records are kept in one location but the papers may relate to the activities of many different departments. Sometimes a centralized records department must handle materials relating to customers as well as to business operations. In this case, all customer material is filed according to the names of the customers—sometimes in a separate alphabetic filing system. Then, all matters dealing with the operation of the business are filed by subject in a subject system.

The subject filing system brings together all material from such areas as advertising, sales, personnel, taxes, insurance, and office procedures. These materials are often needed for reference over a longer period of time than customers' correspondence. Holding them in a separate subject file means that important records can be kept without transfer for as long a time as desired.

Arrangement of a Subject File

A subject filing system contains the same elements as an alphabetic correspondence file.

A subject filing system contains the same elements as an alphabetic correspondence file—equipment, guides, folders, and procedures—which you studied in Chapter 5. The guides of a subject file may appear in one, two, or three positions, depending on the number of headings and subheadings in the outline of subjects for the activities or departments of the business. For example, primary guides might be used in first position to indicate the subjects representing the main headings of the outline. Auxiliary guides might appear in second position to represent subdivisions of each main heading in the outline. If the subdivision headings in the outline are in turn subdivided, guides in third position could carry suitable captions.

All folders in a subject file may be of one type with captions consisting of subject headings only; or folders of a second type may be included for names of individuals and businesses.

Miscellaneous folders similar to those used in an alphabetic file generally are not used in subject systems. Each paper or other document is coded according to its subject title and is filed directly in its properly labeled folder. Tabs on folders used in a subject file are usually third-cut or half-cut.

Outline of a Subject File

The best technique to use in starting a subject file is to develop a detailed outline. Six divisions of a subject filing system are shown in Illustration 10-1. When the file in the illustration was established, a very thorough study was made of the titles under which papers would be requested from the file by those who were to use it. As a result of this study, it was decided that papers were to be filed under six major titles or headings. These six headings were then arranged in alphabetic order on the outline. After further study, it was decided to use twenty subheadings under the main headings. These subheadings were arranged in alphabetic order on the outline within the six primary sections.

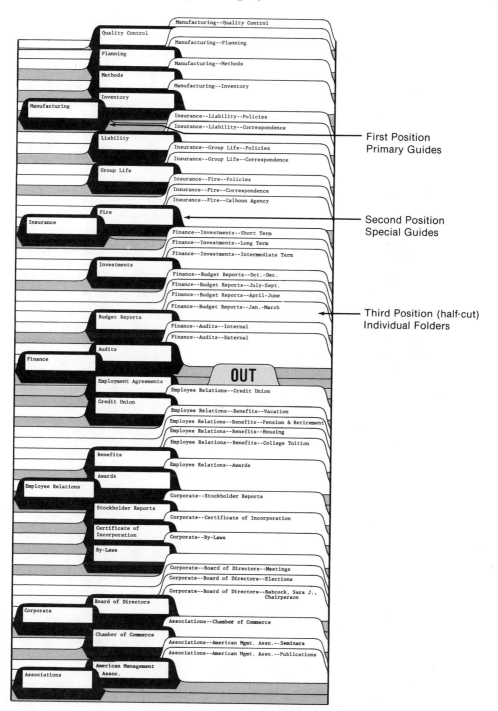

Manufacturing--Quality Control
Quality Control
Manufacturing--Planning
Planning
Manufacturing--Methods
Methods
Manufacturing--Inventory
Inventory
Manufacturing
Insurance--Liability--Policies
Insurance--Liability--Correspondence
First Position
Primary Guides
Liability
Insurance--Group Life--Policies
Insurance--Group Life--Correspondence
Group Life
Insurance--Fire--Policies
Insurance--Fire--Correspondence
Insurance--Fire--Calhoun Agency
Fire
Insurance
Second Position
Special Guides
Finance--Investments--Short Term
Finance--Investments--Long Term
Finance--Investments--Intermediate Term
Investments
Finance--Budget Reports--Oct.-Dec.
Finance--Budget Reports--July-Sept.
Finance--Budget Reports--April-June
Finance--Budget Reports--Jan.-March
Budget Reports
Third Position (half-cut)
Individual Folders
Finance--Audits--Internal
Finance--Audits--External
Audits
Finance
Employment Agreements
OUT
Credit Union
Employee Relations--Credit Union
Employee Relations--Benefits--Vacation
Employee Relations--Benefits--Pension & Retirement
Employee Relations--Benefits--Housing
Employee Relations--Benefits--College Tuition
Benefits
Employee Relations--Awards
Awards
Employee Relations
Corporate--Stockholder Reports
Stockholder Reports
Corporate--Certificate of Incorporation
Certificate of
Incorporation
Corporate--By-Laws
By-Laws
Corporate--Board of Directors--Meetings
Corporate--Board of Directors--Elections
Corporate--Board of Directors--Babcock, Sara J.,
Chairperson
Board of Directors
Corporate
Associations--Chamber of Commerce
Chamber of Commerce
Associations--American Mgmt. Assn.--Seminars
Associations--American Mgmt. Assn.--Publications
American Management
Assoc.
Associations

Illus. 10-1, Portion of a Subject Filing System

It was recognized that a third subdivision could be set up if necessary. These third-level divisions could be used if the amount of material filed in the subdivisions already identified would be large. For example, under "Finance" there would be many budget reports. A logical subdivision of budget reports could be made by dividing the year into quarters. If the reports were prepared daily, weekly, or monthly and were frequently requested in these forms, the titles "Daily," "Weekly," or "Monthly" could have been used as subheadings. However, the reports for this company were prepared quarterly, so quarterly was the logical breakdown.

The third subdivision would also be helpful if certain subtopics were requested frequently but separately from the other papers in the subdivision folder. For example, also under "Finance," the subheadings "Audits" and "Investments" both had logical subdivisions that might be requested separately. Other subdivisions were studied and, where useful and needed, subdivided.

The third subdivision could also be used for individual name folders. These would be added to the system whenever correspondence with a person concerning a given subject was very active and/or if there was a large amount of correspondence. For example, under the subheading "Board of Directors," an individual folder for the chairperson, Sara J. Babcock, was included.

The headings and subheadings on the outline were then studied to see if the titles used were satisfactory. Classification terms, in order to be useful for headings and subheadings, should be logical, practical, simple, easily used, and readily expanded into further subheadings if necessary at a later time. After this study was completed, the headings in the system shown in Illustration 10-1 were outlined as follows:

I. Associations
   A. American Management Association
      1. Publications
      2. Seminars
   B. Chamber of Commerce

II. Corporate
   A. Board of Directors
      1. Babcock, Sara J., chairperson
      2. Elections
      3. Meetings
   B. By-Laws
   C. Certificate of Incorporation
   D. Stockholder Reports

III. Employee Relations
   A. Awards
   B. Benefits
      1. College Tuition
      2. Housing

      3. Pension and Retirement
      4. Vacation
   C. Credit Union
   D. Employment Agreements

IV. Finance
   A. Audits
      1. External
      2. Internal
   B. Budget Reports
      1. January-March
      2. April-June
      3. July-September
      4. October-December
   C. Investments
      1. Intermediate Term
      2. Long Term
      3. Short Term

      V. Insurance
           A. Fire
               1. Calhoun Agency
               2. Correspondence
               3. Policies
           B. Group Life
               1. Correspondence
               2. Policies
           C. Liability
               1. Correspondence
               2. Policies

     VI. Manufacturing
           A. Inventory
           B. Methods
           C. Planning
           D. Quality Control

The primary guides were placed in first position.

The primary guides in the illustration—Associations, Corporate, Employee Relations, Finance, Insurance, and Manufacturing—were placed in first position. After the first primary guide, Associations, the two subdivisons of Associations—American Management Association and Chamber of Commerce—were used as captions on the two auxiliary guides for this section of the file and were placed in second position.

The individual folders were then prepared with half-cut tabs because of the long captions frequently required for a subject filing system. The captions for the individual folders were complete so as to indicate their exact location.

Auxiliary guides and individual folders were then prepared for the rest of the subheadings of the outline and were placed in their proper location in the file.

Several additional points should be noticed while studying Illustration 10-1:

1. When a folder is removed from the file, an OUT card (or OUT guide) is substituted in the same position as the individual folder. In Illustration 10-1, note the OUT guide in place of the folder for Employee Relations—Employment Agreements. If desired, an OUT folder can be used instead of an OUT guide. When an OUT folder is used, materials accumulating while the original folder is out of the file can be held in the proper location. These materials can then be placed in the original folder when it is returned to the files.

2. The months of the year can be used to extend sections in a subject filing system. In Illustration 10-1, the section "Finance—Budget Reports" has a different folder for each quarter of the year and the captions on the folders indicate this breakdown. Dated folders can be used in this same way when needed. An alphabetic breakdown can also be identified in the same manner. If additional folders with the same subject headings are required in other sections, a second folder can be labeled with a number 2; a third folder, with 3; and so on.

3. In the "Insurance" section, there are three folders for holding correspondence. These were added to this subject filing system because there had been a volume of correspondence concerning each of these three types of insurance.

Letters filed in these correspondence folders are first coded by writing subject titles on them. Then they are coded by names of correspondents in the usual manner, that is, by underlining the key unit and numbering the other units to establish the index order of the names.

No miscellaneous folders are needed in this subject system. If, however, miscellaneous folders are desired, they can be added immediately after the last folder in the appropriate sections and labeled with the captions identifying the sections. Miscellaneous titles in subject systems are avoided whenever possible because of the probability of error when filing and finding. If a new subject is important enough to be added to a subject system, a new folder should be made for it whenever possible.

Section 2   Subject Filing Procedures

Filing Correspondence in a Subject File

There are several methods for filing correspondence in a subject system. Some subject files are established primarily to provide up-to-date information on a topic. In this case, the information about a topic is more important than a specific document. Correspondence in such a file is stored in the same folder as all other documents pertaining to the same topic.

There are several methods for filing correspondence in a subject system.

In other subject files, the main purpose is to arrange a variety of materials according to only a few specific topics. In such a file, main captions are prepared for each major topic, and subheadings are prepared and captioned according to the type of material filed. Examples of such materials are catalogs, contracts, correspondence, employees, invoices, and raw materials.

When document-type records (such as sales slips) are of most importance in one phase of filing and correspondence-type records in another phase of filing, using two systems might be the best approach. The first system might be a subject-document system; the second, a subject-correspondence system.

Similar procedures are used in filing materials in a subject file whether the materials are documents or correspondence.

Filing Procedures in a Subject File

To illustrate filing procedures, a subject correspondence file is used in the following discussion.

Inspection. Each incoming letter should be checked to see that it has been released for filing.

A master record of the subject captions and the kinds of correspondence filed in each of the folders should be available.

Coding. In many cases the correspondence is coded by an executive or a secretary before it is sent to the records department. If a letter has not been coded in this manner, the files operator must read it carefully to determine the subject classification to be used as a basis for coding. If the subject appears in the letter in a form identical with that on the caption of the folder in which the letter should be filed, the coding may be done by underlining the subject wherever it appears in the letter. In Illustration 10-2, the subject of the letter is indicated on line 2 of the first paragraph: "Personnel—Recruiting." This title is one of the titles in the latter part of the subject filing system partially shown in Illustration 10-1. Because of its location within the letter, the subject for coding could be underscored. In most cases, however, it is necessary to code the letter by writing the subject classification at the top of the letter or in the upper right corner. The units in the subject title are coded by numbering them to indicate their position or rank in the index order.

To prevent errors in coding, a master record of the subject captions and the kinds of correspondence filed in each of the folders bearing these captions should be available at all times in the records department. This master record may be in the form of a typewritten outline with explanatory comments, in the form of a card index file with all subject captions arranged alphabetically, or in both forms. Unless some type of supplementary record is kept, two files operators may use two different subjects for coding letters of the same type. More differences of opinion arise regarding the coding of letters for a subject file than for any other type of file. Thus, in addition to using a master record, it is advisable to have one person take responsibility for making final decisions on subject coding problems.

Cross-References. A cross-reference should be prepared if more than one subject is involved in the same piece of correspondence. In Illustration 10-3, the information on the cross-reference sheet indicates:

1. That the letter was received from the Greater Cincinnati Chamber of Commerce and discussed a seminar on the recruiting of personnel.
2. That the letter was filed in the folder bearing the caption Personnel—Recruiting.
3. That the cross-reference should be filed in the folder captioned Associations—Chamber of Commerce so that anyone looking in that folder for the correspondence concerning the seminar for recruiting personnel will know that the letter is in the Personnel—Recruiting folder.

In some businesses a photocopy is made of the original letter, and the copy is filed in the cross-reference location. When this is done, a cross-reference sheet is not prepared. The coding of the letter remains the same so that it is evident where the copies are filed.

CROSS-REFERENCE SHEET

Name or Subject *Associations--Chamber of Commerce*

Greater Cincinnati Chamber of Commerce

Cincinnati, Ohio 45202-5790

Date of Item *September 6, 19--*

Regarding *Seminar for employee/recruiting*

Personnel

SEE

Name or Subject *Personnel--Recruiting*

Greater Cincinnati Chamber of Commerce

Cincinnati, Ohio 45202-5790

Authorized by *Sandra Garcia*   Date *9/9/9--*

illus. 10-3, Subject Cross-Reference Sheet

Greater Cincinnati
Chamber of Commerce

SEP 7 19-- A.M.

September 6, 19--

Ms. B. Jean Henderson, President
BJH Industries
4300 South Shores Avenue
Cincinnati, OH 45201-3456

Dear Ms. Henderson

You are cordially invited to attend a seminar for those
employers recruiting personnel to the Greater Cincinnati
area. The seminar is sponsored by the Greater Cincinnati
Chamber of Commerce Executive Recruitment Committee.

The seminar will be held Thursday, October 11, 19--, from
9:00 a.m. to 2:30 p.m. at the Greater Cincinnati Chamber of
Commerce Presentation Center, Second Floor, 120 West Fifth
Street.

A bus tour of Greater Cincinnati will follow the seminar,
during which time lunch will be served.

A maximum of 40 persons can be accommodated, so make your
reservations as soon as possible. Enclosed is a reservation
form for your convenience. If you have any questions, please
call the Chamber and ask for me.

Sincerely

Jayne P. Meyer

Jayne P. Meyer
Recruitment Committee Director

cw

Enclosure

Where a good way of life
keeps growing better

120 West Fifth Street Cincinnati, Ohio 45202-5790 513/579-3100

illus. 10-2, Incoming Letter with Subject
and Cross-Reference Coding

Sorting. After all material has been coded, it should be sorted first according to the main subjects of the file and second by the first subdivisions. This means that if the file is based on an outline consisting of five main headings, the first sorting is on the basis of such headings. For each of these sorted groups, the second sorting is based on the subdivisions of the main heading in the outline.

Placing Materials in Folders. The first basis for arrangement of materials in a subject correspondence folder is the alphabetic order of the names of the correspondents so that all correspondence with one person or company is grouped together in the folder. Different pieces of correspondence for the same correspondent are arranged within that group by date, with the most recent date in front. Material that is placed in an individual folder is arranged in the same manner as that in an individual folder for an alphabetic name file; that is, the paper showing the most recent date is filed in front of others within the group.

Arrangement of materials in a subject correspondence folder is the alphabetic order of the names.

Index to Subject File

A subject system is difficult to keep under control, but such a system can hold papers and other records efficiently. In some subject systems, alphabetic primary guides are used (A, Ba, Bu, etc.) in a manner similar to an alphabetic correspondence file. This makes filing and finding easier under certain conditions. A popular way to control a subject file is to prepare an index card control file and use it along with the subject system. This procedure requires preparing cards that show descriptions of each major subject in the system and also list the subtopics under each subject. For example, it is useful to prepare a control card for each correspondent showing the correspondent's name and the subject title or titles under which the correspondent's papers are filed.

A popular way to gain control over a subject file is to prepare an index card control file.

There are many different types of subject systems, each designed to serve a particular purpose. Some follow a dictionary arrangement so that all main topics beginning with the letter "A," for example, are located behind a primary guide showing "A," just like a dictionary. Others are more like an encyclopedia where main subject headings are determined along with their many subheadings as in Illustration 10-1.

Subject Sections in Alphabetic Filing Systems

Subject sections can be added to alphabetic filing systems whenever and wherever they are needed without disrupting the efficiency of the alphabetic system. However, this is true only when correspondence that is to be filed by subject title is properly coded before being filed. Material to be filed by subject must be recognized by code clerks, and the subject title must be underlined if it appears in the paper. If it does not appear in the paper, the subject must be written and underlined on the upper right-hand side of the paper. Preparation of a separate listing of the subject titles being used will assure that all papers are properly coded.

Questions for Discussion

1. What is a subject filing system?

2. How does a subject file compare with an outline?

3. When is it advantageous to use a subject filing system?

4. Where might we frequently find a subject file in use?

5. In what ways is a subject filing system similar to an alphabetic correspondence filing system?

6. Why does a subject file generally not have miscellaneous folders similar to those in an alphabetic file?

7. What is the first step in setting up a subject file?

8. How is an OUT guide used in a subject file?

9. How is a letter coded for subject filing?

10. What is the purpose of the master record of the subject captions and the kinds of materials filed in each of the folders bearing these captions?

11. When should a cross-reference be prepared in subject filing?

12. What three items of information are available from a cross-reference sheet?

13. If a photocopy is made of an original document, is a cross-reference sheet necessary? Where is the photocopy filed?

14. After materials have been coded, how should they be sorted?

15. How are materials placed in a subject correspondence folder?

16. What is the purpose of maintaining an index to a subject file?

Filing Problems

1. An executive file in the personnel office of a certain company contains information grouped under the following general subject captions:

Employee Testing	Job Evaluation
Sources of Potential Employees	Employee Training
Employee Selection Devices	

The following subdivisions are used often enough to require separate folders in the file:

Application Blanks	Labor Unions
Combination Tests	Factor Comparison Evaluation
Visual Aids	Planning for Training

Employment Agencies—Private
Point System Evaluation
Former Employees
Follow-Up on Training
Achievement Tests
References Submitted by
   Applicants
Labor Scouts
On-the-Job Training
Employment Interviews
Wage Evaluation
Administration of Training
Colleges
Trade Journals
Company Courses
Personal Investigations

Selection of Evaluators
Present Employee Recommendations
Job Grading Evaluation
School-College Courses
Intelligence Tests
High Schools
Instructional Materials
Job Ranking Evaluation
Physical Examinations
Aptitude Tests
Selection of Trainees
Walk-In Applicants
Supervisory Training
Employment Agencies—Government
Social Interest Tests
Teacher Education
Advertisements

Prepare, on an 8½″ × 11″ sheet of paper, a master record of the subject captions and the subdivisions that logically fall under these captions. Arrange both the subject captions and the subdivisions in correct alphabetic order.

2.   The files in the office of the purchasing agent of a manufacturing concern need to be rearranged. The purchasing agent wants to use a subject filing system similar to the one shown in Illustration 10-1. Prepare a master record of the primary guides, secondary guides, and folders in alphabetic order on 8½″ × 11″ sheets of paper.

The primary guides have the following captions:

Office Equipment
Office Furniture
Office Supplies

The secondary guides show the following subtopics:

Dictating Machines
Chairs
Ribbons
Typewriters
Bookends
Copying Machines

Binders
Desks
Pens
Bookkeeping Machines
Carbon Paper
Calculators

Bookcases
Ink
Addressing Machines
Paper
Calendars—Calendar Pads
Duplicators
Miscellaneous Supplies
(Place this guide at the
end of the Office Supplies
section.)

The folder tabs have the following captions:

Offset Duplicators
Accounting Desks
Battery-Operated Dictating
   Machines

Check Binders
Metal Bookends
Perpetual Calendars
Conference Desks

Nylon Post Binders
Thermographic Copying Machines
One-Time Carbon Paper
Duplicator Paper
Metal Plate Addressing Machines
Secretarial Desks
Bond Paper
Folding Chairs
General Use Carbon Paper
Ledger Binders
Tape Dictating Machines
Interoffice Paper
Executive Desks
Storage Binders
Magnetic Ink
Typewriter Paper
Plastic Belt Dictating Machines
Ball Pens
Diazo Process Copying Machines
Address Labels
Spirit Carbon Paper
Transcribing Desks
Cement and Glue
Stencil Duplicators
Airmail Paper
Clerical Desks
Staplers
Plastic Bookends
Offset Pens
Metal Post Binders
Listing Calculators
Second Sheet Paper
Drawing Ink
Electric Typewriters
Desk Calendar Pads
Spirit Addressing Machines
Newspaper Binders
Marking Ink
Wood Bookends
Tissue Paper
Display Calculators

Photocopy Carbon Paper
Xerography Copying Machines
Addressing Machine Ink
Typewriter Ribbons
Typewriting Desks
Accounting Books
Telephone Book Binders
Dye-Transfer Copying Machines
Executive Chairs
Catalog Binders
Diaries
Leather-Covered Bookends
Memo Calendar Pads
Pencil Carbon Paper
Billing Machine Desks
Photocopy Paper
Indelible Ink
Letterhead Paper
Disc Dictating Machines
Paper Clips
Clip and Spring Binders
Carbon Paper Packs
Photocopy Machines
Ceramic Bookends
Fluid Duplicators
Receptionist Desks
Adding Machine Paper
Secretarial Chairs
Carbon Paper Ribbons
Stamp Pad Ink
Calculator Desks
Cartridges, Ball Point
Wrapping Paper
Prong Binders
Manual Typewriters
Wall Calendars
Facsimile Copying Machines
Duplicator Ink
Nonrefillable Ball Pens
Ring Binders
Adding Machine Ribbons
Appointment Calendars

Job 9   Subject Correspondence Filing

At this time complete Job 9 in OFFICE FILING PROCEDURES, Fifth Edition. The instructions and supplies for this job are included in the practice set.

CHAPTER 11

Numeric Systems, Procedures, and Codes

It has been said that we live in the age of numbers. We have identification numbers for ourselves, our bank accounts, our charge accounts, and our possessions. As a student you may have a student number in school. As a worker you will have a social security number and may also have an employee number. In your personal life you may have a driver's license number, an automobile license number, a credit card number, and a savings account number. Often you will buy parts for something you own or new items by number from mail order catalogs or stores. All these items—and many others—have been classified numerically and are listed and stored (filed) by number.

Customers Are Satisfied when Information Is Close at Hand

A number is frequently the only identification needed to locate a desired item. The name of the item and its size, color, and other distinctive characteristics are all summarized in a single number, unique to that one item. If the number is known, the item can be located quickly.

For example, from the number of your automobile license, a police officer can obtain all the details about your car by a call to the central station.

A single number can also provide detailed information about a person. For example, from your driver's license number, one can quickly and easily find out your age, address, driving record, and other information from the motor vehicle registration files. Whether you are a student in school or an employee of a large corporation, your student number or your employee number is all that is needed to locate information about you in the files.

Section 1 Numeric Filing Systems

A filing system that stores records by number rather than by name is a numeric filing system.

A filing system that stores records and other information by number rather than by name is a *numeric filing system*. Such filing systems are used in many everyday business and personal situations. For example, filing by number may be considered (1) when the filing system is large and the names of many people and objects are similar or (2) when it is necessary to maintain secrecy.

Nature and Uses of Numeric Filing

Under certain conditions, numeric filing is efficient, quick, and accurate because a number is much easier to read than a long series of words. A number is, therefore, easier to locate in a file drawer or on a shelf. We all know that banks identify the checking accounts of their depositors by numbers. An individual account number is assigned to each depositor. This number, along with the number of the bank itself, is printed with a special ink on a set of blank checks before the checks are given to the depositor to use. After a check is written and cashed, the bank number assures its return to the right bank, and the depositor's number assures that the amount is subtracted from the right depositor's account.

Social security numbers are used as identification for an increasing number of purposes, including income tax returns. Examples of situations in which numeric filing is used to advantage are:

1. Charge accounts for gasoline purchases and for department store buying, credit cards, and many other types of transactions involving credit, all of which are identified by number.
2. Orders for merchandise from a mail-order house, which places its items by number on the stockroom shelves and lists its items by number in its catalog.
3. Orders for automobile replacement parts to be sent by manufacturers.
4. Premiums on life insurance policies that are filed by policy numbers.
5. Factory jobs that are identified by numbers.
6. Installment loans and mortgages.

7. Legal cases, which are assigned consecutive numbers in the order in which they are initiated.
8. Jobs undertaken by building contractors.
9. Districts or territories, such as sales districts or distribution areas.
10. Medical case histories, which are usually filed by patient number.
11. Student records filed by student number—frequently social security numbers.
12. Mailing lists arranged and filed by ZIP Code numbers.

Letters and other correspondence relating to many of the examples of numeric filing listed above are frequently identified by the same numbers as those assigned to their related documents. This method keeps all information concerning a single topic, individual, or transaction together.

Numeric Correspondence File

A numeric correspondence file usually consists of four parts.

For convenience and secrecy, correspondence itself may be coded and filed by number instead of by name. This is referred to as a *numeric correspondence file*. The chief disadvantage is that a numeric correspondence system requires the keeping of four types of records. This is far too time-consuming for most modern offices where complex manual (hand-operated) systems are avoided whenever possible.

A numeric correspondence file usually consists of four parts:

1. A main file in which guides and folders bear numeric captions. (See Illustration 11-1.)
2. A supplementary index card control file in which names or subject titles are arranged alphabetically.
3. A miscellaneous alphabetic file in which are kept: (1) new materials about new people or subjects for which the volume of future materials is not anticipated to be extensive enough for the immediate assignment of a number; or (2) materials from past correspondents or on subjects that have not yet reached the activity requiring a separate folder and an assigned number.
4. An accession book containing a consecutive record of assigned numbers. (See Illustration 11-2.)

Main File. In the main numeric file, each important topic or name of a correspondent is given an individual folder that has only a numbered caption. The folders are numbered in sequence, beginning with a predetermined number such as 100 or 1000, with little or no regard for the alphabetic order of names. (See Illustration 11-1.)

An alphabetic card control is essential.

Index Card Control File. Since guide and folder tab notations show only numbers, an alphabetic file card control is essential to the operation of a numeric file. The card control consists of an alphabetic arrangement of the names of the correspondents and of subjects. The names are typed on cards, which are filed behind alphabetic guides in a

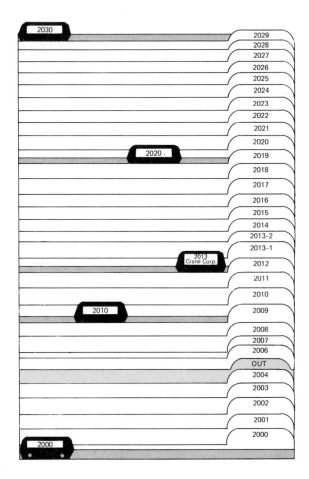

illus. 11-1, Numeric Correspondence File

special card drawer or in a file box. Each card gives the name of a correspondent or a subject title and shows the number of the folder that has been assigned to the name or subject. If the number of the folder given to a company has been forgotten, the files operator can consult the card index control file to get the number of the folder.

Miscellaneous Alphabetic File. If the volume of material concerning a certain topic or from a particular person or company is small, infrequent, or inactive, the material is kept in a separate miscellaneous alphabetic file. But when the volume of information from that person or company or on that topic increases sufficiently to warrant the opening of an individual folder, the folder is given the next unassigned number. All materials to, from, or about this topic or correspondent are always placed in this folder, with the most recent material in front.

A number may be assigned to a subject or a group classification. For example, a topic such as "Applications for Employment" could be given the number 2000. This number would appear on the file folder in which applications for work are filed. The kind of numeric filing system in which folder 2000 would be held could be similar to the system shown in Illustration 11-1. Within such "Applications for Employment" folders, the materials are filed in alphabetic order according to the names of the applicants, and all letters and other materials pertaining to each application are arranged by date, with the latest date in front.

Accession Book. Many users of a numeric system keep an accession book. An *accession book* contains a consecutive record of numbers assigned to folders. One form of accession book is shown in Illustration 11-2.

NUMBER	NAME	DATE
1208	Payroll Register	Feb. 1, 19--
1209	Corwin A. Adams Co.	Feb. 3, 19--
1210	Monthly Production Reports	Feb. 3, 19--
1211	Rogers Collection Agency	Feb. 4, 19--
1212		
1213		

illus. 11-2, Accession Book

Advantages and Disadvantages of Numeric Filing

There are many advantages to a numeric filing system. The most important are:

1. All papers pertaining to a certain job or to related activities are brought together.
2. A certain degree of privacy is possible because only numbers are visible to someone looking at the files. Ordinarily neither names nor titles are written on the guide or folder tabs.
3. Numbered folders or cards that are out of place can be located more rapidly than is possible in most alphabetic systems.
4. Almost unlimited expansion is possible in a numeric filing system.
5. Cross-references are not needed in the numeric section of the files because they are conveniently located in the alphabetic card index.
6. Identifying information by number makes it easier to use mechanical equipment to store and retrieve information from the files.

In spite of the advantages of numeric filing, there are disadvantages to consider, the most important of which are:

1. Numeric filing systems are indirect systems in that the files operator, before filing or seeking correspondence, must first consult an alphabetic index card control file to determine the proper code number for each correspondent or subject.
2. Numeric files provide only for active correspondents in a correspondence file. Alphabetic files are still necessary for miscellaneous folders to accomodate materials received in such limited quantity that individual folders are not necessary.
3. When the numbers in a numeric file become too large, transpositions (reversing the order of the digits) can happen easily. For example, it is more difficult to remember the exact order of a number such as "47213" than a word such as "Moped."
4. Although misfiled papers do not occur frequently, when they do occur, they may be more difficult to detect. For example, a document coded with the wrong number may be hard to find.

**Numeric
File with
Subject
Guides**

*A numeric file
with subject
guides can be
used with many
types of records.*

Correspondence files represent only one of the many uses of a numeric filing system. Many types of other materials are held in numeric filing systems. Numeric systems with subject titles are used for many kinds of records, such as invoices, sales brochures, and price lists. Executive filing systems and accounting systems frequently use a combined form of numeric codes and subject titles on guide and folder tabs. Illustration 11-3 shows a numeric file with subject guides. Although the arrangement of the guides and folders is similar to the numeric correspondence file shown in Illustration 11-1, there are a few important differences:

1. The primary guides in first and second positions in Illustration 11-3 are numbered by 5's because this is a very active file and several folders bearing the same basic numbers are needed to store the large volume of material. These additional folders are identified by adding a hyphen and numbering them in order (see folders 3009-1, 3009-2, 3018-1, 3018-2, and 3018-3).
2. The special guides are third-cut and are placed in third position. The double-width guide is used because subject titles tend to be longer and thus need more space. There are five special guides in this system to provide for very active topics that require frequent filing and retrieval.
3. Individual folders and OUT guides are placed in fourth position.

Section 2   Numeric Codes for Subject Filing Systems

*Subject filing is
a major part of
many numeric
systems.*

Subject filing is a major part of many numeric systems; therefore, it is important to discuss further some of the ways in which businesses use numbers with their subject systems.

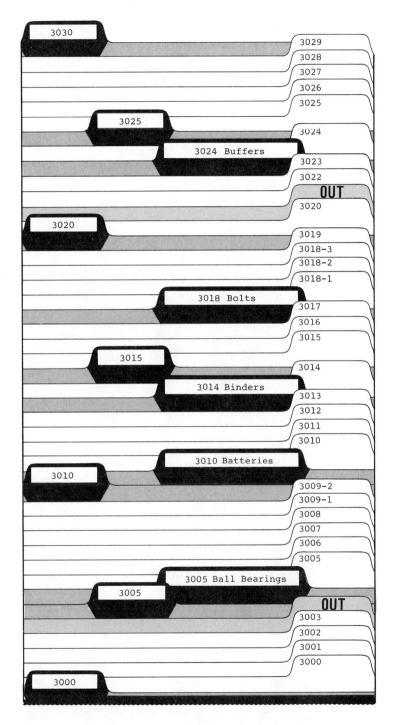

illus. 11-3, Numeric File with Subject Guides in Third Position

Numeric Subject Filing

Files are organized primarily by subject, but numbered notations are used.

The use of numeric codes for subject files has increased during the past several years. This increase has undoubtedly been caused in part by the rapid adoption of mechanized office data processing and word processing. Punched cards and other computer-produced records are more easily processed by number; electronic computers operate through numbers; and reference to information is increasingly being done through the use of various numeric systems. Even when there is a clearly labeled alphabetic name on a card or a record, the number of that card or record must also be known.

In many situations the files are organized primarily by subject, but numbered notations on guide and folder tabs are used just as they sometimes are used in alphabetic name files. The simplest type of numbering is that shown in the example on page 151 in which the subject titles are the same as those used on page 131 of Chapter 10. The numbered notations may be used as follows:

1. As a part of the subject captions to facilitate filing. Subject titles are frequently quite long and seldom appear in their exact form in correspondence. Considerable time can be saved, therefore, if numbers instead of words are used in coding and in locating folders in the files.
2. As a substitute for subject captions. When only numbers are used for captions, then subject headings, divisions, or subdivisions that are closely related can be grouped together in the files even though the subject titles do not fall in the same alphabetic section. When this plan is followed, a supplementary card index file, arranged alphabetically by subjects, is necessary and is used in a manner similar to that for numeric correspondence files.

Coordinate indexing is recommended only for a large subject file.

One example of using only numbers for captions is called *coordinate indexing* and was designed by the Office of Aerospace Research, United States Air Force. It is recommended only for a large subject file that contains many items, each covering several subjects rather than just one subject per item and requiring extensive cross-referencing. A legal research department for a large company is one example of a place where a coordinate indexing system could be used.

Three things are necessary for a coordinate indexing subject file:

1. A simple numeric coding according to the subject.
2. A word list containing the filing words (subject titles) and alternate words to enable the files operator to locate the key title under which the subject is coded.
3. A word card file consisting of one card for each key title and the indexing numbers of all filed items containing information covered by that title. This serves as the cross-reference notation necessary to locate one or more items pertaining to a particular subject.

No.	Heading	No.	Division	No.	Subdivision
100	Accounting				
		110	Audits		
				111	Cash Payments
				112	Cash Receipts
				113	Management Statements
				114	Payroll
		120	Budgets		
				121	Branch
				122	Corporate
		130	Costs		
				131	Administrative
				132	Manufacturing
				133	Office
		140	Credit		
				141	Secured
				142	Unsecured
		150	Expense		
				151	Administrative
				151	Executive
				151	Office
				152	Marketing
				152	Advertising
				152	Research
				152	Sales
		160	Financial		
				161	Bonds
				162	Investments
				163	Stocks
		170	Taxes		
				171	Federal
				172	Local
				173	State
200	Administration				
300	Construction				
400	Engineering				
500	Insurance				
600	Legal				
700	Manufacturing				
800	Marketing				
900	Office				
1000	Personnel				
1100	Public Relations				
1200	Purchasing				

Decimal-Subject Filing

A simple numbering system is adequate for most subject files. When the outline on which a subject filing system is based is more complicated or detailed, however, a decimal system is advantageous.

*When the out-
line of a subject
filing system is
detailed, a deci-
mal system is
advantageous.*

Perhaps the most widely known and used decimal system is that devised by Melvil Dewey. It is used by libraries to classify books, catalogs, pamphlets, and all related materials. Dewey's system divides all human knowledge into nine main groups and one general group. The arrangement of numbers and subjects is as follows:

000	General Works	500	Natural Science
100	Philosophy	600	Useful Arts
200	Religion	700	Fine Arts
300	Sociology	800	Literature
400	Philology	900	History

These major groups, in turn, are divided into nine subdivisions and one general division. For example, the "Useful Arts (600)" section has these subdivisions:

600	General	650	Commerce
610	Medicine	660	Chemical Technology
620	Engineering	670	Manufactures
630	Agriculture	680	Mechanical Trades
640	Domestic Economy	690	Building Trades

These sections are further subdivided into groups of ten. Then, by the use of decimals, the subdivisions can be continued indefinitely.

The Dewey Decimal System, or some adaptation of this system, can be employed to advantage in business filing when provision for expansion in the files must be made and when detailed subdivisions in a filing system are needed. For example, referring to the simple numbering system for the outline on page 151, "Accounting" was assigned number "100." The subdivision "Administrative" (following "150 Expense") was numbered "151," and under this the subheadings "Executive" and "Office" were also numbered "151." Using a decimal-subject system, the arrangement would be numbered as follows:

```
100   Accounting
    150   Expense
        151   Administrative
            151.1   Executive
            151.2   Office
        152   Marketing
```

To be efficient, such filing systems must be carefully organized and the files operators must be thoroughly familiar with the subject outline on which the system is based.

**Direct
Decimal-
Subject
Filing**

The principal advantages of the direct decimal-subject system over the alphabetic system for certain kinds of materials are illustrated by the Yawman and Erbe direct subject filing system shown in Illustration 11-4. It is possible to group related materials in this file, as shown by the series of folders in Section 705. These folders, in a straight alphabetic

Yawman & Erbe of California Corp.

illus. 11-4, Direct Decimal-Subject Filing

Coding in a decimal-subject system is easier and faster than in an alphabetic system.

system, would be spread from the "A" to the "G" sections of the system. Also, coding papers for the decimal-subject system is easier and faster than coding in an alphabetic system because only the code numbers need to be written on file materials. It is advantageous to have decimals showing on guide and folder tabs so that numbers and titles can be identified as a unit.

Other Coding Systems for Subject Filing

Duplex-Numeric Code. Several other number-based and related systems for subject titles are in common use. One of these is known as Duplex-Numeric. The example at the top of page 154 indicates the nature and use of the system.

This system is capable of indefinite expansion and can be used to advantage when subject classifications are numerous and detailed or when an alphabetic arrangement would be impractical. For example, in an architect's office, a file would logically follow the sequence of the erection of a building. The system is extensively used in law offices, where the client is assigned a number and every case handled for the client is assigned an auxiliary number based on the client's number.

Subject Outline	Primary Guide Notations	Secondary Guide Notations	Tertiary Guide Notations	Folder Notations
Accounting	10			
Expense		10-5		
Administrative			10-5-1	
Executive				10-5-1-1
Office				10-5-1-2
Marketing			10-5-2	
Advertising				10-5-2-1
Research				10-5-2-2
Sales				10-5-2-3
Financial		10-6		

Duplex-Alphabetic Code. If letters are substituted for numbers in the Duplex-Numeric system, the method is known as Duplex-Alphabetic. In the example used for the Duplex-Numeric system, the Duplex-Alphabetic caption for "Accounting" would be "A"; for "Expense," "A-e"; for "Administrative," "A-e-a."

Alphanumeric Code. Another system, the Alphanumeric, is a combination of the two preceding systems in that capital letters are used for the main headings of the outline; numbers are used for the first divisions of the main headings; and small letters are used for the subject subdivisions. For example, "Executive" would be "A-5-a-1." In other words, letters and numbers are alternated to determine the captions.

Illustration 11-5 indicates the application of five different systems of coding the same items in a portion of our subject outline. Notice that some of the coding systems are not adapted to the subject outline given in the first column. The simple numeric outline is not adequate, and some of the duplex outlines appear cumbersome. However, these systems are very useful in certain situations.

Section 3   Special Methods of Numeric Filing

Numbers added to an alphabetic system help to reduce misfiling.

We have discussed the assigning of numbers to various materials to help avoid misfiling. Numbers, when added to an alphabetic system, provide a quick check that a particular document is at least in the correct general location. Illustration 11-6 on page 156 uses a straight numbering system for each primary guide. The first guide, "A," is numbered "1"; the second primary guide, "An," is numbered "2"; the third primary guide is "3"; and so on throughout the major divisions of the file. All folders behind a particular guide have the same number as the primary guide; hence, "Adams" is number "1" as is "American Can."

Subjects and Subdivisions	Simple Numeric Code	Decimal Code	Duplex-Numeric Code	Duplex-Alphabetic Code	Alpha-Numeric Code
ACCOUNTING	100	100.	10.	A	A
Audits	110	110.	10-1	A-a	A-1
Cash Payments	111	111.	10-1-1	A-a-a	A-1-a
Cash Receipts	112	112.	10-1-2	A-a-b	A-1-b
Management Statements	113	113.	10-1-3	A-a-c	A-1-c
Payroll	114	114.	10-1-4	A-a-d	A-1-d
Budgets	120	120.	10-2	A-b	A-2
Branch	121	121.	10-2-1	A-b-a	A-2-a
Corporate	122	122.	10-2-2	A-b-b	A-2-b
Costs	130	130.	10-3	A-c	A-3
Administrative	131	131.	10-3-1	A-c-a	A-3-a
Manufacturing	132	132.	10-3-2	A-c-b	A-3-b
Office	133	133.	10-3-3	A-c-c	A-3-c
Credit	140	140.	10-4	A-d	A-4
Secured	141	141.	10-4-1	A-d-a	A-4-a
Unsecured	142	142.	10-4-2	A-d-b	A-4-b
Expense	150	150.	10-5	A-e	A-5
Administrative	151	151.	10-5-1	A-e-a	A-5-a
Executive	No Number Available	151.1	10-5-1-1	A-e-a-a	A-5-a-1
Office		151.2	10-5-1-2	A-e-a-b	A-5-a-2
Marketing	152	152.	10-5-2	A-e-b	A-5-b
Advertising	No Number Available	152.1	10-5-2-1	A-e-b-a	A-5-b-1
Research		152.2	10-5-2-2	A-e-b-b	A-5-b-2
Sales		152.3	10-5-2-3	A-e-b-c	A-5-b-3
ADMINISTRATION	200	200.	20.	B	B

illus. 11-5, **Comparison of the Various Codes Used in Subject Filing Systems**

This use of numbers aids the files operator in returning materials to the same section of the file, but it does not aid in placing the material in proper order within the major sections.

Up to a certain number of digits, the use of additional numbers increases the accuracy of locating the precise spot in the file for each item. Subject filing can therefore be made more accurate through the use of a coding system similar to one of those presented in Illustration 11-5. Beyond a certain number of digits, however, numbers become more difficult to read and remember accurately. This difficulty increases the possibility of misfiling. To reduce the memory load and improve accuracy in numerical filing, various methods are available. These methods include terminal digit filing, middle digit filing, and the use of color coding.

As numbers get larger, they become more difficult to read and remember.

Esselte Pendaflex Corporation

illus. 11-6, Numbers with Alphabetic Name Filing

**Terminal
Digit Filing**

Terminal digit filing is a method of numeric filing designed to reduce the possibility of misfiling because of the difficulty encountered in reading and remembering large numbers. In *terminal digit filing*, the numbers are assigned in the same manner as described for consecutive digit filing, but the numbers are read from right to left in small groups beginning with the terminal group, hence the name *terminal* digit filing.

In terminal digit filing, the last series of digits is considered first.

Terminal digit filing is used when numbers contain five or more digits. In the number 531932, for example, the digits could be separated into two groups of three digits each or three groups of two digits each. Frequently the groups within numbers are separated by hyphens, 53-19-32. The two-digit groups are filed in this manner:

3	2	1
Final	*Secondary*	*Primary*
53	19	32

The files operator first locates the drawer containing those materials or records whose numbers end with 32. A search is then made down the guides in that drawer for guide No. 19. Lastly, the material is filed in numerical order in back of the number 52. Numbers of less than six digits are brought up to that figure by adding zeros to the *left* of the number. For example, the number 93841 would be written 093841.

Terminal digit filing is used in filing such items as checks, mortgages, letters of credit, insurance policies, hospital case records, purchase orders, and various government documents.

Terminal digit filing has several advantages over consecutive digit filing. These are listed below.

1. Filing errors are more easily avoided because only the primary digits need be considered in locating the drawer and only the secondary digits need be considered in locating the guide.
2. Records are more easily obtained because the most current materials are more evenly distributed throughout the files. New numbers are assigned in consecutive order, but each new number will be in a separate drawer. (For example, if 349682 is the next number to be assigned, 34-96-82 will be filed in a different drawer from 34-96-81.) If several files operators are working at the same time, they are less likely to need the same file drawer at the same time.
3. Sorting and handling of records is more efficient because the first sort is by only two digits. Time savings of 25 to 50 percent have been realized by some companies that have changed to terminal digit filing.

Middle Digit Filing

Middle digit filing is a modification of terminal digit filing. In *middle digit filing,* the middle series of digits is considered first, then the series at the left, and lastly, the final series (the series at the right). The primary guides are prepared for the middle series of digits.

In middle digit filing, the middle series of digits is considered first.

In using the middle digit system, the number 531932 would be filed in this order:

2	1	3
Secondary	Primary	Final
53	19	32

The files operator would first locate the drawer or primary guide for those materials or records whose primary digits are 19 and search down the guides for guide No. 53. The materials would then be filed in the proper order according to the number 32.

Middle digit filing has the same advantages and uses as terminal digit filing. In addition, the following advantages are claimed for it.

1. If the filing system is being changed over from a consecutive digit system, it is easier to change to middle digit filing than to terminal digit filing because entire blocks of 100 numbers are moved as a single group.

For example, all records numbered 74-26-00 through 74-26-99 remain in the same sequence after the move and can therefore be moved at one time.

2. In terminal digit filing it is necessary to consider 10 different places to find 10 documents in consecutive order; in middle digit filing, only one place is necessary, each place representing 100 consecutive numbers, as the folders are already arranged in consecutive order.

3. If the company prefers to assign the numbers in blocks rather than individually, it is possible in middle digit filing to have the entire block filed in one place. For example, a sales organization may wish to assign all records with the middle digits of 50 to a main branch in Vermont, all records with the middle digits of 51 to Massachusetts, and so on. In middle digit filing, 100 different folders could have the middle digit of 50 and all would be located in the same section of the files.

Comparison of Consecutive, Terminal Digit, and Middle Digit Sequences

The following table compares the sequence of the number on seven documents filed in consecutive, terminal digit, and middle digit files. The same numbers are used in the three columns.

Order of Filing	Consecutive Number Filing	Terminal Digit Filing	Middle Digit Filing
1	8-23-38	46-23-21	13-19-28
2	13-19-28	23-48-21	57-19-28
3	13-23-28	13-19-28	08-23-38
4	23-48-21	57-19-28	13-23-28
5	23-48-35	13-23-28	46-23-21
6	46-23-21	23-48-35	23-48-21
7	57-19-28	08-23-38	23-48-35

Both the terminal digit and the middle digit methods of storage and retrieval are popularly used with open-shelf filing. Illustration 11-7 shows a portion of one terminal digit system. When open shelves are used for active files storage, the guide and folder tabs extend from the side of the guide or folder. This permits the folders to stand with the folded portion of the folders down. The papers in the folder itself then rest on their long edge.

In the illustration, the number of the first folder in the lower shelf is 50-25-54. Notice, for this system, the top number 54 is the terminal group and represents the shelf location. In a drawer file, this would be the drawer number. The bottom numbers are the two middle digits, 25,

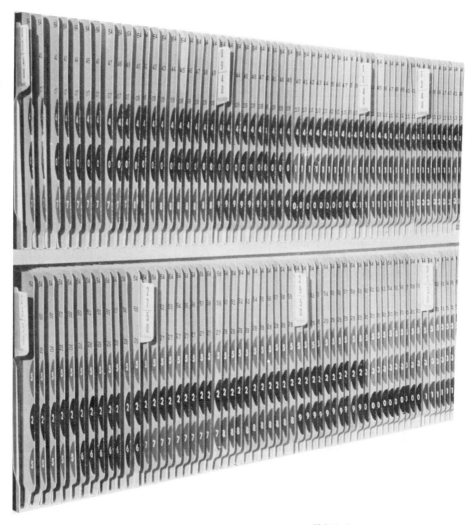

V.R.E., Inc., Malvern, Ohio 44644

illus. 11-7, Open-Shelf Terminal Digit File

and represent the guide number. The first two digits, 50, identify this specific folder and are printed in the middle of the number series. This arrangement of printing numbers is done so that a glance by the files operator across the top digits of the tab will easily indicate a folder that is on the wrong shelf. This is so because all folders whose terminal digits are 54 should be together in a section or drawer of a filing system. Likewise, a glance across the bottom numbers can detect a folder out of group sequence, because all folders whose middle digit is 25 should be in the same section of ten folders.

The tabs on the guides have two pairs of numbers—25/50 on the first guide visible to us. The top two numbers, 25, identify the middle digits of the number; the bottom two numbers, 50, identify the first folder number of the subdivision. Guides are located every 20 folders.

A similar system can be used with middle digit files. Using a middle digit system, the number 50-25-54 is arranged so the shelf or drawer is labeled with the middle digits, 25; the guides are labeled with the first two digits, 50; and the folders are arranged by the final two digits, 54. With the format used for Illustration 11-7, the top numbers on the guide are 50 and the bottom numbers are 54 if the design of one guide for every 20 folders is continued. The folder numbered 50-25-54 follows 50-25-52 and 50-25-53.

Use of Color in Numeric Filing

There are many color systems in use for numeric filing systems.

Color coding is frequently used in numeric filing systems as an aid in quick identification of groups of numbers and in identification of mis-filed folders. There are many color systems in use for numeric filing systems. One system uses a different, clearly identifiable color on the tab of each folder. The color used is determined by the *next to last* digit. In this system, each group of ten folders is one color with a second contrasting color for the next ten folders. If ten colors are used, the color group will repeat itself in only one group out of each ten groups of ten folders.

In the terminal digit system used in Illustration 11-7, each folder has three color labels. These labels show as half circles (or "half moons"), one below the other on the lowest half of each folder tab. Ten different colors are used, each color representing a particular digit from 0 through 9. The colors are assigned to the folder according to the file code numbers of the document. The system is designed so that if a folder is misplaced on the shelf, its color code will be different from those on either side of it. Just a glance will make it obvious to the files operator that the folder is in the wrong location.

Just where the color is applied to the tab depends on the design of the filing system. In some systems, the entire tab is colored; in others, a thin strip of color covers the top of the tab. Other methods use a colored plastic clip over a particular number on the tab or have a particular number printed in the appropriate color. In each case, the files operator must know and understand the exact color coding being used. It is reported that the use of color could reduce misfiling by up to 80 percent.

Numeric-Name System

In the system shown in Illustration 11-8, made by the Shaw-Walker Company, numbers are printed on the folder tabs, which are wide enough to accommodate gummed labels indicating the name or subject of the folder. By showing both a number and a name, additional identity is given to each folder and makes filing and finding faster and surer.

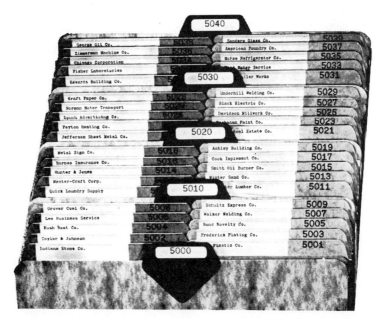

Shaw-Walker

illus. 11-8, Numeric-Name System

Another feature of this system is that even numbers are given to folders with tabs on the left side and odd numbers are given to folders with tabs on the right.

In Illustration 11-8, notice that the arrangement is determined by the numeric sequence, not by the alphabetic sequence of names. Thus, the system is primarily numeric and indirect, requiring a supplementary alphabetic card file for identification purposes.

Soundex Alphanumeric Filing System

There are many possible variations of alphanumeric filing systems. One such variation is the Soundex System, manufactured by KARDEX Systems, Inc. The Soundex System is designed to bring all names that sound the same but are spelled differently (such as *Patin, Paton, Patten,* and *Patton*) into one section of a file by assigning alphanumeric codes to the names on the basis of pronunciation rather than spelling.

Soundex is a highly specialized system and is typically used in large filing departments with special problems that the system is designed to solve. A files operator who is assigned to the operation of such a system is given careful in-service training. For that reason Soundex and similar systems are not covered in detail in this book.

1. What is a numeric filing system?

2. List ten situations where numeric filing may be used to advantage.

3. What four parts does a numeric correspondence filing system usually include?

4. In a numeric file, how does the alphabetic order of names affect the assigning of numbers?

5. Describe the arrangement of the numeric correspondence file in Illustration 11-1, page 146.

6. Explain the use of the index card control file.

7. Why is a miscellaneous alphabetic file used in a numeric filing system?

8. What is the purpose of an accession book?

9. What are the advantages of a numeric file?

10. What are the disadvantages of a numeric file?

11. Describe the arrangement of the numeric file in Illustration 11-3, page 149.

12. What is a numeric subject file?

13. How are numbers used in a subject file?

14. What is a decimal-subject file?

15. When would the Dewey Decimal System be used in business filing?

16. Describe the general nature of the Duplex-Numeric Code.

17. In what way is the Duplex-Alphabetic Code similar to the Duplex-Numeric Code?

18. What is the Alphanumeric Code?

19. How is a number read for filing in terminal digit filing?

20. What are the advantages of terminal digit filing over consecutive digit filing?

21. In what way does middle digit filing differ from terminal digit filing in the reading of numbers?

22. What is the advantage of using color coding in numeric filing systems?

Filing Problems

1. A. Assume that individual folders are to be opened in a numeric file for the names in the following list in the order in which the names are shown. Type or write each name on a separate 5″ × 3″ index card or on a slip of paper cut to that size. Keep the names in the order listed. Assume that the accession book indicates that the next number to use is 813. Assign a number to each name and write that number in the upper right-hand corner of the card.

   B. After you have typed the 40 cards and assigned the numbers, arrange the cards in alphabetic order in preparation for filing in the supplementary index card control file.

   C. Prepare an answer sheet similar to the one illustrated below. Type or write the numbers 1 to 20 in a column at the left of the sheet and 21 to 40 in a column down the middle of the sheet. After the numbers, list the folder numbers assigned to the names in the order in which you have arranged the names.

```
Name _____
Problem _____/_____ Date _____
1. 849          21.
2.              22.
3.              23.
4.              24.
5.              25.
6.              26.
17.             37.
18.             38.
19.             39.
20.             40.
```

Dancer Ski Resort	Duo-Fast Corporation
Albert J. Reuters	Reuter-Schmidt Manufacturing Co.
A-1 Box Corporation	East Street Laundry
DuVal's Collection Agency	Archie T. Nesbitt, M.D.
D'Arcy Department Store, Canton, Missouri	Mid-West Snow Removal Co.
	B-4 Six Club
Gerry South & Sons Plumbing	George St. John, Catering
A & D Towing Company	D'Arcy Department Store, Elkton, Florida
Mid-Way Motel	Tiny Tot Clothes
Bark River Fishing Bait	I-Dent License Plates
Cecil MacMurray Book Mart	R A Enterprises, Inc.
Reuter's Bowling Lanes	Tar Paper Manufacturing Co.
Nesbit Coats Emporium	Duvall Gas Stop
East Side Beauty Salon	U-C-Us Landscaping
C-Thru Glass Company	Zero Base Freezer Lockers
Gee Wizz Pizzas	Nonstop Auto Repair
St. Patrick's Day Club	A-A Electric Utility
Rae-Lynn Bridal Shoppe	D'Arcy Department Store, Canton, Minnesota
Zabel Realty	The 1920 Club
Southeast Orange Groves	McMurray's Salad Dressing
Gerry's Barber Shop	

2. A. Assume that each of the following 50 numbers is the numeric code for a document that has been removed from the files. The files are arranged according to a consecutive digit system. Type or write each number on a separate 5″ × 3″ index card or on a slip of paper cut to that size. Type the digits in each number in pairs by typing a hyphen after the second and fourth digits.

   B. After you have typed all the cards, arrange them in the proper order for consecutive digit filing. Your first number will be 08-24-01, the lowest number; it will appear after No. 1 on the answer sheet.

   C. Prepare an answer sheet similar to the one illustrated in Problem 1, except that you will need 50 numbers instead of 40. After the 50 numbers on the answer sheet, list the numbers on the cards in the order in which you have them arranged.

08-24-12	12-48-46	21-35-40	12-41-20	08-24-11
12-41-25	30-18-01	43-44-25	21-52-02	21-51-13
12-48-37	43-22-35	12-45 08	68-30-21	36-48-15
21-35-13	63-22-25	68-30-25	44-54-22	28-13-22
28-02-26	12-50-01	44-55-22	21-31-13	43-13-03
30-24-02	30-49-15	63-31-46	39-31-10	50-55-38
37-31-46	48-20-46	43-15-12	43-35-25	48-18-30
43-30-36	12-44-01	08-24-01	63-18-25	28-13-35
50-54-14	30-24-08	44-50-14	68-36-13	37-31-39
68-30-45	50-55-30	28-40-12	63-50-18	36-48-16

3. A. Using the same index cards that you prepared for Problem 2, rearrange the numbers for a middle digit file. Your first number will be 28-02-26; it will appear after No. 1 on the answer sheet.

   B. Prepare an answer sheet similar to the one illustrated in Problem 1.

4. A. Using the same index cards that you prepared for Problem 2, rearrange the numbers for a terminal digit file. Your first number will be 30-18-01; it will appear after No. 1 on the answer sheet.

   B. Prepare an answer sheet similar to the one illustrated in Problem 1.

Part 5
Special Storage and Retrieval Systems

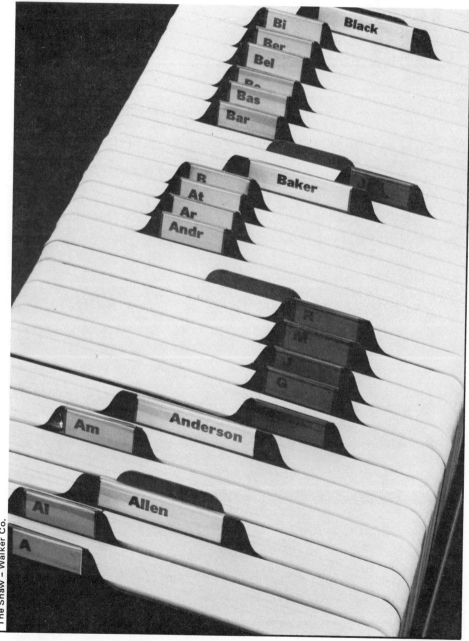

The Shaw – Walker Co.

CHAPTER 12

Card Record Filing Systems

Card record filing systems are used when fast, efficient reference is needed.

When fast and efficient reference to current information is needed, some kind of card record filing system is undoubtedly in use. Card record systems are vital to operations in many organizations. It is essential to efficiency, therefore, that office personnel understand the principles of card filing, as well as the types of systems used and the equipment available.

Getting Work Done Is Easier with Organized Files

*Cards are used
extensively for
storing a variety
of information.*

Cards are used extensively by business, industrial, professional, and governmental organizations. Cards are also used in libraries, schools, hospitals, and homes. Business and industrial organizations store on cards a variety of information, such as stock records, payroll records, personnel records, shipping and receiving records, and accounting records. There is no end to the kind of information stored in card record systems.

Libraries make use of cards in the card catalog file. This familiar card file logs all the books stored in the library. The cards are arranged alphabetically and are grouped by title, by author, and by subject. The librarian refers to these cards as title cards, author cards, and subject cards. Illustration 12-1 shows a typical card catalog file, which consists of 5″ × 3″ cards filed in a standard closed vertical card file.

illus. 12-1, Card Catalog File in a Library

Schools and colleges often keep student permanent records on cards. Hospitals, doctors, and dentists keep patient information on cards. At home, recipes are often kept on cards and filed in a small card file box. After your study of numerical filing, you may have arranged your record or tape collection by number. In that case, you refer to a supplementary, or cross-reference, card file to find the number assigned to a particular record or tape.

There are many methods of using cards to show a great variety of reference information or to carry statistics that are vital to business operations. Some of the many commonly used systems of card filing have already been described and illustrated in previous chapters of this text. In Chapter 2, an alphabetic card file for names and addresses is described and illustrated. In the chapters on geographic, subject, and numeric correspondence filing, other card indexes are described as auxiliary parts of the systems. But these represent only a few of the total uses of card systems.

Cards come in a variety of sizes, colors, and designs. The size and style of card that best fits the requirements of the job to be done is the one selected for use. Whether 5″ × 3″ cards are used to list customers' names, addresses, and telephone numbers, or 8″ × 5″ cards to keep a current inventory record of materials or supplies, or 14″ × 12″ ledger cards to keep a current record of how much money customers owe your company, one thing is certain: card record systems play an important role in the total record control system of an organization.

Storage Features of Card Record Systems

Cards are stored on edge or flat.

Because there are many types of card records, the equipment to house the cards varies to a considerable degree. Much specialized equipment is available that provides a variety of storage and retrieval alternatives for those who plan card record systems. In general, however, there are two classes of equipment: (1) equipment designed to hold cards in a vertical position and (2) equipment designed to hold cards in a horizontal position.

In the *vertical position*, the cards are stored on edge in an upright position. Vertical guides are used to mark sections in the file drawer in a manner similar to that used in all types of correspondence files.

In the *horizontal position,* the cards are stored flat in an overlapping arrangement. When the cards overlap, the lower, or sometimes the upper, edge of each card is visible when the tray in which the cards are held is pulled out from the cabinet. For this reason, horizontal card files are often called *visible card files* or *visible files*. Illustration 12-7 shows a visible card file with one tray pulled out in a posting, or recording, position.

Reference and Posting Features of Card Record Systems

Card record files may be used either for reference or for posting purposes. A *reference card file* is one from which information is retrieved, such as addresses or current merchandise price lists. The supplementary card file used in a numerical correspondence file is a good example of a reference card file. You refer to the auxiliary, or supplementary, card file to find the number assigned to a particular folder in the system. The card catalog file already mentioned and illus-

A reference card file is one from which information is retrieved.

A posting card file is one in which current information is recorded on the file cards.

trated in Illustration 12-1 is a reference file also. The file is used to retrieve information that will help you locate a particular book in the library.

A *posting card file*, on the other hand, is one in which current information is recorded on the file cards, either by hand or by machine. An accounts receivable records file (money owed a company) is an example of a posting card record file. Clients' names are listed on large ledger cards and amounts due and paid are recorded on the ledgers either by hand or with a posting or bookkeeping machine. Stock and inventory records are posting files, also. Information is posted on these cards as stock is received, used up, or ordered.

Reference and posting card files can be arranged either in a vertical or a horizontal position. The arrangement of the cards depends on how the file is being used. For example, the visible horizontal file makes an ideal posting file. Because the cards are filed flat, it is easy to find the cards and to make manual entries on them without removing the card from the tray file.

Following are two typical vertical card record systems: an alphabetic card system and a subject card record system. Both files are vertical card files; however, the alphabetic card record shown in Illustration 12-2 is a *reference* card file, while the subject card file in Illustration 12-3 on page 171 is a *posting* card file.

Section 1 Vertical Card Files

The development of a vertical card record system requires (1) a guide plan and (2) suitable equipment. In general, the plan used for a system of guides in a vertical file may be as standard as that used for correspondence files. Thus, a guiding plan can be a standard alphabetic, geographic, subject, or numeric plan; or it can provide combinations of any of these standard plans.

Alphabetic Systems for Card Files

The vertical card file shown in Illustration 12-2 is an example of an alphabetic system of guiding as applied to records relating to names of firms or of individuals.

In the illustration, notice that the system includes the following sections:

1. Primary alphabetic section guides are located in first position and show single-unit notations from "A" to "A1."
2. Special guides for commonly found names are given prominence by having tabs double-width covering the second and third positions in the file drawer.
3. Common name sections are further subdivided by guides in fourth position for commonly found second units in names.

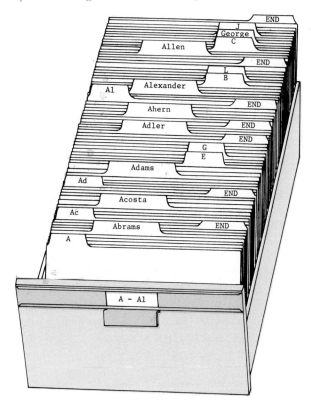

illus. 12-2, Alphabetic System for Card Files

4. "END" guides are shown in fifth position. These are used to mark the close of particular name groups within a given alphabetic section. "END" guides eliminate the need to search through a number of cards in order to locate the close of a special section and the resumption of the major alphabetic sequence. For example, the last index card bearing the name "Abrams" would be filed before the "END" guide; and the card following this "END" guide would show a name such as "Abramson, T.L."

Alphabetic systems for card files are used extensively to hold records relating to names of customers, personnel, or suppliers of goods and services. Alphabetic systems are also used in conjunction with files that are primarily concerned with subject titles, with geographic locations, or with numeric correspondence files.

Subject Systems for Card Files

The subject system shown in Illustration 12-3 is used to hold stock record cards for items held for sale by a filing equipment and supplies dealer. In this system, there is a card for each type of stock that is carried. These cards are designed to show such information as how many

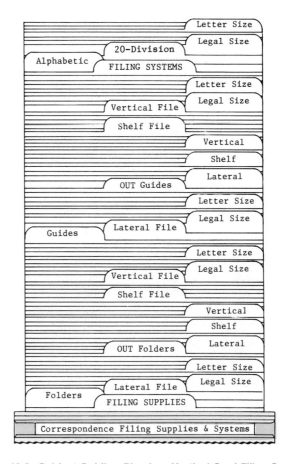

illus. 12-3, Subject Guiding Plan in a Vertical Card Filing System

units of a particular item are on hand, how many units to order, when to reorder, and from whom to reorder.

A person seeking a particular card in such a subject system would (1) locate the desired drawer in the system by scanning the drawer labels; (2) within the drawer, scan the primary guides and locate the desired major division; (3) scanning from left to right across the drawer, find the location of the block of cards that would include the one wanted. Searching for the particular card within the block of cards would involve flipping through the cards and locating the one bearing the desired title—all cards being arranged in alphabetic order according to names of items held in stock.

In a large stock record system, numeric notations in the form of stock record numbers usually are included as titles on cards and the final arrangement of cards is one of numerical order.

Subject systems that have been organized in much the same manner as the one shown in Illustration 12-3 are commonly used to control many types of business, industrial, and scientific records. Subject systems may be used for storage record cards, purchasing and stock records, inspection and maintenance records, quality control data, and material control systems.

Equipment for Vertical Card Files

A variety of equipment is available for use in vertical card filing. Whether they are address cards, computer cards, magnetic cards, or ledger cards, all find their way into suitable housing. Equipment for vertical card records may be stationary, portable, or power-driven.

Equipment may be stationary, portable, or power-driven.

Stationary Cabinets or Shelves. Stationary cabinets like those shown in Illustration 12-1 are commonly used for both large and small filing systems. More recently, equipment for holding card systems in large open bins or on stationary shelves has been developed and is widely used. In Illustration 12-4, shallow trays holding cards are placed in rows on stationary shelves. The trays hold depositors' record cards, which are controlled by guides bearing such captions as those you have already seen in Illustration 12-2.

Permission by Supreme Equipment & Systems, Corp., Brooklyn, New York

illus. 12-4, Card Files

In this card file section of a metropolitan bank, more than 600,000 signature cards are held for frequent reference. This system was installed by the Supreme Equipment & Systems Corporation.

Portable Trays and Bins. Portable open trays or open bins on casters are helpful to file users to hold card records that are needed at different work stations.

Power-Driven Movable Shelf Equipment. Most interesting of all equipment for card records is the power-driven movable shelf equipment. When this type of equipment is used, cards are held in shallow trays that are placed on movable shelves. The shelves are mounted on a framework held inside a cabinet shell, and the framework is geared to revolve in a manner similar to the motion of a Ferris wheel. Any particular shelf can be brought into and held at a working position by pressing one of a series of push buttons mounted on a panel in front of the machine operator. Illustration 12-5 shows a power-driven movable shelf unit. Each shelf holds card trays in a side-by-side arrangement.

Wheeldex, Division of LeFebure

illus. 12-5, Power-Driven Card File Units

Each tray also holds a set of guides in addition to required cards. These trays can be removed from the shelves, but usually the operator can refer to or otherwise process the cards without taking a tray out of the shelf area.

Illustration 12-6 shows details of a push-button control panel and of a shelf holding a series of trays for an alphabetic card system. The panel

Wheeldex, Division of LeFebure

illus. 12-6, Push-Button Control Panel for a Power-Driven Card File Unit

controls the shelves of the unit shown in Illustration 12-5.

The advantage of power-driven equipment over manually operated equipment varies according to conditions existing in particular types of business operations. For example, in some companies, reference to card records is infrequent, while in others, card records are vital to operations and are referred to continually. Also, in some organizations, relatively few card records are needed, while in others, card systems are complex and voluminous. Thus, as business conditions vary, the relative value of power-driven equipment for card systems varies. When records are required in volume and/or are very active, power-driven equipment has these advantages:

1. A large volume of cards is held in compact, easily accessible form.
2. Working time is saved by bringing cards to the operator's station rather than by moving the operator from the work station to the filing area.

3. Use of floor space is improved because records can be held in tiers rising to heights that would not be possible to use with manual equipment.
4. Desired information is transmitted rapidly because cards are retrieved quickly. Therefore, service to customers or to company personnel is more efficient.

Signals for
Vertical
Card Files

Signals clearly
mark the
more im-
portant data.

Card record filing systems can be made more efficient through the use of equipment and methods for signaling the more important data that are held in the system. By means of signaling devices, different types of information or data can be more clearly marked and thus be more readily located and summarized when needed. Here are a few examples of the many types of signaling devices available for office use:

1. Insert slips can be put into the hollow tabs of guides to mark major or special sections of the system. The slips are available in various colors. Printed forms can be purchased from dealers, or blank forms can be used on which desired notations are typed.
2. Cards of different colors can be used. For example, in a personnel file, cards of one color can be used for men and those of another color for women. Also, a manufacturing business that sells to both wholesalers and retailers might use cards of one color for wholesalers and cards of a second color for retailers.
3. Small, colored movable signals may be attached to the tops of the file cards so that the position as well as the color classifies the information on the card. In a credit file, for example, a red signal can be attached in a particular position on a card to indicate that an account is one month overdue. A black signal can be attached in another position to indicate that an account is two months overdue. In this manner, a credit manager can tell at a glance the number of delinquent accounts and the age of each account. Furthermore, credit references can be checked much more easily than if each card had to be pulled from the file and read in detail to secure the desired information.

Section 2 Visible Card Files

Types of
Visible
Systems
and
Equipment

There are three major types of visible record systems, and each is distinguishable because of certain features found only in that particular type of system. The systems are: (1) visible card files, (2) loose-leaf visible books, and (3) vertical-visible files.

Brief descriptions of each system include the following features:

1. Visible card files are formed by a series of cards held in a flat position in shallow trays, with each card positioned so that one or more edges are always visible.
2. Loose-leaf visible books are formed by cards or sheets of paper held flat and set in a staggered position, allowing an edge of each card or sheet always to be visible.

3.   Vertical-visible files are formed of cards specially cut to permit an upper, angle-cut corner to be seen at all times when cards are held in vertical rows across the width of a wide drawer or tub-like container. The margin of each card on the right side is also visible because of the offset positioning of cards in the rows.

Systems for Visible Card Files

Visible card files can be controlled by any of the systems used in filing.

In visible card files, the primary guiding notations appear on labels that are inserted into holders on the outside of the drawers or trays in a cabinet. Captions on these labels show the range of the group of cards held in each tray.

Inside the tray the visible edge of each card shows an identifying mark that assists in finding cards and keeping them in an orderly arrangement. The mark of identification corresponds to the major system used in a particular file, whether it is alphabetic, numeric, geographic, subject, or a combination of these.

Illustration 12-7 shows the structure of a typical visible card filing system. In the illustration, notice that one of the shallow trays held in the cabinet has been pulled out in a position for reference or for posting purposes. Also observe that the cards in this tray have been opened so that a particular section is exposed, the section being composed of a face of one card (in vertical position) and a face of another (in horizontal position). The two faces of each card are used to hold a single record in common.

KARDEX Systems Inc.

illus. 12-7, Visible Card Cabinet

Cards held below the open section are in an overlapping position that allows the lowest line on each card to be seen, thus providing the visible element in this type of card system. The overlapping factor is shown in Illustrations 12-8 and 12-9.

Acme Visible Records, Inc.

illus. 12-8, Lock-In Chain and Progressive Signals for Visible Card Records

Visible card files can be controlled by any of the systems known and used in filing. Any of the following types of titles can be used as captions: personal names, names of stock items, dates, decimal or serial numbers, geographic names, and subjects. Two such systems are indicated in Illustrations 12-8 and 12-9.

The segment of a system given in Illustration 12-8 indicates that a numeric system is being used. This is evident because the visible edge of each card shows a number in the left corner and these numbers are arranged in sequence (385, 386, 387). Had this been an alphabetic system, the descriptive titles that follow the numeric ones would have been listed in alphabetic order and the numbers would have been out of sequential order. The system indicated in Illustration 12-9 shows that this file is governed by an alphabetic arrangement in which descriptive titles are arranged in alphabetic order.

Acme Visible Records, Inc.

illus. 12-9, Transparent Signals for Visible Card Records

**Signal
Systems for
Visible
Records**

*Visible records
can be signaled
to show a great
variety of
summary
information.*

One of the most useful and distinctive features of visible records is that they can be signaled (marked) to show a great variety of summary information. When visible cards are so signaled, many vital facts can be determined without a detailed examination of all the data on a whole card or a series of cards. Signal marks can be made on the cards by hand, or signal devices can be selected from a variety of types manufactured of metal or plastic materials.

Signals can be used to show such information as: (1) the amount of stock on hand at any given time (stock record cards); (2) the volume of sales or the percentage of quota on sales (sales record cards); (3) the number of overdue accounts and the length of time each is overdue (credit and collection cards); and (4) the date for follow-up on any matter concerning accounts, contacts, and so forth.

Illustration 12-8 shows the lower visible edges of three cards and the types of signaling devices used to flash notice of vital information to persons who scan these cards. Two types of signals are shown. Those (4 in number) closest to the description titles (for example, Bench Grinder) are called "Lock-In Chain" by their producer, Acme Visible Records, Inc. These are colored, movable plastic strips which are fixed in slots at the lower edge of the card and can be moved up and down to signal vital information of one kind or another as desired. The signals to the right of the Lock-In Chain ones are known as "Progressive" signals by the manufacturer (Acme) because they can be moved by a sliding motion progressively from one notation to another; for example, from one month to the next or from one number to the next. These signal marks are used to show a variety of spot information of vital importance to those who refer to the cards. For example, the cards shown in Illustration 12-8 are concerned with an inspection schedule in a preventive maintenance system. In this, the Lock-In Chain signals are used to signal the week during which an inspection will be made of Bench Grinders. Progressive signals are used to show the month during which the inspection must be made. Thus, it is signaled that Bench Grinders will be inspected during the first week of February. When this inspection has been completed and data have been posted to the cards, the signals will be moved to show the week and month for the next inspection.

Illustration 12-9 shows a typical signalling device used in many visible record systems. The signals consist of strips of plastic material, which might be either clear or opaque, colored or plain, depending on the particular use to be made of them in the signal system. These plastic strips are fitted into the lower edge of the card and under the flap of the pocket in which the card is held. Strips can then be moved along a horizontal path to desired locations on the face of the card. In the cards illustrated, signals are used to show the weekly supply on hand of each item of stock. As the supply is lowered, the signal is moved to a lower number to flash this fact to those who refer to this card to determine when to reorder a particular item. Many variations of this type of stock control record are widely used in business and industrial organizations.

Loose-Leaf Visible Systems

Loose-leaf cards or sheets that are held in prong binders or ring binders are widely used where voluminous data must be kept in a relatively small space. An advantage of this system is that the binders are portable.

Loose-leaf visible cards are available in several forms. Some binders hold cards so that bottom edges are visible. Others hold them so that top edges show, while still others are arranged so that the side edges are visible.

The types of records kept in loose-leaf form are as varied as those kept in visible card files. They include cards for records of stock, data on purchasing, accounting or record-keeping data, and many other types of records.

Vertical-Visible Files

Essentially, vertical-visible files represent a combining of the vertical and the visible systems of filing cards by holding specially cut cards in vertical position across the width of tub-like containers. (See Illustration 12-10.) In this arrangement, one visible edge of a card is formed by a diagonal cut having been made across the upper corner of the card. A second visible edge results from each card being placed in an overlapping position in relation to other cards held in the same row. An unusually wide cabinet called a "tub" is the receptacle used to hold rows of vertical-visible record cards.

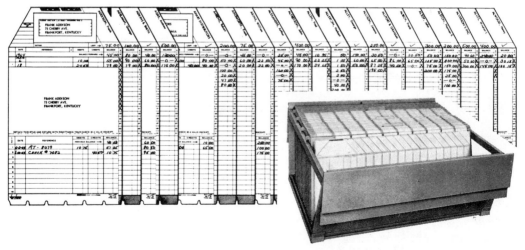

Acme Visible Records, Inc.

illus. 12-10, Vertical-Visible Card File

Vertical-visible files can be signaled to show a variety of key data.

Like all other visible record systems, vertical-visible ones can be signaled to show and to feature key data of one kind or another. The kinds of data that can be held on cards can take any of a number of forms so that signal devices are found in great variety. For example, cards can be used in conjunction with integrated data processing systems by having edge-punched common language strips form a part of the card. These can show on a visible part of the card, or the card can be marked to show that a common language tape is included with it. Colored signals can be clipped to any visible surface to indicate such data as a summary total, a due date, a reorder date, etc. Also, cards of different colors can be used to indicate types of major items being handled by records in the system.

Data Drawer–Wilson Jones Company

Data Drawer Holding Computer Printouts

This *Data Drawer,* produced by Wilson Jones, is an adaptation of visible equipment that permits computer printout reports to be held in an easy-to-use visible cabinet.

Wheel Equipment and Systems for Card Records

In addition to the type of equipment that holds cards in trays that can be set into mechanically powered units, cards are also affixed directly to wheel-like frames that are manually or motor operated. These are known as *wheel files* and are made in a variety of forms. They have the advantage of being relatively simple to operate and yet capable of showing all faces of cards for posting or for reference purposes.

*Wheel files are
simple to operate
yet capable of
showing all
faces of cards for
posting or
reference.*

Wheel files are generally of two types: (1) The open wheel type (without cabinet enclosure) has cards attached in vertical position. The whole file is rotated into a desired position by hand action. (2) The enclosed wheel file is held in a cabinet equipped with a work-station shelf area. Cards are brought into alignment with the shelf area by manually turning the wheel on which cards are affixed.

The open wheel system shown in Illustration 12-11 is a portable unit that holds 2,000 cards (6″ × 3″) and an A-Z index of 60 divisions. Both larger and smaller units are available in this type of equipment for cards of varying sizes and in quantities varying from 1,000 to 7,000.

*Photograph Courtesy of Bostitch
Division of Textron, Inc.*

illus. 12-11, Open Wheel File for Card Records

The cards and guides that are used in all types of wheel files are cut and perforated so that they can be fitted around the twin rails that are formed around the core of the revolving central section of the wheel.

When the wheel is turned to a desired position, cards are spread into a wide "V" section. This permits either direct reference to a given card or reference and posting without having to remove the card from the wheel. Posting is possible because the revolving central core is not free-wheeling; it is held under limited pressure by a ratchet-like arrangement within the central section of the unit. Illustration 12-11 shows the posting or reference position of a wheel file.

Many kinds of "quick reference" data are kept in open wheel systems. Among these are name and address lists, inventory records, wage rates, price lists, and item location lists of various kinds.

Some of the larger enclosed wheel files operate in the same manner as that described for the portable open wheel type. Enclosed units usually hold more cards of larger sizes than those held in portable open wheel types. Enclosed wheel equipment usually is of "desk height" and includes either a shelf-like work station, or can be operated from a desk station. (See Illustration 12-12.)

Some wheel files turn like a carrousel.

If there are advantages to a wheel file that turns like a Ferris wheel, what about one that turns like a carrousel or a merry-go-round? That kind of wheel equipment is available, too. Illustration 12-13 shows a Rotascan card file. Notice the carrousel-rotating shelves. Tiers of shelves can be added as they are needed. Space is compact. The equipment provides the added advantage that more than one person can have access to the file at one time.

Wheeldex, Division of LeFebure

illus. 12-12, Enclosed Wheel File for Card Records

Rotascan Retrieval Systems

illus. 12-13, Carrousel-Rotating Wheel File for Card Records

Factors Affecting Choice of Card Record System and Equipment

What is the best system and the best equipment for card records? Obviously there is no simple answer to this question. A choice of system and equipment for card records requires consideration of many factors such as these:

1. What kinds of card records are needed?
2. How and by whom will the cards be used?
3. What is the volume of cards to be stored?

4. How much cash is an organization willing to invest in the system?
5. What systems and equipment are available?

Knowledge, liberally supported by experience, is required to build the best card record system for a particular organization. The more knowledge you have about card record systems and equipment, the better equipped you will be to handle the challenges of card filing in your own work.

Questions for Discussion

1. What are three kinds of information kept on cards and by whom?

2. What are two general classes of equipment for card record systems?

3. How does a posting card file differ from a reference card file?

4. Describe a typical guiding plan for an alphabetic name card system.

5. Why are END guides used in card files?

6. What are three types of records for which subject guide plans for card files might be used?

7. What is the difference between stationary and portable card record equipment?

8. What are some advantages in using power-driven equipment for files?

9. Would a power-driven file be a good choice of equipment for a library card catalog file? Why or why not?

10. How can colored movable signals be used to advantage in vertical card systems?

11. Why are signals an important feature of visible card systems?

12. What are two reasons for using loose-leaf visible systems?

13. What particular advantages do vertical-visible systems have over other types of visible equipment?

14. What are two common uses for a wheel file?

15. When selecting a card record system or equipment, what five important factors should be considered?

CHAPTER 13

Word Processing and Micrographic Filing Systems

The huge amounts of information needed to run modern businesses require mechanical and electronic filing and retrieval.

More and more information is needed to run modern businesses. Management needs additional information to make better and quicker decisions. Government agencies continually require more information from businesses and individuals. Tax laws are becoming more complicated and require that more records be kept by the public. New laws, such as those related to employee hiring, promotion, assignments, and pay, require large volumes of records.

This huge accumulation of information requires precise filing techniques and very rapid retrieval. Manual methods to create, process, store, and retrieve this quantity of information are in many cases too slow and costly to satisfy the needs of business operations. It has, therefore, been necessary to develop mechanical and electronic machines to help with the creation, filing, and finding tasks. This chapter will describe some of the data processing, word processing, micrographic, and other related systems designed to help control this growing volume of information.

Coding and indexing are still vitally important.

It is important to note that with the use of these newer systems, the tasks of coding and indexing information are still vitally important. The information created and processed by each system must be prepared accurately for machine processing. The equipment is merely a tool to speed up the processes of filing and finding. In fact, many of the cards, papers, magnetic tapes, and films produced by electronic means and by micrographics must still be stored and retrieved by methods similar to those used to control materials produced by and held in systems like those already studied. The main changes are in the form of the record (for example, magnetic tape and microfilm), not in the indexing systems.

Section 1 Data Processing

Data processing refers to the manipulation of information.

The term *data processing* refers to the manipulation of information, a process that has been done since people used chisels and stone tablets to keep records. As the volume of and need for these records increased, faster and more accurate tools were invented to record and process the information. Pen and paper, typewriters, adding machines, computers, and the small pocket calculators many of us use are all examples of these tools.

The major impact of these data processing tools and systems on files operators is in the form of the records produced and in the increased use of automated equipment for sorting and retrieving the records.

The development of smaller, more powerful, yet less expensive equipment (the minicomputer, for example) has made it possible for even the smallest business to have its own equipment. When a businessperson prefers not to purchase or lease a data processing system, the manager can use a data processing center. There, for a fee, the computations can be completed and returned to the business ready to use.

Punched Card Systems

Punched card systems record information in the form of holes.

Nature and Use of Punched Cards. *Punched card systems* are systems that record information in the form of holes in cards and that use machines to "read" the holes and process the information thus read. The leading manufacturers of punched card machines are International Business Machines (IBM) and the Sperry Univac Division of the Sperry Corporation.

Both the IBM and the Sperry Univac machines use a standard card that has 80 vertical columns. (See Illustration 13-1.) In addition, IBM has designed a 96-column card for use with its small low-cost computer.

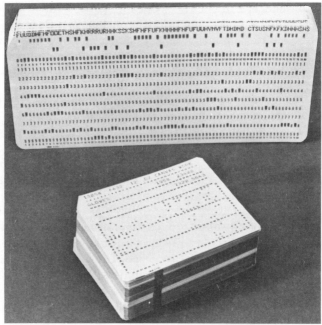

IBM Corporation

illus. 13-1, Punched Cards

Each column on a card can accommodate one or more punched holes. Each column that is punched represents a single number or letter. Information is punched into the card according to a standard arrangement, with certain columns on the cards reserved for the recording of specific information. For example, several columns on the card may be reserved for the name of an employee; another group of columns, for the employee's address or department number; still other columns, for important information about the employee. Each of these groups of columns is called a *field*. For example, the group of columns containing the employee's address would be one field. The meaning of the punched holes can be printed at the top of the card for visual reading, if desired.

There are many ways by which information is punched into cards. Various types of office machines record the information and verify the accuracy of what was recorded in the form of punched holes. An introductory book on data processing will give details for those interested.*

Punched cards are unit records.

Punched cards are also known as *unit records* because each card contains one unit of information, and each card is handled as a single item or record unit. As such, the cards can be sorted into alphabetic or numeric order either by hand through reading the information printed on the top of the card, or by a machine called a *sorter*. The sorter operates somewhat along the same principles as terminal digit filing, sorting from right to left only one letter or number at a time.

Information regarding prospective customers, for example, might be punched into a series of cards, one customer on each card. The cards can then be sorted according to postal ZIP Codes, sales representatives' territories, or the cities and states in which the prospective customers live. Since hundreds, and even thousands, of cards can be sorted by machine in one minute, this operation is much faster than hand filing and retrieving.

Punched cards are placed in long trays or drawers.

Punched Card Filing. Punched cards are placed in long trays or drawers held in specially constructed cabinets. Illustration 13-2 shows open-shelf filing using three indexing systems: (1) in the lower two rows, *numeric filing*, a system that is frequently used for parts inventory records; (2) in the second row from the top, *alphabetic filing*, a system that is used for such material as customer name and address cards; and (3) in the top row, *grouped card sets*, a system that is used for such applications as sales records where individual cards are less important than a collection of all sales for a particular department or a particular item.

Each tray or drawer bears a label on which is written a description or a code showing the contents. The labels are similar in use to labels on the front of file drawers in cabinets. A variety of specially constructed equipment is available for punched card filing systems, all designed to assemble systems comparable to those used for index card systems.

---

* A good book in this area is: S. J. Wanous and Gerald E. Wagner, *Fundamentals of Data Processing* (2d ed.; Cincinnati: South-Western Publishing Co., 1981).

TAB Products Company

illus. 13-2, Punched Card File

The desired card or cards may be retrieved in the same manner as other material by locating the proper drawer or tray by the label card, then scanning the guides in the drawers, and finally by reading the printed coding on the top of each card until the proper card is found. When many cards are needed, or when printed coding is not placed on the top of the cards, all cards from the appropriate section of the tray or drawer may be placed in the sorter and mechanically located.

If a listing of the information punched into the cards is desired, the sorted cards may be fed through a *tabulator*. The tabulator reads the holes punched into the cards and prints out the information on paper or cards. It is capable of reading all or selected information punched into the cards, depending on what information is needed. The tabulator also normally performs computations of addition and subtraction.

Filing of tabulator print-outs can take many forms.

Tabulator Printout Filing. Filing of tabulator printouts can take many forms. If the printout is in the form of individual records such as invoices, the records are indexed and filed in folders in the same manner as other similar-sized documents. Alphabetic, numeric, or combination indexing systems are used. On the other hand, if the printout is on a large continuous form, the material is usually bound into a specially designed report-type folder and is labeled on the back like a book or on a tab-like file folder or guide. The folders can be placed in a vertical file shelf or drawer or placed on tracks in hanging folders. One such system is shown in Illustration 13-3. Note the indexing written by marking pen on the printout package. Special report folders with attachments for hanging are used in this open-shelf system. The indexing is alphabetic (subject), but numeric indexing or a combination of alphabetic and numeric can also be used.

TAB Products Company

illus. 13-3, Tabulator Printout File

Electronic Data Processing   *Electronic data processing* (EDP) refers to the processing of information with the speed of light by using electronic means. EDP systems have affected filing work not only because of the vast amounts of data that are developed and must be stored for future use, but also because of the various storage mediums used. Information produced by EDP must be available immediately when needed.

Storage Mediums. Data storage mediums for electronic data processing systems include punched cards and printout forms as well as magnetic tape, magnetic disks, magnetic drums, and magnetic cores.

The stored information is not visible on the magnetic mediums (tape, disks, drums, and cores), since information is recorded in the form of magnetized spots that create electrical impulses which can be "read" only by special machines. The magnetic tapes are similar to those used in an ordinary tape recorder in a home or office.

It is vital that indexing and coding be carefully planned before the recording process begins.

A large volume of data can be stored on magnetic tapes, disks, drums, and cores. Since information recorded on these magnetic devices cannot be read without being printed out, it is vital that the indexing and coding of such information be carefully planned before the recording process begins. The location of information is commonly called its *address* when reference is made to the magnetic storage devices. A set of instructions prepared for a computer is called a *program*, and the person who prepares the instructions is called a *programmer*. The programmer must be thoroughly familiar with all phases of the actual business application that must be processed as well as with the capabilities of the machine.

Payroll work is one type of business activity that lends itself to EDP. All the involved steps of preparing a payroll, including the preparation of the paychecks themselves, can become highly automated under this system. As a by-product, a considerable amount of information regarding an employee may be stored on magnetic tape and supplied whenever needed. For example, if a directory or list of employees and their work locations is needed, it is easily obtained automatically from a printout of the tape through the use of electronic data processing equipment.

Storing EDP Information. When magnetic tape is being stored, great care must be taken to see that no dust or dirt collects on the tape. In addition, the temperature and humidity in the storage area must be carefully controlled.

In order to make identification easy, a visible label must be placed on each tape as it is being prepared. This label serves the same purpose as the drawer label in regular files. Many companies employ a files operator, called a *tape librarian*, whose job is to maintain control over the magnetic tapes and to see that they are stored properly, correctly charged out, and returned.

Magnetic tapes are filed on end in various specially designed cabinets or on specially designed shelves. Illustration 13-4 shows one such installation in a large insurance company. Note the use of consecutive numeric indexing in this company. Other numeric systems and various alphabetic systems, including subject indexing, are also used.

The security of data processing files is vital.

The security of data processing files is a vital responsibility of the files operator. The theft or destruction of one reel of tape could possibly cause the company to put many valuable hours of work into reproducing lost information. Many security devices are designed to help safeguard this information. Among these devices are lead carrying and storage cases; locks to make use of the reel of tape impossible without the proper key or combination; security guards at the entrance to the storage area; and the preparation of duplicate tapes, called *back-up tapes*, to be safely

Spacesaver Corporation
Ft. Atkinson, Wisconsin

illus. 13-4, Computer Tape Storage File

stored in another location. Illustration 13-5 shows one method of security storage of magnetic tapes in a specially built safe. The tapes are labeled with a band around the reel using alphabetic or numeric indexing for quick and easy retrieval.

As discussed earlier, computer printouts are placed in specially designed binders and are filed on shelves or in file drawers designed for that purpose. The binders are labeled on the outside cover, on the back, or on tabs in the same manner as correspondence folders. (See Illustration 13-3.)

Data-Safe is a registered trademark
of Diebold, Inc., Canton, Ohio

illus. 13-5, Security Storage of Magnetic Tapes

EDP systems eliminate a large amount of hand filing.

It is obvious, then, that a large amount of hand filing of certain types of materials is completely eliminated when an EDP system is installed. Nevertheless, the machine must be told how to do everything. The main difference in records control is *where the information is filed* and *through what means*. As long as information must be retrieved, a knowledge of filing procedures is necessary. Filing systems for EDP tape or punched cards or paper tape must be as complete and as efficient as systems used for index cards or for correspondence and other documents. The indexing systems used are the same as those used for other records—alphabetic, numeric, or a combination of the two.

Word Processing

Word processing is a combination of equipment, methods, and systems that converts ideas into the printed word.

The newest mechanized system to affect information preparation, storage, and retrieval is word processing. The American National Standards Committee, of Washington, D.C., defines word processing as ". . . the transformation of ideas and information into a readable form of communication through the management of procedures, equipment, and personnel." *Word processing*, therefore, is a combination of equipment, methods, and systems that converts ideas into the printed word. The machines used (dictating, typing, and copying) have made information *processing* easier, but in some respects they have made information *handling* (filing, storage, and retrieval) more difficult because documents are put on many different kinds of magnetic mediums as well as on paper.

Word processing is rapidly joining data processing so that numerical information processing as well as words are combined into one system. Minicomputers, as well as large computers, have been connected to word processing equipment to produce, store, and recall information of many types. This results in what many call an integrated data processing system.

Integrated data processing systems transfer information from one machine to other machines automatically.

Integrated data processing (IDP) is a system of machine control based on the ability of certain office machines to transfer information to other machines automatically. Such a system follows this basic rule: *Do it only once.* This means that the exact information should be captured on some type of common language medium the first time the information is prepared. The next time this information is needed, it is automatically written from its common language (machine-readable language) form.

Storage Mediums. Many common language mediums are used with word processing and IDP. Understanding these mediums will help you understand how to file and retrieve the information when needed. We have already discussed computer tape and punched cards in the section on electronic data processing. The following storage mediums are also used in word processing.

Punched Paper Tapes. Punched paper tape is one type of common language medium. The tape can be prepared automatically by a small attachment to a specially designed electric typewriter, adding machine, cash register, printing calculator, or other common business machine. As the operator types the original document, the paper tape is automatically punched. The next time the same information is needed, the tape is fed back into the device on the typewriter or other machine and an exact duplicate copy of the original is prepared automatically. Punched paper tapes are treated as unit records.

The system is used for a number of business operations. For example, bank checks that have the name and address of the depositor printed on each check are frequently prepared on paper tapes. When the customer wants more "personalized checks," a notice is returned to the bank requesting the checks. Frequently the bank encloses the tape in a pocket of an order blank that is sent to the depositor with the set of checks. The customer keeps the order blank and tape until more checks are needed. The order and the tape are then sent back to the bank with the order. The bank (or a service bureau employed by the bank) inserts the punched tape into a machine. Information about the depositor identical to that on the present checks is automatically reproduced on a new set of checks.

Magnetic Tapes. Some word processing machines use magnetic tapes to store information. These tapes are similar to computer tapes but are much shorter and narrower. Many are contained in cassettes exactly like those used on a home cassette tape recorder. Illustration 13-6 shows a typical cassette with subject labels.

Magnetic Cards. Magnetic cards are approximately the size of a punched card but are designed to store information as magnetic spots instead of punched holes. Magnetic cards (called *mag cards*) hold considerably more information on each card than punched cards and, like punched cards, are considered unit records.

Diskettes. Diskettes are small, flexible sheets of magnetic material on which relatively large amounts of data can be stored in magnetic form. These are popularly referred to as *floppy disks*. Like punched cards, mag cards, and others, they are treated as unit records because generally only one topic or record is on each disk.

Internal Storage Mediums. The term *internal storage mediums* refers to a variety of storage devices attached to or part of the word processing equipment. Large quantities of information can be recorded inside the equipment. This information can be retrieved instantly whenever the machine is keyed with the address (location) of the infor-

National ®, a subsidiary of
Dennison Mfg. Co.

illus. 13-6, Magnetic Tapes with Labels

mation. The machine is instructed to either type, print, or display the information on a video screen. The video screen is similar to that of a home television screen. The popular *memory typewriter* is an example of word processing equipment with internal storage. Information is stored on magnetic mediums inside the memory typewriter. Although it has only limited storage space, the typewriter types out the stored material, as requested, on letterhead paper, invoices, ordinary blank sheets, or however instructed.

Information stored on magnetic mediums cannot be read until it is either printed out or displayed.

Indexing and Storing Word Processing Information. Obviously, information stored on magnetic mediums cannot be read by the person needing the information until it is either printed out on paper or displayed on a cathode ray tube (CRT) such as a television (video) screen. In order to be printed or otherwise displayed, the information must be located.

Punched paper tapes are usually kept in folders in a master file. The folders housing the tapes are constructed with small pockets into which the prepunched tapes are inserted—frequently with a printed paper copy of the contents of the tape. The operator simply removes the prepunched tape from its pocket and feeds it through the machine. The tape is then replaced in the pocket of the folder and filed until needed again.

Similar machines also produce edge-punched cards as well as paper tape. Edge-punched cards perform the same function as paper tape. In addition, they are more convenient to file. Each tape must be placed in a special pocket, whereas cards are rigid and can be filed in a manner similar to that used for ordinary file cards. Illustration 13-7 shows a folder with a pocket into which a punched paper tape has been inserted. Folders with punched paper tape, or edge-punched cards, can be filed alphabetically or numerically exactly like other paper records or cards.

Magnetic tapes are also indexed alphabetically or numerically. Illustration 13-8 shows a vertical drawer file, a carrousel for the top of a desk, and a floor stand—all used for storing active magnetic cassette tapes. These devices are expandable as more storage space is needed. In addition, tapes are stored in individually indexed boxes in vertical drawer files similar to card files, or on large circular rotating files for easy access.

Shaw-Walker

illus. 13-7, Filing Punched Paper Tapes

Magnetic cards are filed on edge like regular card files, or in see-through plastic pockets designed to hold documents and cards together. Alphabetic or numeric indexing systems are used for rapid and accurate retrieval. Notebook folders are popular, also, for holding cards and tapes.

Diskettes are becoming very popular for storing information since they are small, flexible (hence, called "floppy disks"), and easily stored. Illustration 13-9 on page 196 shows the use of labels on floppy disks. The labels could be color coded if desired. Color coding is popular for indexing all types of word processing mediums.

Illustration 13-10 on page 197 shows various file storage methods for floppy disks: a loose-leaf notebook, a vertical file drawer with hanging folders, and a vertical file drawer with hanging folders that contain the printout material as well as the diskette. Notice the guides in the

National ®, a subsidiary of Dennison Mfg. Co.

National ®, a subsidiary of Dennison Mfg. Co.

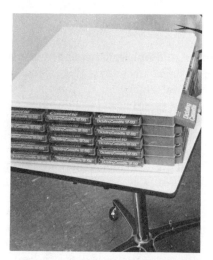

National ®, a subsidiary of Dennison Mfg. Co.

illus. 13-8, Storing Magnetic Tapes

drawer file are the same as those used for correspondence and other document files. A carrousel such as the one shown in Illustration 1-1, page 4, can also hold floppy disks.

To aid in retrieving information on internal storage (storage of information within the machine), the address (storage location) is: (1) recorded on index cards, (2) typed on a standard sheet of paper, or (3) in large installations, stored in the machine on another magnetic tape, disk, or card for printout or video display when needed.

Avery Label Co.

illus. 13-9, Labeling Floppy Disks

An auxiliary index is very important.

Since subject and numeric filing are used extensively with both word processing and data processing documents, an auxiliary index is very important. By first referring to the index for the proper address, retrieval is quick and accurate. In the index, material is listed by common titles and cross-referenced under other likely titles. Through this procedure, any one of many titles can be used to locate a specific document rapidly and accurately.

Section 2 Micrographics

Microfilming is a process of filming documents to reduce their size.

Microfilming is a process of photographing documents so as to reduce the size of the original to a very small (micro) size. These miniature pictures are generally taken on 16 mm (millimeter) or 35 mm film. For special types of work, 105 mm or a variety of other sizes is used.

Micrographics includes filming, filing, and retrieval of information.

A broader term than microfilm is *micrographics*. It is more commonly used; it is preferred by specialists; and it is more descriptive by not limiting our thinking to just filming. *Micrographics*, then, is a total information system, including filming but also including the filing and retrieval of information.

Filming

The records control area involving micrographics is frequently part of the records management function. As a result, files operators become involved in several important activities concerning micrographics. Most of these activities are similar to the filing responsibilities already dis-

*National ®, a subsidiary of
Dennison Mfg. Co.*

*National ®, a subsidiary of
Dennison Mfg. Co.*

*National ®, a subsidiary of
Dennison Mfg. Co.*

illus. 13-10, Storage Methods for Floppy Disks

The coding and arranging of documents before filming is of great importance.

cussed; for example, coding the records for filing, preparing labels and guides, selecting cabinets and shelves, filing the materials, and quickly retrieving what is needed. Once records are filmed in a particular order, they always remain in that order; therefore, the coding and arranging of documents before filming is of great importance.

Many times files operators are asked to help film records. They are frequently trained to use the cameras on the job. There are a variety of cameras designed for microfilming, but they fall into two basic kinds. The exact type selected depends on the nature of the material to be filmed and the uses to be made of the film after it is created.

Rotary cameras are used for many common types of business papers.

Rotary cameras are the most frequently used cameras. They are easy to operate, accept popular-sized documents, and are very fast when the documents are fed to the machine automatically. Rotary cameras are used for many common types of business papers such as correspondence, invoices, bank checks, and school transcripts. (See Illustration 13-11.)

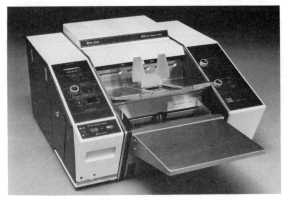

Bell & Howell

illus. 13-11, Rotary Camera

Planetary cameras are used especially for filming large documents.

Planetary cameras are the second basic type and operate somewhat differently from the rotary cameras. The papers are usually hand fed, one sheet at a time; but a greater variety of document sizes can be photographed and the picture shows details more clearly. Planetary cameras are popular especially for filming large documents such as blueprints, engineering drawings, and bound books, newspapers, and magazines. A smaller planetary camera is available for photographing smaller documents requiring the filming of fine detail. (See Illustration 13-12.)

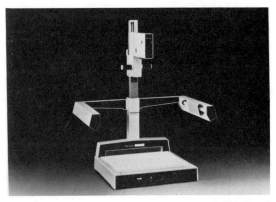

Bell & Howell

illus. 13-12, Planetary Camera

Variations of the rotary and planetary cameras are used for photographing different information. For example, a type of planetary camera can create microfilm directly from computer tapes without producing a paper printout first. This is called *Computer Output Microfilming* (COM). Another is called a "step-and-repeat" camera for filming a series of images all on the same piece of film.

Reading and Printing

Film is placed in a projector for viewing or reading.

A hard copy is any copy that can be read without a viewer.

After the film has been developed, it is placed in a projector for viewing or reading. This projector is called a *reader-viewer,* or just a *reader.* (See Illustration 13-13.) If the user wants to print out a copy of the picture, a reader-printer is used. (See Illustration 13-14.) After seeing which document is wanted, the operator obtains a print, called a hard copy, by merely pressing a button or switch on the reader-printer. The term *hard copy* refers to any copy that can be read without the use of a viewer or other magnifying device. A reader-printer can reproduce the document to any one of various sizes—smaller than the original document, the same size as the original, or larger than the original. Some readers are small enough to be portable and are very inexpensive. They can be carried in a briefcase and can be used whenever and wherever necessary. Reader-printers are larger than readers and are not portable.

Bell & Howell

illus. 13-13, Reader-Viewer

Bell & Howell

illus. 13-14, Reader-Printer

Microforms   Microfilm can be created and/or used in many formats. These formats include roll film, aperture cards, microfiche, and microfilm jackets. Although most of these formats begin as roll film, their end use may be different. It is in describing this end use that the term "microform" applies. (See Illustration 13-15.)

Minolta Corporation

illus. 13-15, Common Microforms

Roll microfilm is a length of microfilm on a reel, spool, or core.

Roll Microfilm. The most popular, and least expensive, form in which microfilm is produced is roll microfilm. *Roll microfilm* is simply a length of microfilm on a reel, spool, or core. It appears similar to motion picture films and is generally in rolls of 100 feet, although other lengths are used.

Large quantities of information are recorded on each roll microfilm. The information is recorded serially, in the exact order in which it is placed into the camera. It is suited to recording books, newspapers, and other lengthy documents that do not need updating frequently. The recording of correspondence, bank checks, invoices, entire computer runs, and other daily transactions are popular roll film contents. In order to update a roll of film, the entire roll must be photographed again or the new transactions must be photographed and spliced (cut out and glued) into the existing roll. Splicing destroys the legal acceptability of microfilm in many cases.

Retrieval requires that documents be indexed, coded, and arranged before they are filmed.

Retrieval of specific documents or other information from all microforms requires that the documents be indexed, coded, and arranged in correct filing order before they are filmed. Guides, called *targets* or *flash targets*, in microfilm are prepared and filmed at the beginning of each group of records. The targets are prepared with print that is large enough to be eye readable without magnification by a reader. Targets serve the same purpose as the guides and folder tabs of a regular filing system and contain alphabetic, numeric, date, or short subject titles. The targets are also readily seen as the film is moved rapidly across the screen of the viewer. When information is coded correctly before filming, it is mostly self-indexing.

Other more sophisticated coding systems are available to index filmed materials for use with complicated searching equipment. For example, counting devices (counters) are used to measure the number of feet of film run through the reader. This counter is similar to an automobile's odometer, which measures the number of miles the car has traveled. By recording the counter reading, a particular document can be located rapidly.

In another indexing system, each document is automatically numbered as it is filmed. This number, now part of the microfilm frame, serves as the address of the document. In the same way, magnetic codes can be placed on the film and automatically "read" by a special attachment on the reader. By use of a keyboard, the code can be requested and the reader will move rapidly to that location.

Microfilm and regular filing are similar.

Microfilm filing and regular filing are very much alike. Roll film is placed in small individual boxes. A label (similar to that on a file folder) is prepared and glued to the cover of the box. The boxes are placed in drawers, on shelves in a cabinet, or on a rotatable carrousel for active use. Drawers and shelves are also labeled in the same manner as in conventional filing systems.

Aperture cards contain holes in which frames of microfilm are placed.

Aperture Cards. An *aperture card* is a card containing an aperture, or hole, cut into the card that provides a place for one or more frames of microfilm. Aperture cards are unit records, like punched cards, and are referred to as *unitized microforms*. The microfilm frames are cut from roll microfilm after the roll is developed. Frames are then placed into the apertures provided in the card. (See Illustration 13-16.)

Aperture cards are usually cards of the size to be used in a card punch and sorter. Through the use of a card punch, holes are created for use in machine identification of the card and its microfilm image(s). Then the aperture cards can be filed and retrieved through the use of a mechanical sorter. When properly labeled, they may also be filed and retrieved manually. Aperture cards have been used extensively for engineering drawings but are also popular for X-rays and some business records.

Indexing and coding of aperture cards follows the same procedures as for other cards. The aperture cards can be produced in color or contain color lines to aid in quick visual retrieval and refiling. They are generally housed vertically in boxes, on shelves, or in specially designed drawers. Guides and drawer labels aid in the same manner as for other paper files. Cards may also be filed in pockets of standard-sized folders containing related documents. Machine sorting is a common method of

Eastman Kodak Company

illus. 13-16, Aperture Cards

card retrieval. As more images are placed on the card, however, the room for the punched holes is reduced, making machine retrieval less effective.

Microfiche is a transparent rectangle of film on which images have been photographed.

Microfiche. Another unitized microform is the microfiche. A *microfiche* (pronounced *micro feēsh*) is a transparent rectangle of film onto which from 60 to 98 small images have been photographed. Illustration 13-17 shows a microfiche being read. The standard size of a microfiche is 6″ × 4″. Many advances have been made in microfiche. One is the development of what is called *ultrafiche*. One 6″ × 4″ ultrafiche film will hold images of thousands of papers. Microfiche is a common product of computer output microfilm (COM).

Next to roll microfilm, microfiche is the most popular type of microform and is growing in use rapidly. It is used for the storage of related documents, such as a pamphlet, a parts catalog, a customer mailing list, or patients' medical histories. The publishing of book reports, magazines, catalogs, and newspapers on microfiche is called *micropublishing* and is becoming common.

The "header" is used for identification of the fiche.

A filing code and other information usually is lettered across the top or bottom margins of a microfiche film. This is called the *header* and is used for identification of the fiche without having to use a reader-viewer. Color coding can be used to aid in filing and retrieving microfiche. Color may be a horizontal band across the entire header, one or more vertical strips at the top of the fiche, or the entire fiche may be placed in a color-coded envelope. Color is usually used in conjunction with other coding systems.

illus. 13-17, Using a Microfiche Reader

All varieties of alphabetic and numeric indexing systems are used in filing microfiche.

A microfiche jacket is frequently used instead of the actual microfiche.

Microfiche Jackets. Although not a microfiche in the strictest sense, another unitized record, a *microfiche jacket,* or *microcard*, is frequently used instead of the actual microfiche. The jacket is made of two panels of very thin transparent film-like material. Lines of adhesive join the panels horizontally, dividing them into three or more strips into which microfilmed images are inserted. (See Illustration 13-18.) The images to be inserted are cut from roll microfilm and slid (either as individual images or as strips of images) into the channels of the jacket. The insertion is done either by hand or by using a specially designed machine.

National ®, a subsidiary of Dennison Mfg. Co.

illus. 13-18, Microfilm Jacket

Images no longer needed may be removed from the channels of the jacket and, if desired, new images may be inserted to update the information already placed in the jacket. Illustration 13-19 shows a microfilm jacket reader-loader. Microfiche jackets are usually the standard 6″ × 4″ size but other sizes are available.

Jackets are frequently used instead of actual microfiche because the special "step-and-repeat" camera process needed for microfiche is expensive and takes up a lot of office space. The jacket process uses regular roll film and can use the more compact rotary camera. Microfiche jackets and microfiche can be viewed in a special reader or in many readers made to accept a variety of microfilms. A hard copy of any image in the jacket can be obtained by using a reader-printer. Microfiche jackets are indexed in the same manner as microfiche.

Bell & Howell

illus. 13-19, Microfilm Jacket Reader-Loader

Values of Microfilm   Microfilming techniques and forms have developed rapidly in recent years. As a result of these developments, many values are claimed. Duplicate copies can be made of rolls of film, microfiche, or aperture cards in less than one minute on small office-type copiers. Prints of microfilm images are made even faster, and prints can be made larger or smaller than the original document to make copies easier to read and handle.

As much as the contents of a five-drawer file can be recorded on two 100-foot rolls or one 200-foot role of film. This amounts to approximately 20,000 8½″ × 11″ documents on the rolls. Thousands of 8½″ × 11″ documents can be placed on one 6″ × 4″ ultrafiche. Frames for about 350 microfilmed documents can be mounted in a five-inch high stack of aperture cards. This storage technique makes possible the saving of enormous amounts of floor space and great numbers of filing cabinets. As much as 98 percent of the space can be saved.

Although documents reduced to microfilm save considerable filing space, microfilm cannot be economically used for space savings alone because the cost of the microfilm equipment may be greater than the cost of the space saved. In an active file, when the original filing arrangement is accurate, microfilm simplifies and speeds up the retrieval of information by making it impossible to refile an item incorrectly. It must be remembered that microfilm captures not only the records but all of their defects as well. Records must be carefully and correctly arranged before filming.

Microfilm also offers security for valuable records in that copies are sent rather than originals. Cross-references are easily handled by photographing extra copies whenever they are desired. Microfilm is durable in that it can be kept indefinitely and when used does not show wear and tear as the original document would.

Microfilm, especially microfiche, can be mailed to other locations at a minimum cost. Microfilm systems can be adapted to both high- and low-volume offices.

Applications of Microfilm

Microfilm is useful as a method of processing and retrieving information on an active basis.

Specific uses of microfilm have been mentioned for the various microforms. Microfilming was once used exclusively as a method of protecting vital records or as a means of saving space. Today it is even more useful as a method of processing and retrieving information on an active basis.

Almost all types of businesses now use micrographics. The largest users include utilities (gas, electric, water), financial institutions (banks, investment companies, savings and loan associations), insurance companies, government agencies (federal, state, local), military agencies, transportation companies, educational institutions, libraries, manufacturing firms, retail and wholesale distributors, and hospitals.

Questions for Discussion

1. Why have mechanical and electronic machines been developed to help with the creation, filing, and finding tasks?

2. What has been the effect of these newer systems on the coding and indexing process of filing?

3. What is the major impact of data processing tools and systems on files operators?

4. Why are punched cards known as unit records?

5. How are punched cards stored? How are punched cards retrieved?

6. In what ways are tabulator printouts filed?

7. How has electronic data processing (EDP) affected filing work?

8. What data storage mediums are used for EDP systems?

9. Why must indexing and coding of information be carefully planned before the recording process on magnetic mediums is begun?

10. What is the job of a tape librarian?

11. Who is responsible for the security of data processing files?

12. What is word processing?

13. What storage mediums are used with word processing and integrated data processing systems?

14. How are the following items stored for retrieval?
    a. Punched paper tape
    b. Magnetic tape cassettes
    c. Magnetic cards
    d. Diskettes (floppy disks)

15. Why is an auxiliary index important in filing word processing and data processing documents?

16. What is microfilming? What is micrographics?

17. In what activities might files operators become involved concerning micrographics?

18. What is a hard copy?

19. What is roll microfilm?

20. What are targets as used in microfilming? What purposes do they serve?

21. What is an aperture card? How are such cards filed?

22. What is a microfiche? What is a microfiche jacket?

23. What is the header? How is it used?

24. What are some of the values of the use of microfilm?

Part 6
Records Control

The Shaw – Walker Co.

CHAPTER 14

Equipment Used in Records Control

Section 1 Selecting Filing Equipment

Variety of Equipment

Selecting the best style of filing equipment for controlling records is an exciting and challenging task. Exciting because the greatest growth in filing and records control has been in this area of equipment design and supplies. The old, traditional files have taken on a new look to meet the increasing demands placed on them and to fit into the new open, or landscape, office designs.

The use of automated electronic equipment has not decreased the volume of paperwork as many thought it would. Rather, the new technology has created a greater volume of paper and other media records to be stored and controlled. A variety of new and different types of equipment has been created to house the different magnetic mediums produced by the electronic office systems. You have already seen some of the paperless records and housing for them illustrated in Chapters 1 and 13.

Browse through such magazines as *Modern Office Procedures*, *The Office*, *Administrative Management*, and *Office Products News* and see for yourself the variety of filing equipment and supplies advertised there. No matter how staggering the volume of records or the kinds of records kept, filing equipment is available to store and protect them. From cardboard boxes to computerized storage of file data, filing equipment in a wide range of sizes, shapes, capacities, costs, and colors is available (1) to speed up information storage and retrieval processes, (2) to cut down on the number of misfiled records, (3) to reduce the amount of record storage space, and (4) to complement a new office design or layout.

Challenge of Selection

How do you choose from the variety of filing equipment? Therein lies the challenge! The selection of filing equipment, like the selection or purchase of any item, requires an investigation, or at least a consideration, of three basic purchase factors: needs, wants, and cost. In other words, examine what your particular records control system requires. In light of all that is available to you, what do you want for your system?

*The three basic
purchase factors
are: needs,
wants, and cost.*
And finally, how much can your organization afford to spend? The importance attached to these factors will depend on the knowledge, experience, and personal taste of the person making the selection. Each person or organization has its own set of priorities, needs, and values, and it is difficult to know what has been sacrificed or compromised when these three factors are considered and juggled about.

All would go well if we entered into every purchase or acquisition with a clear, objective mind, having fully explored our needs, wants, and bankbooks. Unfortunately, few people are that objective in balancing the three purchase factors—needs, wants, and cost. Sometimes these factors work together, and sometimes against one another as the ultimate decision to buy is reached. Let us look at these purchase factors further.

Needs. The selection of filing equipment begins with needs—future needs as well as present needs. Every organization has its own individual and specific requirements as to the kinds of records it must control and how these records are to be used. It is rare that you will find any two filing systems exactly alike. Before equipment and supplies can be selected for any given office, you need to know such things as:

1. What kinds of records are to be filed and controlled.
2. How frequently each kind of record will be handled—constantly during the day or only every once in a while.
3. How many people will be working at the files.
4. What volume of material will be handled in a given period of time—every six months or every year.
5. Which method of filing will be best suited to the material that will be filed—straight alphabetic, geographic, subject, numeric, or some combination of these systems.
6. What type of charge-out and follow-up system will be most satisfactory.
7. What transfer plan will be used.
8. Will records control be centralized, departmentalized, or handled through a combination of these plans.

Not all of these matters will have to be considered in every situation, but in general all of them should be considered at one time or another before a system can be properly planned and controlled.

Wants. Before you can want something, you must first be aware of what is available. For example, you must know what a rotary file is before you can want one. It is in the area of wants that this chapter will be of most value to you. Space prohibits the coverage of every piece of filing equipment, but you will become familiar with the basic types of filing equipment that you can expect to find in the office. As you learn the basic types of filing equipment, you will become aware of the choices and alternatives provided by the wide variety of filing equipment and supplies available. For example:

1. When various types of filing cabinets are considered for installation, it might be determined that some three-drawer cabinets should be purchased so that they could be used as counters. Other two-drawer cabinets might be selected for use as desk-side units.
2. Open-shelf units might be selected in preference to vertical cabinets because the records to be handled are of the semiactive variety.
3. Guides with hollow tabs might be purchased if a system is to be constructed for a particular office.
4. For a relatively small but very active file for an executive, a subject guiding system might be found most suitable, and hanging folders might be used because of the increased accessibility this type of equipment can give.

Cost. Cost is the factor that makes the ultimate equipment purchase a reality. No matter how carefully you have checked your needs and investigated equipment styles, the filing system and equipment cannot become a reality without money. Whether it is a $100 vertical filing cabinet or a $100,000 computer assisted microfilm retrieval (CAR) installation, cost plays an important part in the selection process. Since labor accounts for about 80 percent of filing costs and equipment accounts for only about 20 percent in most filing systems, it is good business to select equipment that will reduce the time and energy used by records assistants.*

Keep in mind the benefit-cost ratio presented in Chapter 1. It is a good reminder that business expects a fair return on the dollars it invests. The purchase cost factor requires a look not only at the cost of the equipment but also at the resulting benefits to be obtained from the equipment.

Section 2 General Types of Filing Equipment

You have already seen a variety of equipment for storing cards in Chapter 12. You have also seen some paperless record storage equipment in Chapter 13. The remainder of Chapter 14 deals principally with general types of equipment available to hold correspondence and documents. The adaptability of this equipment to house a variety of other office mediums and records is included. Reference is made, also, to equipment used for special records not already mentioned in the textbook.

The computer and related systems will be considered because they are important aids to gathering and retrieving information. This trend in records control means that increasing skill will be required of files operators in the future. They must be familiar not only with filing principles, but also with a variety of new equipment.

---

*This trend is reflected in a recent study conducted by the Milwaukee Chapter of ARMA (Association of Records Managers and Administrators). Further references to this study are made later in this chapter.

Although sometimes used in combination with one another, most filing equipment fits into one of the following ten categories:

1. Vertical cabinets.
2. Open-shelf files.
3. Lateral cabinets.
4. Rotary files.
5. Mechanized files.
6. Mobile files.
7. Hanging folder equipment.
8. Equipment for specialized records.
9. Desk-top and desk-side equipment.
10. Equipment for computer filing.

Vertical Cabinets

The vertical file cabinet is the most widely used piece of filing equipment.

Vertical cabinets are rectangular shells in which are held a series of large, bin-like drawers constructed so papers can be filed in a vertical position with writing facing forward toward the files operator. Illustration 14-1 shows two-, three-, four-, and five-drawer vertical file cabinets.

The vertical file cabinet is the most widely used of all filing equipment. According to a survey conducted by the Milwaukee Chapter of ARMA, over 80 percent of the respondents used vertical file cabinets. The standard vertical file cabinets have been updated and look quite different from their traditional gray ancestors. The cabinets now come in a wide variety of colors and contemporary wood veneers to fit into most modern office designs. If you have ever pulled out too many drawers at one time and had the cabinet tip over, you will be glad to know that vertical cabinets may be equipped with an interlocking device that prevents the files operators from pulling out more than one drawer at one time.

Shaw-Walker

illus. 14-1, Two-, Three-, Four-, and Five-Drawer Vertical File Cabinets

Because cabinets are available in various sizes, they can be adapted for use in a number of ways:

1. One- and two-drawer units may be used near desks to provide easy reference to very active papers.
2. Three-drawer cabinets may be used as work counters and as dividers between sections in an office.
3. Four- and five-drawer cabinets may be used as blocking partitions in an office area. Frequently, units of these sizes are selected because active and semiactive materials can be handled in the same cabinets. (This procedure is described in Chapter 7.)

Some cabinets are made of very heavy metal, and the cabinet shells are insulated to provide some degree of fire protection for valuable papers and documents. Heavy cabinets are also made with combination locks and with the reinforcement necessary to permit their use as safes for the storage of vital and valuable documents and papers.

Vertical cabinets have the advantages of providing closed, convenient, and relatively compact storage space in drawers that can be organized under any of a variety of systems for guiding purposes. Vertical cabinets are most useful when individual papers are being handled rather than when entire folders are to be taken from the files.

The principal disadvantage of vertical cabinets is their bulk. They occupy a great deal of floor space; and, when very active files are in operation, they require wide aisles to allow the pulling out of the file drawers. As a result, much floor space is lost.

Although the vertical cabinet is still the most popular piece of filing equipment in the office, the Milwaukee survey indicated a decreasing trend in anticipated use of the vertical file cabinet in the future. Other types of filing equipment are gaining in popularity. Read on.

Open-Shelf Files

Folders are placed on open shelves with the tabs along the side edge.

In an effort to minimize some of the disadvantages of filing certain types of records in vertical cabinets, various forms of shelf filing equipment have been developed and are widely used. The Milwaukee ARMA survey showed that almost 74 percent of the firms responding made use of open-shelf filing. One third of the respondents anticipated more use of open-shelf files in the future.

The equipment and supplies used with shelf filing differ from those used with vertical filing cabinets because folders are placed on open shelves with the visible portion of each folder along the side edge rather than across the top. Thus, tabs on both guides and folders must be cut so that their notations show vertically (down the side) rather than horizontally (across the top).

On the open-shelf file in Illustration 14-2, tabs on the folders are shown in a combined alphanumeric filing order. Captions on the folders are written in a vertical style.

TAB Products Company

illus. 14-2, Open-Shelf File with Removable Sections

Folder-supporting devices of one kind or another are usually included as part of an open-shelf filing system. The supporting device pictured on the file cart opposite the open-shelf file are small bin-like sections that can be removed by the operator. Such sections are used to hold guides and folders in an upright position as well as to serve as dividers and carriers of file materials.

Very active papers are not usually held in shelf files mainly because entire folders must be pulled out of the shelf area before papers can be filed or found. Furthermore, guide and folder notations are not as readable as are those on top-tabbed guides and folders in vertical cabinet filing systems. Therefore, semiactive materials are more apt to be held in shelf files. Some types of insurance papers, case histories in hospitals, legal papers, and contract job records can be most profitably held in shelf files.

In general, the advantages of shelf filing over cabinet filing are:

1. Floor space is saved because room for the pulling out of drawers is not needed; therefore, aisles between shelves can be narrower than aisles between vertical cabinets.
2. Direct access to folders is easier because these are held on open shelves and are always visible.
3. Costs for shelf filing equipment are much less than those for vertical cabinet filing since the shelf equipment is relatively simple in construction.

The disadvantages of shelf filing over cabinet filing are:

1. An entire folder must be withdrawn from a shelf before any action can be taken to find or file papers.
2. Open shelves do not provide adequate protection from dust.
3. Notations on folders and guides are not as readable as those on the top edges of guides and folders in vertical cabinets.
4. Open shelves are not always neat in appearance.

Lateral Cabinets

Lateral cabinets contain pull-out drawers that hold papers in a lateral position.

A lateral file is one in which folders and guides are held in pull-out drawers constructed to hold papers in a lateral direction. Lateral cabinets are constructed in either of two styles: (1) with drawer fronts that can be opened to expose the contents of the drawer, as in a shelf file, or (2) with drawer fronts that are fixed parts of file drawers and thus move as the drawers are being pulled out of the cabinet area, as in a vertical file cabinet. This factor is important because the system of guides and folders varies with the type of drawer being used in a lateral cabinet. A lateral file with solid drawers can use only top-tabbed guides and folders (see Illustration 14-3), while a lateral file drawer with a sliding front panel can be equipped with both top-tabbed and side-tabbed guides and folders (see Illustration 14-4). The contents of the drawer with top- and side-tabbed guides and folders can be arranged so that the tabs can be read either from right to left or from left to right. This factor can be used to advantage to gain maximum working space when several lateral units are being placed in a filing area.

The lateral cabinet shown in Illustration 14-4 shows two open drawers and five closed drawers. In the top part of the upper open drawer, six primary side-tabbed guides are visible. Between these primary guides are sets of top-tabbed folders. The two tabs in the lower part of the drawer are tabs of OUT guides. The drawer has not been pulled forward out of the cabinet shell, but this is the action that is taken in order to get access to the folders in this file. The closed drawers are opened by pulling the front panel up and sliding it back into the body of the cabinet shell. The two card file sections shown below the open correspondence drawer are auxiliary parts that can be ordered and fitted into the space that usually would be occupied by a single correspondence drawer.

Esselte Pendaflex Corporation

*Permission by Supreme Equipment &
Systems Corp., Brooklyn, New York*

**illus. 14-3, Five-Drawer Lateral Cabinet
with Solid Drawers**

**illus. 14-4, Lateral Filing Cabinet
with Sliding Front Panels**

Cabinets with exchangeable sections are advantageous when there is a need for combination files in an office.

A comparison of lateral cabinets with vertical cabinets and shelf units shows that the laterals require less floor space than do the verticals because less aisle space is needed to accommodate the opening and closing of drawers. Since shelf units do not require any aisle or floor space for drawer action, these are the most economical in terms of floor area required. Top-tabbed guides and folders used in solid drawer laterals are similar to those used for vertical files and are usually considered better than the side tabs needed for shelf files. Guides and folders in lateral cabinets equipped with sliding front panels can be tabbed on the side edge or across the top or in both positions. For very active files, this is an advantage to be gained from the greater visibility of all guides and folders held in open-front, pull-out drawers.

Rotary
Files

Rotary units are composed of a series of circular shelves that rotate.

The production of rotary units for holding correspondence and related materials is a developing phase of the office equipment manufacturing industry. In essence, rotary units are composed of a large outer shell within which a series of circular shelves are rotated in somewhat the manner of a lazy-Susan server. On the rotating shelves, guides and folders are set and carried as spokes are carried on a wheel; or folders and guides may be set into rectangular bin sections formed as separate units on the "floor" of the rotating shelves.

Illustration 14-5 shows a multi-media filing carrousel. Rotary files are available in a variety of styles. They can be from one to six tiers high. Some are available with casters so that they can be moved to various work stations around the office. If record security is a need, cabinet enclosures that can be locked are available, as shown in Illustration 14-5.

Some of the advantages of free-standing rotary files are:

1. Savings in floor space are realized.
2. Tiers can be adapted to hold any size record from 5″ × 3″ card to computer printouts.
3. Tiers or entire carrousels can be added as they are needed.
4. Easy access to files by several files operators is possible because the open tiers are highly visible and each moves independently.

Rotascan Retrieval Systems

illus. 14-5, Multi-Media Filing Carrousel with Cabinet Enclosure

Mechanized Files

The two general types of mechanized filing equipment are electronic and power-driven files.

The process of transforming certain types of files into mechanical delivery systems is a continuing phase of progress in the field of records control. Primarily, mechanized equipment is centered around some type of mechanical system that locates parts of a filing system and delivers these to a console (work station).

The use of power-driven equipment does not eliminate the need for processing papers in the usual manner before they are placed in the files. However, mechanized systems do provide great accessibility to papers and documents by an operator stationed at the console of a mechanized unit. They are of definite value when the factor of equipment cost is secondary to the need for facility and speed in handling very active records.

There are two general types of mechanized filing equipment: electronic files and power-driven files.

Electronic Files. The larger and more sophisticated mechanized files, known as *electronic files*, are equipped with optical scanning devices that locate precoded folders and/or precoded tub-containers that hold folders and other types of file materials.

The Minitrieve unit shown in Illustration 14-6 consists of (1) a console (work station), which is located at the front of the unit, and (2) a vault-like enclosure in which records are stored behind the console. The operator seated at the console is referring to a folder taken from a tub that has been delivered to the console by the process described below.

Illustration 14-6 shows the two sections of the Minitrieve electronic file in detail. Within the vault area there are two facing banks of metal file tubs separated by an area occupied by an electronically operated conveyor (center, rear in picture). Upon a code signal from the operator at the console, the conveyor moves to a desired tub, which is drawn onto the conveyor and then moved forward into reference position at the console. After the desired paper, document, or folder has been removed or reviewed, the operator presses a button labeled "Restore"; the tub then is moved back to its original place in the vault area.

For complete control of records held in any of the mechanical types of equipment, there must be guiding plans, identification of filed materials, charge-out of papers or folders borrowed, and transfer of semiactive and inactive materials.

Systems like the Minitrieve shown in Illustration 14-6 have the following advantages over manually operated systems:

1. Storage space utilization is increased considerably because units can use space from floor to ceiling in a storage area.
2. Push-button speed in retrieval is far superior in relation to any other mechanical or manual method.
3. Papers and documents can be kept in security control because of the completely enclosed area in which they are held and the access by a single operator.

*Permission by Supreme Equipment &
Systems Corp., Brooklyn, New York*

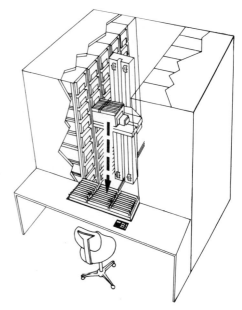

*Permission by Supreme Equipment &
Systems Corp., Brooklyn, New York*

illus. 14-6, MINITRIEVE—Console and Storage Sections in an
Electronic File

Units the size of the one in the illustration, and larger, are being included in the construction plans of some of the newest office buildings in metropolitan areas.

Power-Driven Equipment. The basic reason for using any of the various types of power-driven equipment is to move shelves or trays of records into working positions by electronic means. In power-driven equipment, records are brought to the operator rather than having the operator move from place to place to consult records located in various sections of an office or of a building.

Power-driven equipment for correspondence and document files is made in diverse forms with varying mechanical features as well as with unique types of delivery systems.

Power-driven units such as that shown in Illustration 14-7 usually hold about 18 shelves in a vertically moving suspension system that is controlled by a push-button panel located at or near the work station in front of the cabinet area. By using this control, an operator can select any of the shelves in the unit and have it delivered to reference position by machine action. Notice that guides and folders are side-tabbed so that the operator, being in front of the machine, can search at eye-level across the length of a file drawer for a needed folder.

Acme Visible Records, Inc.

illus. 14-7, Power-Driven Unit for Correspondence and Document Filing

Power-driven equipment is also produced in units smaller than those previously described and illustrated. Small units of the Ferris-wheel rotary type can be selected from a variety of units which are fitted to hold cards or correspondence-type materials. Illustration 12-5, page 173, shows one of these units used for holding card records.

Mobile Files

Mobile files on rollers eliminate the conventional aisles between ranges of file shelves.

Mobile files are formed by having a series of file sections mounted on rollers. This makes it possible to move any section of the files along a fixed track. The theory behind the mobile file is to eliminate the conventional, nonproductive aisles between ranges of file shelves. Illustration 14-8 shows a bird's-eye diagram of the conventional shelf arrangement, with an aisle between each range of shelves. Illustration 14-9 shows how to double the number of shelf units in the same storage space by eliminating the aisles.

Spacesaver Corporation
Ft. Atkinson, Wisconsin

illus. 14-8, Conventional Shelving Arrangement

Spacesaver Corporation
Ft. Atkinson, Wisconsin

illus. 14-9, Spacesaver Mobile File Arrangement

Both electric and manually operated mobile shelf systems enable a full bank of shelves to move easily and quietly along tracks on the floor so that one or more aisles are created only where they are needed at the moment. Illustration 14-10 shows such a mobile file unit. The operator easily moves the entire range of shelves until an aisle is created where the record is located.

Although it is a great space saver, the mobile file may be a poor choice for a system that is very active and used by many people. Much time could be lost waiting to create the aisle that you need to locate a particular record.

Spacesaver Corporation
Ft. Atkinson, Wisconsin

illus. 14-10, Mobile Carriage System

Hanging Folder Equipment

Hanging folder equipment suspends folders from rails or rods.

The hanging folder (or suspended folder) method of holding papers represents a very adaptable and widely used form of records control. There are two types of hanging folder equipment. One type has folders constructed with metal or plastic strips across the top edge of the front and back parts of the folders. The strips extend beyond the sides of the folders and fit over parallel rails that run on both sides of the file drawer (see Illustration 14-11). The folders are suspended over the strips. In this suspended position, folders are more easily moved and more readily accessible than are folders in standard vertical or lateral cabinets. Illustration 14-11 shows hanging folders in a lateral cabinet. This same kind of system can also be used in vertical cabinets by adding parallel rods to the sides of a file drawer not originally so equipped.

Courtesy of Westinghouse
Architectural Systems Division

illus. 14-11, Hanging Folder System in a Lateral Cabinet

Another type of hanging file equipment consists of a cabinet that has rods instead of shelves extending the full width of the cabinet. The folders have hook-like extensions on the front and the back. These extensions fit over the rods so that the folders hang from the rods. (See Illustration 14-12 on page 222.)

Robert P. Gillotte & Co., Inc.

illus. 14-12, OBLIQUE Hanging Folder System for Hospital Records

There are many uses for hanging folder systems because (1) materials of different sizes can be held more efficiently in suspended folders than in the more stationary vertical folders; (2) hanging folder systems are flexible and folders can be easily moved, or opened, or replaced; (3) some types of hanging folders can be indexed more completely than is possible with other types of folders and, therefore, records are more accessible in a hanging or suspended folder system.

Equipment for Specialized Records

Control programs are necessary for many types of specialized records.

Up to this point, equipment and systems have been considered for correspondence, documents, and cards. There are, however, many other types of records that must be held under control programs because they are vital to successful operations either in an entire organization or in a department.

Catalogs and Directories. Catalogs and directories are representative of a type of reference material used in many business, industrial, and service organizations. These records may be found in bound-book form or in loose-leaf binders, or they may be in transcribed form and written on cards that are filed in either visible or vertical card systems.

When records of the catalog type are in active use in their original form, rotary filing units are frequently used to hold and carry these bulky books. The rotary units are much easier to handle and much more accessible for use by a number of workers at the same time than would be the case if such materials were held in cabinets or on book shelves. Also, when catalog-type material is transcribed onto cards and the cards are held in large visible books, these also may be used to greatest advantage when held in rotary units.

When catalog-type material is semiactive or when it is used occasionally by only a few workers, it may be kept in bookcases or in vertical filing cabinets. When held in these ways, catalogs may be marked and filed according to several plans: (1) by firm name—with a supplementary card index file listing in alphabetic order the items or subjects included in each catalog; (2) by number—with an alphabetic card file of firm names and the subjects included in each catalog; (3) by subject—with an alphabetic card index listing of firm names.

Cross-references may be made in the catalog card index, just as they are made in any other card system, by listing on one card the places where related material can be found.

Bulky Materials. Many of the important records that are kept by business and industrial organizations are not written on standard size cards or sheets of paper. Because of this, special indexing and filing problems are encountered. Among these types of records are X-rays, maps, blueprints, tracings, duplicator plates and stencils, some types of forms, and computer printouts.

Many of these records are too large or too bulky to be held in standard file equipment, but most can be satisfactorily stored in hanging folders that are large enough and strong enough to hold large sheets or bulky objects. A system of this type frequently is used by hospitals to hold such large items as X-ray film and other related data. Illustration 14-12 shows a hanging folder system for such records. Each of the folders in this system is equipped with a vertical tab that holds a numbered insert slip to identify the folder. The numeric system of guiding is used on an open file so that hospital records will be filed by an indirect system and thus held in an impersonal manner as well as in a unit form. This requires that a master index be kept which shows personal names in alphabetic order and lists the folder numbers assigned to those persons. The cabinet that holds such a master index is seen in the lower right corner of Illustration 14-12.

Desk-Top and Desk-Side Filing Equipment

Two of the more important work areas that require planning and equipping for records control are the desk and related work stations. In such areas as these, filing systems are limited to rather small units.

Desk or work station filing systems are limited to rather small units.

Frequently, it is difficult to control these types of filing systems because of their "personalized" nature and the rate of turnover of papers held in these systems.

One major step in controlling desk and auxiliary files is to start with a carefully planned system held in suitable equipment. A second step is to maintain order in the system by continuously weeding out unwanted papers and constantly transferring other papers to less active sections of the filing system.

Illustration 14-13 shows a type of equipment specially designed to serve as a desk-side or work-station-side unit. Notice that this one-drawer lateral unit is equipped for a hanging folder system and that folders face forward toward the operator. This system has two major advantages as a desk auxiliary file: (1) Hanging folders are easier to handle than are "fixed-position" folders and (2) all folders face the person who is referring to the file so that all parts of the guiding system are visible. Therefore, filing and finding time is reduced to a minimum.

illus. 14-13, A Lateral Desk-Side Filing Unit

In Chapter 12 you have already seen the popular wheel files used as desk-top and desk-side filing units. Rotary files are also used as desk-top or desk-side files. Illustration 14-14 shows such a desk-side filing unit. The lower tiers of rotary files may be removed for use as desk-side files.

Systems for guiding desk records can be as diverse as those used for any phase of business operations. However, subject and alphabetic guiding plans are those most frequently used for the control of executive records.

Photograph courtesy of Methods Research Corp., Farmingdale, NJ

illus. 14-14, Rotary Desk-Side Filing Unit

Other types of useful auxiliary units are available in portable or stationary styles. One such unit is the sorter and temporary file shown in Illustration 14-15. This is designed as an auxiliary unit for holding current papers at a ready position for a period of time so that the retrieval of very active papers will not require a search of the general files. Notice that hanging folders are side-cut to permit reference to letters or documents without having to remove them from the file. Papers are filed from the top of the file but are removable from the side. These features add greatly to the usability of this particular type of equipment.

Equipment for Computer Filing

Computer filing is a blend of data processing and micrographics.

Will computer filing outmode the filing systems and equipment as we now know them? It is not likely, because: (1) there are many situations where paper (hard copy) records are necessary; (2) only the larger organizations can afford and justify the expense of a computer installation for records control; and (3) where computers and new office technologies are being used for information storage and retrieval, filing needs have not been eliminated, but have merely changed.

Computer output microfilm (COM), for example, is a process of transferring information from the computer directly onto microfilm or microfiche, eliminating the paper (hard copy) printout. Instead of filing the paper document, the files operator must now be concerned with filing the microforms for fast and easy retrieval. Alphabetic, numeric, and color coding are as much a part of filing computer tapes, disks, cassettes,

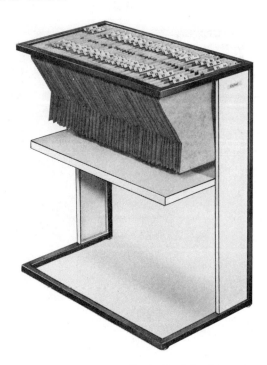

Esselte Pendaflex Corporation

illus. 14-15, Sorter and Temporary File

and magnetic cards as they are of filing paper records. Most of the filing equipment already used in the office is easily adapted to house, retrieve, and refile these new office forms.

Computer assisted microfilm retrieval (CAR) is a more advanced blend of data processing and micrographics. The advantage of CAR is that it has an added retrieval feature. With CAR, the computer is used to automate the retrieval function. Documents are stored on microfilm, but the index to the documents is stored in the computer. The microfilm retrieval terminal shown in Illustration 14-16 is electronically linked to a computer. The basic principle of CAR is to store information on microfilm (notice the microfilm file at the left of the retrieval terminal in Illustration 14-16) and to use the computer to organize the index for speedy retrieval. The retrieval terminal is capable of locating, displaying on a reader, and printing copies of records and COM documents from both roll film and microfiche formats.

When the files operator needs a particular document, the operator places the microfilm cartridge into the retrieval terminal and keys the computer. A signal is then sent from the computer to the film retrieval terminal, instructing the terminal to retrieve a particular image from the film file.

Eastman Kodak Company

illus. 14-16, Microfilm Retrieval Terminal

This kind of installation is costly. With a cost range from $50,000 to $150,000, the system is practical only for large numbers of active records that remain active for long periods of time. For example, high input volume of more than 4,000 pages a day and more than 100 retrievals a day might justify such a system.

Questions for Discussion

1. What are the three basic purchase factors to consider in selecting filing equipment?

2. What information is required in order to arrive at the filing equipment needs of an organization?

3. What are the various types of filing equipment available?

4. Are filing cabinets useful in ways other than for storage of papers? In which other ways are they used?

5. What are some of the advantages and disadvantages of shelf filing?

6. What main advantages does lateral filing have over vertical cabinet filing?

7. What are some advantages of free-standing rotary files?

8. What is the principal difference between an electronic filing unit and a power-driven filing unit?

9. What advantages are there in using mechanized files as compared with using manually controlled files?

10. Would you use mechanized files for semiactive papers? Explain.

11. What is one principal advantage and one principal disadvantage of a mobile file system?

12. What are some advantages of using hanging folder equipment?

13. What are some of the types of specialized records for which filing systems and equipment must be provided?

14. Why are rotary cabinet units sometimes very useful for holding catalog and directory types of materials?

15. Why are desk files difficult to control?

16. What are some types of desk-side or work-station-side filing units?

17. Why is it unlikely that computer filing will outmode filing systems and equipment as we now know them?

18. Is it practical for all organizations to install a COM or a CAR records control system? Why or why not?

CHAPTER 15

Maintaining and Improving Records Control Systems

From your first office job on, you will be concerned with filing problems. Even if your job is only partly in the records keeping area, there is a good chance that you will come face to face with both of the following problems: (1) You will be the only operator of an existing filing system that may be woefully weak. (2) You will be expected to do whatever is necessary to file all office papers and to find the ones that are needed, when they are needed. In other words, it will be up to you to use (and repair) an existing "system" or to develop a new system and keep it in operating condition.

Locate, correct, and prevent filing problems.

With this in mind, material in this chapter is designed to help you keep a filing system under control. The chapter also includes ideas and suggestions about methods that can be used to locate, correct, and prevent filing problems.

If on your first job you find yourself to be the sole possessor of a so-called "filing system," what should you do about it? Well, an old saying is, "Circumstances alter cases"—and they do. Not all situations are alike. However, because you have studied this textbook and have used the practice set, you will know what is needed to operate and to control a records system. Use this knowledge to help yourself work out of problems and into control. Find out why things are not as they should be. Think about your problems. Form a plan for solving them. Don't trust yourself to remember the details of problems; write your thoughts down in outline form. Fill in details as the problems become evident. Then you will be able to remember what the problems are and why they need attention. Act on the solutions on which you have decided. Be sure, however, to get your supervisor to approve what you propose to do before you go all out on your improvement program. Don't expect everything to fall into place in a short time. And above all, don't give up.

You may, of course, start working in an office where a good records control program has been developed. If so, learn all you can about the operations of this system. In such a situation, you are likely to find that there will be a handbook, called a *manual*, in which the filing system is described and the routines are detailed. By all means, read this manual and follow it *to the letter*.

It is probable that where there is a good filing system, there is also a well-trained and efficient supervisor. If you work with such a person, you are indeed fortunate. Cooperate fully with your supervisor and faithfully follow his or her advice.

An efficient files operator is a valued worker.

When you know how to use the records system, you will be a valued worker. You should then be able to enjoy your job because it is interesting and because you are performing a service that is vital to the success of the company that employs you. The more proficient you become and the more you learn about records control, the more likely you are to be promoted to higher jobs.

The remaining parts of this chapter are designed to give you ideas and show you procedures that can be used to make you an efficient and effective files operator.

Section 1   Procedures for Good Records Control

A good records program does not "just happen."

A good records program does not "just happen." It must be carefully planned and then acted on. In order to have a successful operation, attention must be given to all procedures. You can use the list that follows as a guide when you are considering improvements in any phase of your filing system and its operating problems.

Shaw-Walker

illus. 15-1, Organized Records Make Your Job Easier

1. Records control routines should be carefully planned and strictly followed. Even though filing is only a part of general office or secretarial work, a definite amount of time should be made available for it.

2. Papers should be indexed, coded, and processed in accordance with definite rules and routines.

3. Responsibility for directing filing and records control operations should be definite. One person should probably be given this duty.

4. Only personnel assigned to perform records work should be allowed to operate the filing system.

5. A manual of procedures (a guide) should be available and should be kept up-to-date. The manual should include such technical material as:

   (a) A general description of the records control system and its various parts or divisions.
   (b) A list of indexing rules to be used.
   (c) A description of the coding practice to be followed.
   (d) A description of charge and follow-up procedures.
   (e) A definition of procedures to be followed prior to and during transfer time.

6. The files should not be overcrowded with papers and folders. Attention should be given to the following matters:

   (a) Room for expansion should be provided in all file drawers and on all file shelves.
   (b) Unneeded papers should be screened out during the scanning and coding phase of operations.
   (c) Material already in the files should be scanned on a continuous basis and uncalled for papers should be removed whenever possible. (Such a "weeding out" requires knowing which folders and/or papers are used for reference and which are not. One way to recognize unwanted material is to make a tally mark on the "up" edge of a paper or a folder each time it is requested. A lack of tally marks indicates a "dead" folder or letter.)
   (d) Papers should be transferred from active files into semiactive or storage ones according to a carefully developed transfer program.
   (e) Papers should be eliminated according to a plan for the destruction of records.

7. Equipment and supplies used in the control program should be selected after careful study has been made of the need for them and their probable uses.

8. A plan for charging and tracing borrowed materials should be in operation.

9. Order should be maintained in all phases of records control by using such accepted practices as the following:

   (a) Notations on guide and folder tabs should be typed or printed in a uniform style.
   (b) Worn folders should be replaced.
   (c) When folders are returned to the files, the folders should be neatly aligned with those already in position. Follower blocks in file drawers should be used to keep folders from sagging. Boxes or blocks should be used to hold papers in a neat arrangement on shelves.
   (d) Torn sheets should be mended and "dog ears" should be straightened.
   (e) Pins and clips should be taken off papers in files.
   (f) Tops of filing cabinets or shelves should be kept clear of all materials.

10. Miscellaneous folders should be checked regularly, and individual folders should be started for active correspondents.

11. Individual folders should be inspected and extended when it seems necessary.

12. Special subject, geographic, and date sections should be added as needed to make the system more efficient.

Preparing and Using a Records Control Manual

It is always advisable to have a records control manual.

Regardless of how large or how small a records department may be, it is always advisable to have a records control manual to be used as a guide by all those who work in the department. This is especially true because of two factors common to all records control work.

First, all such work must be as closely related as possible to the unique practices and standards used in any particular company because each company has certain routines and standards peculiar to its own type of operation. Workers must know these procedures if efficient operations are to result. Also, as procedures are developed or improvements are made in departmental routines, they must be explained in permanent form; otherwise they will be lost, misunderstood, or misused as time passes and personnel changes occur.

Second, a records control manual assembles in summary form a variety of technical information that is vital. Many of the rules and procedures that you have studied in this textbook will be found in company

illus. 15-2, Finding the Right Paper at the Right Time

manuals. But it should be understood that some of the rules and routines given in this textbook must be adapted for use in a particular company. For example, the basic rules for indexing must be used by all who keep records; but a given company might operate in a specialized field that would require an elaboration or extension of one or another of the basic rules for indexing. It is very possible that a company dealing with agencies or branch offices in foreign countries may require a more detailed statement of the basic indexing rule for processing foreign names. Such an extension of the rule would be explained in the company manual.

In summary, records control manuals, or filing manuals, are prepared for the following reasons: (1) to formalize records control procedures used in a given company so that all personnel will be informed and will be able to proceed in a uniform manner; (2) to record technical information in order to guide and train departmental personnel; and (3) to relate general standards of performance to the specific needs of any given organization.

Section 2 Records Control: What Kinds—How Many—When and Why

In this section you are given information that enables you to understand a filing system so that you can use it and repair it as required. You will know *what kinds* of supplies it should have and *how many* are needed. You will also be advised about *when* to do certain things and told *why* they must be done. With this information you will be better prepared to face the two problems mentioned in the first paragraph of this chapter.

The section that follows gives an outline of the things you should know if you are to improve an existing filing system or start a new one. Each point in the outline will be treated more fully in the pages that follow the list.

The You-Must-Know List

1. How guides and folders are described and used as supplies.
2. What kinds of records are held in the system.
3. How active the filing system is.
4. What equipment and supplies are needed for systems of varying activity rates.
5. How many papers should be held in a folder.
6. How much free space there should be in the system.

Explanation of the You-Must-Know List

1. **How Guides and Folders Are Described and Used as Supplies.** Guides and folders vary considerably in thickness, weight, and strength. These variations are defined according to a scale of thickness. This scale is known as the *point system*. One point equals one thousandth of an inch (.001).

Guides and folders are usually made of a composition material called *pressboard* or of a heavy paper called *manila*. The term used to describe the measure of the thickness of pressboard and manila is called *caliper*.

Why are these measurements important? Well, the thicker the guide or the folder, the more space it occupies in a file drawer or on a file shelf.

Guides. Most guides are made of pressboard. They range in caliper measurement from 20 to 35 points. Guides are also made of 18-point manila stock.

Durability is the primary factor to consider when buying guides. Guides used for active to very active files are generally 20- to 25-point pressboard. Eighteen-point manila guides are sometimes used in semiactive files because such guides are less expensive than others. Since they get less use in semiactive files, manila guides are acceptable if they are needed to assist in the finding and filing of papers.

The choice of guides of a particular thickness should be measured not only by durability but also by their relative cost. Guides are expensive. Money can be saved by not "over-guiding" a filing system. Considerable saving can be made if the grade of guides selected is related to the activity of the system that is to be equipped. For example, to equip a semiactive file with an expensive guiding system would be a great waste of money. On the other hand, buying manila guides for an active system would be wasteful. Such guides would wear out quickly and would have to be replaced frequently.

Folders. The caliper of manila folders ranges from 8 to 18 points; that is, from 8 thousandths (.008) of an inch to 18 thousandths (.018) of an inch. The difference between .008 and .018 does not seem very important; but, if your system had only 10 five-drawer cabinets, the .018 folders would use 144 inches of file drawer space while the .008 folders would use only 64 inches—a difference of 80 inches. Eighty inches of space equals more than 3 file drawers 26 inches deep. This much space would be lost if you did not need the heavier folders. Lost space means more cost for filing services. Cost is vital and must be kept as low as possible.

Folders used for heavy-duty purposes, such as the carrier folders that were described in Chapter 6, page 77, are made of pressboard that ranges from 20 to 25 points. Some heavy folders are made with W-shaped bottoms to permit expansion for carrying or holding bulky items.

The caliper of manila folders in general use is either 9½ or 11 points. A paper stock called *Kraft* is also used for file folders. Kraft and manila are comparable in quality and price. Kraft is the darker colored of the two and is less apt to show soil.

2. **What Kinds of Records Are Held in a Filing System.** If you are studying a filing system in order to use it to best advantage, first find out what kinds of records it holds. Is it all correspondence or are other kinds of papers included? If other papers are included, what are they and how do they relate to correspondence? Are related papers filed in the same folders that hold correspondence, are they held in separate folders in the same system, or are they held in a separate filing system?

Related Papers. Some of the types of papers that are related to correspondence and filed in the same folders with it are found in the following offices. In a lawyer's office all papers concerning a case may be held in one folder or in a series of related folders. The papers included may be statements of law or of evidence along with correspondence relating to the case. Files in a personnel office might contain letters of application and references as well as application forms and test results. Purchasing department files holding such papers as price lists and product information may also hold copies of bills of lading and any correspondence relating to any of these matters. All such related papers may be held in the same folder for a particular supplier or in a series of related folders covering the same subject.

Coding Related Papers. The ever-present danger when filing different but related papers is that related papers may not be properly identified and, for that reason, may be misfiled. In order to minimize this danger, a common number or name must be assigned to all related papers. This identification must be used as a code to be marked on all related papers. This code can be a name, an order number, a job number, a case number, or a title.

If dates do not appear on papers being coded for related filing, a date stamp can be used to mark the current date on such papers. Then each paper can be filed within a group in an identifiable order. Also, the date sequence within the group will be retained.

3.   **How Active the Filing System Is.** You must know how frequently the filing system and all its parts are used each day. Checking the activity of a system requires keeping information on the following activities in the filing department: (1) how many papers are coded, sorted, placed in folders, and removed from folders; and (2) if a perpetual transfer system is being used, how many papers and folders are weeded out or transferred each day.

Each of the above items takes the time of a records assistant, involves paper handling, and is a part of the entire system of records processing.

If you keep a tally on each of these items for about a month, you will know how much activity is involved in your filing system. Also, there is a *very general way* of measuring relative activity so that you can estimate the degree of activity in your filing system. In this scheme there are four levels of activity: (1) very active, (2) active, (3) semiactive, and (4) inactive.

1. A *very active* system is one in which 6 percent or more of the total number of papers in a file are acted upon each day. "Acted upon" means processed in any of the ways that are given in the first paragraph of this section.
2. An *active* filing system is defined as one where about 5 percent of the total papers are handled in a day.
3. A *semiactive* system involves processing from 2 percent to less than 5 percent of all papers.
4. An *inactive* system results from a less-than-2 percent action with papers in the system.

These ranges of files activity are subject to error because, once again, "circumstances alter cases." For example, the kind of equipment used or not used can cause variations in the rates of activity that are measured in terms of percentages. But the rates are useful as a very general indication because they can show how much and what types of equipment and supplies are needed to make a system operate at top efficiency. For instance, if records processing is in the less-than-2 percent range, the system is in the storage or inactive area. There, guides are not needed and containers are boxes rather than drawers or shelves that are much more costly.

4. What Equipment and Supplies Are Needed for Systems of Varying Activity Rates. The activity rate of a filing system determines the equipment and supplies needed.

Very Active Files. A system of this type must be held as closely as possible to the records control center or desk. It can be held in the bin drawer of a desk or in the drawers of a desk-side unit. An A-Z set of primary guides is needed. Folders that are used in a manner similar to that of miscellaneous folders can be added behind each primary guide. Individual folders can be started as required by an accumulation of papers for a person or a firm. These are easily moved to the active system when the need for them in the "hot" file has diminished.

A very active file can also be held to advantage in a sorter that is located near the control desk. After being coded, incoming papers are filed in one of the many types of sorters available. The papers are held for a period of time until the rate of demand for them has decreased and then they are transferred to the active files.

Active Files. The active file is the "heart" of any records control program. It must be carefully planned and maintained in first-class order. It should have the best and most appropriate equipment and supplies.

Active filing systems should not have too many nor too few guides per file drawer or shelf. Having too many guides uses valuable space and can cause distractions in a searching operation. Also, guides are expensive—it is wasteful and costly to purchase too many. On the other hand, searching is more difficult if there are too few guides. This costs money in the form of salaries for unneeded records assistants and wasted time.

How many guides should be used in an active system? Usually the amounts given in the following table are recommended.

Number of File Drawers	Number of Guides Needed	
1	20-25	Divisions of the
2	40	Alphabet
3-4	80	
5-6	120	
7-8	160	
9-12	240	
13-16	320	
17-24	480	
25-36	720	
37-50	1000	

The number of folders that should be used behind each guide varies according to the type of material that is being held in an active system. When there are many individual folders in a system, it usually is advisable to have not more than 6 folders behind each primary guide. Less active systems can take more than this number; 8 to 10 folders are frequently found behind primary guides as files activity is lowered.

Semiactive Files. Semiactive filing systems are the "in-the-middle" ones—not "hot" but not "cold" either. They hold papers that have been transferred from the active system. You will recall that, depending on the way transfer is handled, semiactive files can either be in the same area as the active files or held in the storage files.

If the semiactive files are in the same cabinets as the active files, the semiactive files will be more usable if they are equipped with a set of primary guides. This set does not have to be of the same quality as that used for the active system. Also, the set does not need to have nearly as many guides. An example of this would be: if the active system were held in the 2 upper drawers of a series of 12 four-drawer cabinets, it would need a set of 480 primary guides. These would divide the alphabet into 480 parts. If the semiactive file were held in the 2 lower drawers of each of the 12 cabinets, it would need about 5 primary guides per file drawer, or a total of 120. This is only one quarter of the number needed for the active system.

Semiactive materials frequently are held on shelf filing units rather than in cabinet drawers. If such a system is in the upper level of semi-activity, one primary guide for each 6 inches in horizontal space is recommended.

All of the folders in a semiactive file are used first in the active system and then are transferred to the semiactive one or to the storage files. During this process it is possible to combine several folders holding related material into one folder. This reduces the number of folders that will be held and usually reduces the number of papers to be transferred, because dead materials can be more easily located and removed during the transfer process.

Storage Files. Guides are not used in storage files because the number of times that stored records are requested for reference is relatively low. Because of this, the demand for papers is much less urgent than it is in an active system.

In this situation, miscellaneous folders can be used as guides because they show on their tabs the same notations that primary guides show. Therefore, during the transfer process, when material is being placed in transfer boxes or cases, miscellaneous folders can be moved from the back of alphabetic sections to the front position. There they will serve the same purpose as the primary guides do in the active files.

5. How Many Papers in Each Folder. Regardless of the activity of a filing system, there must be a limit on the number of papers to be placed in each folder. There should be a statement about this in the records control manual, and it must be treated as a rule not to be broken. This rule is especially critical for papers held in miscellaneous folders, which can very easily become filled with far too many papers. Over-crowding creates a particularly serious filing problem because the papers in a miscellaneous folder are from several correspondents and an overfilled folder in this situation can cause a real foul-up. Miscellaneous folders must be checked on a regular basis, and the material in them must be divided into individual folders as soon as possible.

Capacity of File Folders. When the base of a manila folder is expanded to its maximum distance by folding the front flap to the top score mark, it has a base of three quarters of an inch. It is amazing how much paper can be held in this space—150 sheets of 20-pound bond paper will fit in this space. If the weight of paper is lower, much more can be stored—for example, 260 sheets of 13-pound copy paper.

Obviously, anyone who expects to find a record again will not put this much paper in one file folder. How many, then, should be considered as a maximum or a minimum amount? Actually, estimates of these standards must vary with the activity of a filing system.

In *very active files*, papers are not held very long. Because of this, the number of papers per folder is not a problem.

In *active files*, care must be taken not to file too many papers in folders. The standard usually followed is a *maximum* of 50 sheets to each folder. This means that the *average* number of papers in folders will be about 25. This figure might be too high for folders in some active systems. The *relative activity* of a filing system is the most important thing to consider when determining a specific standard for folder capacity.

In *semiactive files,* folders are in the semiactive system because they have been transferred directly from the active system. Therefore, the number of papers to be held in folders has been predetermined (fixed) by the rule used for the active system. However, some material in the active folders can be combined so that it will fit into fewer folders in the semiactive or storage files. Material in individual folders is especially adaptable to reductions of this kind. In such cases, the *average* number of papers per folder in the semiactive or storage files can be extended to about 50. This means that some folders will hold up to 100 sheets without harm to the filing and finding operation.

6. How Much Free Space in the Filing System. At transfer time, or when a new system is being planned, it is very necessary to leave free space in every drawer or on every shelf. If this is not done, drawers and shelves will be bulging with papers long before the next transfer time comes around and therefore the whole filing system will be out of order. Moreover, it will be very difficult to pull folders and to replace them.

At least 4 inches of free space should be left in every 26-inch deep file drawer. An appropriate amount of free space must also be left on shelves holding active or semiactive materials.

Storage boxes and transfer cases holding inactive materials can be filled but should not be crammed with folders and papers. These types of files hold materials that still have reference value, and there must be access to such materials without undue effort and confusion.

Section 3   How Long Papers Should Be Kept

As you learned in Chapter 7, it is very necessary to "clean" the active filing system on a regular basis in order to prevent an overwhelming accumulation of papers (they pile up fast). This is also true of papers held in storage filing systems. There must be a plan to control the final disposition or the final handling of records of all types. Some records will have outlived their usefulness in a relatively short time. Others will have reference value for an indefinite period of time. This means that there cannot be a time at which all records are destroyed. Such action would be a disaster.

In order to avoid destroying useful papers and documents, great care must be taken to consult those whose records are being considered for destruction and to decide with them on a schedule for the destruction of their papers. Usually a *records retention schedule* is prepared and finalized only after a committee of representatives from various departments in an organization has been appointed and has met and planned the entire destruction program. After this has been done, personnel in the records department must adhere to the schedule. This is the final action in the control of records.

illus. 15-3, Enjoy Your Work!

INDEX